Aristotle

on Ethics

'. . . for those attempting to come to grips with Aristotle's *Ethics* in the context of his own work and time, Hughes provides a congenial and helpful introduction'

Mary McCabe, *King's College London*

Aristotle's *Nichomachaean Ethics* is one of the most important and central texts in the history of Western philosophy. It lies at the heart of contemporary moral theory and is essential to understanding the history of ethics.

Gerard J. Hughes provides students with a stimulating, clear and accessible guide to Aristotle's *Nichomachaean Ethics*. He explains the key elements in Aristotle's terminology and highlights the controversy regarding the interpretations of his writings. The GuideBook carefully explores each section of the text, and presents a detailed account of the problems Aristotle was trying to address, such as happiness, responsibility, moral education and friendship. It also examines the role that Aristotle's *Ethics* continues to play in contemporary moral philosophy by comparing and contrasting his views with those widely held today.

Aristotle on Ethics is essential reading for all students coming to Aristotle for the first time and will provide an ideal starting point for anyone interested in ethical thought.

Gerard J. Hughes is Master of Campion Hall at the University of Oxford. He is the author of *The Nature of God* (Routledge, 1995).

Routledge Philosophy GuideBooks

Edited by Tim Crane and Jonathan Wolff
University College London

Rousseau and the *Social Contract*
Christopher Bertram

Plato and the *Republic*, Second edition
Nickolas Pappas

Husserl and the *Cartesian Meditations*
A.D. Smith

Kierkegaard and *Fear and Trembling*
John Lippitt

Descartes and the *Meditations*
Gary Hatfield

Hegel and the *Philosophy of Right*
Dudley Knowles

Neitzsche on Morality
Brian Leiter

Hegel and the *Phenomenology of Spirit*
Robert Stern

Berkeley and the *Principles of Human Knowledge*
Robert Fogelin

Aristotle on *Ethics*
Gerard Hughes

Hume on *Religion*
David O'Connor

Leibniz and the *Monadology*
Anthony Savile

The Later Heidegger
George Pattison

Hegel on History
Joseph McCarney

Hume on Morality
James Baillie

Hume on Knowledge
Harold W. Noonan

Kant and the *Critique of Pure Reason*
Sebastian Gardner

Mill on Liberty
Jonathan Riley

Mill on Utilitarianism
Roger Crisp

Wittgenstein and the *Philosophical Investigations*
Marie McGinn

Spinoza and the *Ethics*
Genevieve Lloyd

Heidegger on *Being and Time*
Stephen Mulhall

Locke on Government
D.A. Lloyd Thomas

Locke on *Human Understanding*
E.J. Lowe

Routledge Philosophy GuideBook to

Aristotle
on Ethics

- Gerard J. Hughes

Routledge
Taylor & Francis Group

LONDON AND NEW YORK

First published 2001
by Routledge
2 Park Square, Milton Park,
Abingdon, Oxon, OX14, 4RN

Simultaneously published in
the USA and Canada
by Routledge
270 Madison Ave,
New York, NY 10016

Reprinted 2003, 2005 (twice)

*Routledge is an imprint of
the Taylor & Francis Group*

© 2001 Gerard J. Hughes

Typeset in Times by Florence
Production Ltd, Stoodleigh, Devon
Printed and bound in Great Britain
by TJ International Ltd,
Padstow, Cornwall

*British Library Cataloguing in
Publication Data*
A catalogue record for this book is
available from the British Library

*Library of Congress Cataloging
in Publication Data*
Hughes, Gerard J.
  Routledge Philosophy GuideBook to
  Aristotle on ethics / Gerard J.
  Hughes.
  p. cm.—(Routledge Philosophy
  GuideBooks)
  Includes bibliographical references
  and index
  1. Aristotle. Nicomachaean ethics.
  I. Title: Aristotle on ethics. II. Title.
  III. Series.
B430.H84 2001
171'.3–dc21   00-051835

ISBN 0–415–22186–2 (hbk)
ISBN 0–415–22187–0 (pbk)

Contents

Acknowledgements   ix
Note on the text   x

1   Aristotle's life and work   1

An outline of his life and times   1
His works and philosophical
   background   4

2   Style, structure and aim of
   the *Ethics*   9

The *Nicomachaean Ethics*   9
Aristotle's aim in writing the *Ethics*   13
Aristotle's Preface (1):
   Why do we do anything at all?   14
Aristotle's Preface (2):
   Realistic expectations   16
Aristotle's Preface (3):
   Suitable students   17

3 The fulfilled life 21

The meanings of *eudaimonia* and *aretē* 22
Fulfilled lives? 24
A central problem: 'Dominant' or 'Inclusive'? 27
Two further agreed characteristics of *eudaimonia* 31
Background: Aristotle's views on the human soul 33
The Function Argument 36
Theōria and being a good citizen 45

4 Moral virtues and moral training 53

The definition of moral virtue 54
Moral training 70

5 Practical wisdom 83

Overview of the issues 84
Practical wisdom and theoretical ability 87
Is practical wisdom like other practical skills? 88
Practical wisdom: about means or about ends? 94
Practical wisdom and moral virtue 106
The unity of the virtues 109
Is Aristotle's account defensible? 112

6 Responsibility 117

'Acting willingly': sorting out common opinions 118
Moral conclusions: the best index of character 129
Responsibility for one's character 133
Decisions and freedom 137
Additional note on 'wanting' 142

7 Moral failure 145

Why is moral failure problematic? 145
Aristotle's solution: one interpretation 148
A more detailed defence 154

8 Relationships with others 167

Aristotelian relationships 168
Is Aristotle an ethical egoist? 172
Flexibility, relationships and justice 179

9 Pleasure and the good life 183

The issues as they appeared to Aristotle 185
Aristotle's comments on the moral arguments 188
The argument from opposites 190
Aristotle's own view: arguments and problems 194
Are some pleasures not really pleasures? 199
Is the fulfilled life enjoyable? 205

10 Aristotle's moral world and ours 211

Culture: acceptance and criticism 211
Virtues and principles 218

Glossary 223
Bibliography 225
Index 229
Index of texts 235

Acknowledgements

The stimulus to write this book came from Jo Wolff. I am much indebted to him for his encouragement at every stage. Especially I must thank Justin Gosling for reading the entire manuscript in draft, and for taking the time to make many characteristically insightful comments. I am also most grateful to one of Routledge's readers, who commented in detail most helpfully and constructively. Where I have resisted any of their suggestions, I have nobody to blame but myself. I should also like to thank Sue Hogg and Graham Pugin for being willing to take the trouble to read some of the more awkward bits and let me know whether people coming to Aristotle for the first time would find it an accessible introduction.

Campion Hall
Oxford
March 2000

Note on the text

For the sake of having one standard system which all scholars use, references to any work of Aristotle are always given according to the page, column and line in Bekker's Berlin Edition of 1831. This edition has the great advantage that each reference is quite unique. Thus, 1147b10 refers to line 10 of the second column on page 1147 of Bekker. Even with no mention of the title of the work, this is unambiguously a reference to the *Nicomachaean Ethics*, Book VII, chapter 3. In this book I have given the standard references, but have also included the Book and chapter of the *Ethics* as an additional help to placing a reference in its context.

The translations here are my own. But since it is always useful to compare different translations of any ancient author, the reader might wish to consult the other translations given at the start of the Bibliography. To make the sense clearer I have occasionally inserted in square brackets a word which does not occur in the Greek, but can be deduced from the context.

Chapter 1

Aristotle's life and work

An outline of his life and times

Aristotle came to Athens in 367 BCE at the age of 17, to go to university. 'University' in this case meant the Academy, the philosophical school founded by the great Plato, who himself had been a disciple of Socrates. Athens was *the* cultural centre of the Mediterranean, and its citizens would have had two reasons for not being immediately impressed by the young Aristotle. He came from the far north of Greece, from the city of Stagira in Macedonia; a country boy, then, doubtless lacking in cultural refinement. In this, the Athenian prejudice would have been misleading. Both Aristotle's parents came from families with a long tradition of the practice of medicine, and his father was court physician to King Amyntas III of Macedon. Court circles in Macedon were not uncivilized, and the value they placed upon education is demonstrated by the very fact of their sending Aristotle to Athens. There was, however, a second reason Athenians would have had for not welcoming Aristotle with wholly open arms.

He was connected with the royal family of Macedon, and Macedon had military ambitions. Amyntas's son Philip II embarked on a programme of militarist expansion which, much to the resentment of many prominent Athenians, led to his domination over much of Greece, and eventually to the subjugation of Athens itself.

Still, for twenty years Aristotle remained at the Academy, studying, debating, writing and teaching. Unfortunately, most of his writings from that time have been lost, and we are able to do little more than make educated guesses about precisely what he studied, and where his own interests lay. But as those years went by, the political situation brought about by the policies of Philip of Macedon rapidly worsened, and the climate in Athens became more and more nervous and hostile. Against this background, Aristotle, whose legal status in Athens was that of a resident alien, found himself regarded with suspicion. Finally the crisis came. Philip battered the city of Olynthus, one of Athens's close allies, into submission; and, a few months later, in 347, Plato died.

Aristotle was thus doubly isolated. Speusippus, a nephew of Plato, took over as head of the Academy. Would Aristotle have hoped that he himself might have got the job? Did his not getting it depend upon the fact that Speusippus was a relative of Plato, or on the fact that to appoint Aristotle would have been impossible in the prevailing political climate? Or was it perhaps that Aristotle's own philosophical views were by this time somewhat out of tune with the prevailing tone in the Academy? Whatever the academic reasons may have been, Aristotle thought it prudent, especially given the hostile political situation, to leave Athens and the Academy. He went to join a group of Platonists at Assos, a city on the north Aegean coast of what is now Turkey. The local monarch, Hermias, was himself interested in philosophy, and the philosophers encouraged him to fulfil the Platonic ideal of becoming a philosopher-king. Aristotle was later to write a hymn lamenting his untimely death (he was murdered) and praising his personal qualities 'for which he will be raised by the Muses to immortality'.

Before that, though, Aristotle had himself married Pythias, and they were again on the move. Philip II invited him to return to Macedonia to become tutor to his son Alexander. Alexander later was to become known as 'the Great' because of his amazing conquests which extended the Macedonian Empire across what is now Turkey, Egypt, much of Western Asia, and on into India. Perhaps Aristotle hoped to inculcate Plato's ideals in the young heir to the throne, but in the light of the brutality of some of Alexander's campaigning tactics, one may wonder just how complete Aristotle's influence on his pupil was.

Alexander left for his campaigns in the east, and Aristotle once again returned to Athens, in 334, under the protection of Antipater, the regent whom Alexander had appointed, and who was one of Aristotle's closest friends. At some point during his time in Macedonia, Aristotle's daughter, called Pythias after her mother, was born, but, tragically, his wife died, perhaps in childbirth. It was probably to help with looking after his infant daughter that Aristotle either married, or lived with (the ancient sources differ on the point), Herpyllis. Whatever his legal relationship with her was, in his will Aristotle was to speak warmly of her devotion to him, and to make careful provision for her support. She also became the mother of his second child, this time a son whom he called Nicomachus.

Upon his arrival back in Athens, Aristotle founded his own philosophical school in a public exercise park called the Lyceum. The students there became known as 'peripatetics' from their custom of walking up and down (in Greek, *peripatein*) as they discussed their philosophical researches. Here in his Lyceum Aristotle taught and pursued his own research happily for the next eleven years. It was the most productive period of his life, and the time of his most enduring achievements. Once again, though, political disaster struck. Alexander died suddenly at the young age of 32. The Athenians at once saw their chance to rid themselves of the Macedonian regent. In a wave of anti-Macedonian feeling, they charged Aristotle with 'impiety', the same catch-all offence which had led to Socrates's execution two generations earlier. Once again Aristotle had to leave, remarking, it is said, that he did so 'lest the Athenians commit a second sin against philosophy'. He survived only a year in exile, and died at the age of 62, in 322.

His works and philosophical background

The two great influences on Aristotle's philosophy were Plato and his own research into biology, especially the biology of animals.

Plato must have been a hard act to follow. He had developed and transformed the philosophical method of Socrates and applied it to an amazingly wide range of problems, including the immortality of the soul, the nature of virtue, the meaning of justice, and the theory of truth. He had attempted to give a theoretical justification for what he regarded as the right way to live both as an individual and as a member of the city-state. In so doing, he had been forced to seek for the foundations of ethics and politics by developing highly original views in metaphysics and in the theory of knowledge. The very scope and style of philosophy itself were those which had become established in Plato's Academy. The framework was to all appearances firmly established. Was there any room for genuine originality?

Recall that Aristotle studied and debated in Plato's Academy for twenty years, from the age of 17 until he was 37. He must surely have been enormously influenced not merely by Plato's method and by the conclusions which Plato and his students believed to be beyond dispute, but also by the places at which Plato's arguments were recognized as deficient, often by Plato himself. It is still a matter of dispute whether the young Aristotle started off by being more in agreement with Plato and ended up being much more critical; or whether he was more critical in his earlier years and only later began to see that there was perhaps somewhat more to be said for his old teacher's views than he used to think. It may also be true that the brilliant young pupil influenced his teacher, and that this influence shows up in some of Plato's later works.[1] Still, at least some things are reasonably clear. Aristotle retained Plato's interests in ethics and politics, and like

[1] The problem is not made any easier by the fact that we cannot with certainty date many of Aristotle's works even to the extent of clearly distinguishing the later from the earlier. In any case many of Aristotle's works are known to be lost. For a short and judicious comment on the problems of saying anything about Aristotle's philosophical development, see T. H. Irwin [1988], ch. 1, §5, pp. 11–13, and the articles referred to in Irwin's notes.

Plato agreed that ethics and politics had ultimately to rest on more general considerations of epistemology and metaphysics. There are also some similarities in method. Plato, following Socrates, often starts his dialogues by eliciting the views of one of his students, and then going on to see how far those views will stand up to criticism. Somewhat similarly, Aristotle habitually takes as his starting points *endoxa*, 'received opinions'. By this term Aristotle means to include views which are held by everyone, or at least by most people, as well as those held by the wise.[2] We should start, then, with what common sense might suggest, or with what earlier philosophers have thought, and then subject those views to critical assessment. Aristotle is more sympathetic than Plato to the thought that most people cannot be wholly mistaken.

The view most popularly ascribed to Aristotle is that he rejected Plato's 'Theory of Forms'. Certainly at one time Plato did believe that, if words like 'beauty' or 'courage' or 'equality' or 'good' were to have any meaning, they must point to the corresponding Forms – really existing, perfect, instances of these properties. Only if there are such Forms as Beauty itself, or Goodness itself, will there be any satisfactory explanation of the way in which we understand the beauty and goodness of this-worldly things, imperfect as they are. Only if these perfect Forms exist will there be any solid basis for morality, or indeed for knowledge itself. So, the popular view has it, Aristotle had no time for such metaphysical speculations, and made a radical break with Plato. This view is a gross oversimplification. First, Plato himself later in his life at least considerably modified the Theory of Forms, if by that is meant the kind of views advanced in the *Phaedo*. Besides, Aristotle is perfectly willing to talk about forms, and on some interpretations even ended up by holding a view of forms not wholly unlike Plato's. Still, there is an important truth behind the oversimplification. The clue lies in Aristotle's interest in biology, which perhaps had been first aroused by his parents with their medical background and practice. Much of the research done by Aristotle and his students consisted in the meticulous examination and classification of animals, fish and insects, and in the attempt to explain why they were

---

[2] *Topics* 100b21; see also *Nicomachaean Ethics* 1143b11–14, 1145b2–7.

as they were, and why they behaved as they behaved. Aristotle was convinced that the explanations were to be found not in some super-sensible world of Platonic Forms, but in the internal organization of the organisms themselves. Their patterns of growth, development and behaviour were directed by an inbuilt purposiveness, different for each species, the nature of which could be called the 'form' of that organism, and could be discovered by patient study and inquiry. More generally, perhaps the nature of every kind of thing could be discovered in a similar way. This quest for the natures of things – for the *phusis* of each kind of thing – is what Aristotle called *Physics*; and the further underlying truths about explanation in general, upon which such inquiries ultimately rested, were what he discussed in his *Metaphysics*.[3]

Here, then, is the original contribution which Aristotle believed he could make towards handling the questions that Plato had raised. Instead of looking to an abstract discipline such as mathematics to provide the ultimate explanation of things, as did the Platonists in the Academy, Aristotle proposed to study in detail the world around him, and to deal with the philosophical implications of that study in an inte-grated way. What, he asks, must be the fundamental characteristics of a world if inquiry into the natures of things in that world is to be possible at all? Like Plato, then, Aristotle seeks to know the ultimate explanations of things; unlike Plato, he thinks that questions about ulti-mate explanations must arise out of, rather than dispense with, mundane questions about how we are to explain the shapes and move-ments and growth of animals, and the regular behaviour of the inanimate parts of nature. In particular, looking at how the different species of organisms are by nature impelled to pursue what is good for them, we can begin to see how values are central to the behaviour of living things. Once we learn to look at ourselves as animals, and to understand how animals function, we can begin to glimpse how biology, with its inbuilt values, can in the case of thinking animals like ourselves lead on to ethics.

---

[3] 'Meta-Physics' probably refers to an inquiry which comes *after* (*meta* in Greek) the direct inquiry into the natures of things, when the inquirer sees that deeper questions must be dealt with.

Aristotle would have thought it astonishing if thinking animals like ourselves had no way of expressing to themselves what was good for them. So, at many points in the *Ethics*, he starts by considering what people usually or frequently think about various questions connected with morality, on the assumption that their views must either be right or at least contain some considerable kernel of truth which would explain why people hold them. But is this assumption a reasonable one to make? Might an entire society not be blind to the rights of women, or accept racist beliefs quite uncritically? Quite in general, does Aristotle's method not amount to little more than repeating the prejudices and unquestioned assumptions of his own culture? Aristotle might reply to this that he has no intention of *merely* repeating the views of the ordinary person, nor of the wise, without criticizing and assessing them. If one asks how this criticism is to proceed, Aristotle would reply that a good first step would be to bring into the open any hidden inconsistencies in common beliefs, and try to sort those out. But, the critic might press the point, even if that results in a coherent account, mere coherence doesn't guarantee *truth*. A person might be consistently racist or sexist and still be simply mistaken, surely? Aristotle might reply to this that even if it is comparatively easy to be consistent within a limited area of one's beliefs (say, about the rights of women), it is much harder to be consistent across a wide spectrum of one's beliefs. One would have to integrate ethics and psychology, physiology, sociology and the rest; and once one tries to do this, at some point the hidden inconsistencies will reappear. Achieving an overall 'fit' between one's experience and one's beliefs is not at all easy; and when it has been achieved, that is as close as one is ever likely to come to the truth. This is a very complex issue, and we shall have to see as we go along whether Aristotle's method seems likely to deliver what he is looking for.

For the moment, at least, this much can be said. Like Plato, Aristotle is concerned to get behind what people might happen to think in order to assess their views, to examine their foundations and their justification. Like Plato, Aristotle is concerned with how individuals ought to live, and how they ought to contribute to their communities. He, too, is concerned with the nature of moral virtues, justice, personal responsibility and moral weakness. Like Plato, he believes that ethics must be rooted in a view of the human soul. But unlike Plato, his conception of what a soul is derives in the first instance from biology, rather than from religious views about the incarnation and reincarnation of a disembodied true self. And this difference has profound implications for morality.

Chapter 2

Style, structure and aim of the *Ethics*

The *Nicomachaean Ethics*

The *Nicomachaean Ethics* is so called either because Aristotle dedicated the work to his young son, or, more probably, because it was Nicomachus himself who edited the work and gave it its final form some years after his father's death. Aristotle also wrote another book on moral philosophy, the *Eudemian Ethics*, which for the purposes of our present study we may leave to one side.[1] I shall here be dealing just with the *Nicomachaean Ethics,* and for convenience I shall refer to it simply as the *Ethics* when there is no danger of confusion.

We know that Aristotle wrote stylish dialogues and other works on philosophy intended for the general

---

[1] Not only are there the two works: to complicate matters further, three of the eight books of the *Eudemian Ethics* are identical with three of the ten books of the *Nicomachaean Ethics*. The more widely held view is that the *Eudemian Ethics* was written first. How to explain the duplicate books? Perhaps three of the books were lost from one of the two works, and were replaced by the three parallel books from the other work (which probably was the *Eudemian Ethics*). However, there is

public. Unfortunately, only some fragments of these have survived, and in any case most of these probably date from Aristotle's first stay in Athens when he was working in Plato's Academy. The surviving works, in contrast, were not intended for the wider public, and most of them could not be described as polished literary creations. More probably, they contain Aristotle's own notes for lectures he was giving, or topics he was working on. The *Ethics* most likely dates from the period after Aristotle had returned to Athens and founded the Lyceum. Like everything else we have from this period, in some places the writing is extremely condensed, and would, presumably, have been explained more at length in the course of the lecture. In other places, the style is more elaborate and the text could have been delivered more or less as it stands. There are also some inconsistencies. Did he perhaps revise what he wanted to say in some places, but did not get round to making the corresponding corrections elsewhere? Alternatively, it might well be that Nicomachus or some later editor was responsible for arranging whatever materials had come down to him from Aristotle, and fitted some bits in as best he could. What has come down to us is at least to some extent a record of work in progress, and we should read it in that spirit. It should encourage us to think about the problems as Aristotle himself was thinking about them. Rather than being daunted by a great man's finished definitive work, we might perhaps think of the questions we might put to a lecturer, or the contributions we might try to make to a seminar.

The *Ethics* will strike the modern reader as, if not exactly chaotic, at least rather loosely written. For a start, the traditional division into 'Books' and 'chapters' is almost certainly not Aristotle's, and we should not allow it to distract us.[2] Some topics run over from one book to another (as for example, friendship straddles the division

no agreement about the relative dating of the two works. The question turns on one's estimate of the significance of the differences between the two works, and which is more plausibly regarded as a revision of the other. A powerful case for questioning the common view that the *Eudemian Ethics* was written first has been put by Anthony Kenny [1978]; his further reflections are to be found in Kenny [1992], Appendix I.

[2] It has been suggested that a Book consisted of the amount of text which would fit onto a single roll of papyrus.

between Books VIII and IX, and the moral virtues are treated in Books II and IV and V). Within a single book, too, successive chapters often seem to hop from one topic to another almost without warning. To some extent this is the result of the editing, but it also reflects the nature of ethics as a subject, comprising as it does several issues which are loosely related to one another rather than tightly interlocking. Still, we should not exaggerate. Whether it is Aristotle's or that of a later editor, there is at least some structure, and an intelligible sequence of topics, along the following lines:

I   What do we aim at in life? What is it that would make living worthwhile? A worthwhile life must surely involve developing our specifically human characteristics to the full. How could we find out what those are? Upon reflection, we can see that what is most characteristically human about ourselves is the way in which thought colours all our lives – not just our intellectual pursuits, but also our feelings and emotions, our choices and relationships.

II   So we start by considering the ways in which thought influences those traits of character which contribute to living a worthwhile, fulfilled life. What are these traits? How do we come to possess them? And how do our characters in turn influence the choices which we make in life, and for which we are held responsible?

III   We need to think about choice and responsibility in more detail. Are we responsible for all our behaviour, and also for the character we have developed?

We can use the examples of individual virtues to illustrate these points. . . .

IV   Discussion of several more examples of virtue.
V   The virtue of justice (which is not quite like the others).
VI   Living a worthwhile life requires not only that we have a well-rounded and balanced character, but also that we have developed the intellectual skills needed to grasp which choices we need to make as we go along. What is it to have a good moral judgement?

VII　How can people responsibly make wrong choices? The connection between good and bad choices and virtues and vices. Pleasure as a possible source of temptation.

VIII　The preceding topics might give the impression that a worthwhile human life might be lived entirely on one's own. On the contrary humans are naturally inclined towards various kinds of friendship.

IX　More on friendship: its justification and its importance.

X　Pleasure again; for surely a worthwhile life must somehow be fulfilling and enjoyable? This leads on to a final discussion of the ingredients of fulfilled life, both for the individual, and for the individual as a member of a community.

So Aristotle's train of thought goes more or less like this: To live a fulfilled life, we need to be guided by emotions which are balanced, and by habits of thought which enable us to see what is and is not relevant to our decisions, and why. In developing these balanced emotions and discerning choices, we are presumably acting responsibly; so we need to know what we can properly be said to be responsible for. (Digression here, to elaborate on the various examples of balanced and unbalanced responses which can be fitted into the above scheme.) Now much of the foregoing depends on the notion of a discerning choice: so we need to discuss how such choices are made, and what kinds of knowledge they presuppose. Again, obviously enough, people are often held responsible for wrong choices. But how can someone knowingly do what they know they should not do? At this point, something of a leap: we have discussed the qualities of the good individual, but what of the individual's relationships to others? Why bother with such relationships, and how do they contribute to a fulfilled life for *me*? When we have answered those questions, we can try to sum up. Ethics has to say something about the fulfilled life, and about the kind of community in which persons leading such a life might hope to function best. Just a sketch of this last point here, since after the *Ethics* comes the *Politics*.

Aristotle's aim in writing the *Ethics*

Plato's most ambitious work on morality was his *Republic*. It included not simply discussions about how an individual should live, but, much more ambitiously, integrated that view into a comprehensive picture of the ideal state. Personal morality, good citizenship, and the best way to organize a state all fit together. Aristotle's aim in writing the *Ethics* and the *Politics* was no different. He hoped to provide an account of how the good person should live, and how society should be structured in order to make such lives possible. Aristotle did not believe that all that was needed for moral education was to give people a true understanding of what was good and noble and morally worthwhile. Understanding is not enough without motivation, which knowledge alone cannot provide. So Aristotle sets out to give an account of moral training as well as moral theory. A detailed discussion of all this can wait until later, in Chapter 4, but the following two texts will serve to give us a preliminary outline of what he is trying to do:

> It is well said, then, that it is by doing just acts that someone becomes just, and by doing temperate acts that they become temperate. Without doing these, no one would have any chance of becoming good. But most people do not perform these actions but take refuge in theory, thinking that they are being philosophers and will become good in this way. They behave a bit like patients who listen carefully to their doctors, but do none of the things they were told to do. As the latter will not be made well in body by such a method of treatment, the former will not be made well in soul by such an approach to philosophy.
>
> (II, 4, 1105b7–18)

> Our present inquiry (unlike our others) is not aimed at theoretical knowledge. We are not conducting our inquiry in order to know the definition of virtue, but in order to become good, otherwise it would not benefit us at all. So we must think about what concerns actions and how we ought to perform them. . . .
>
> (II, 2, 1103b26–31)

Aristotle's Preface (1): Why do we do anything at all?

Aristotle tells us that the first three chapters of the *Ethics* are by way of being a preface to the work as a whole (1095a12). In these chapters, he gives an outline of his approach, indicates the results which might be expected, and describes the kind of student for whom his lectures are designed.

Ethics and politics are concerned with what we should *do*. If we do something (as distinct from have something happen to us, or from a piece of purely reflex behaviour), we do it for a reason. So Aristotle starts off his introduction by making some general observations on the reasons we might give for doing anything. The observations are indeed very general; and that is because he wants to get back to the most basic assumptions involved in ethics. We commonly try to think out problems such as 'Should mother come and live with us, or would she be better where she is?', or 'Can we really blame him for what he did?' and so on. It is much more rarely that we ask 'What should I be doing with my life?', and even more rarely that we ask 'What is the best way to live?' Aristotle thinks that to deal with the more everyday problems, we have in the end to deal with the very general, but very fundamental issues. 'Why do anything at all?' is indeed a strange question; but it might provide a clue to what is needed in order to answer the others. So, he begins:

(1) Sometimes we *make* things (such as a statue, or a chair), and sometimes we simply *do* things (like walking, or discussing philosophy).

(2) Some of the things we do, we do for their own sake (listening to music, or keeping a promise, for instance).

(3) Sometimes, we do something, or make something, for the sake of something else that we want (we read a book in order to learn about Aristotle; we paint a picture in order to enjoy looking at it; we make CDs in order to earn a living).

(4) Sometimes we do things both for their own sake and because they are means to achieving something else as well. (We go for a walk because we enjoy walking, and in any case the exercise is good for our health.)

Reasons are hierarchically ordered: we read a book to learn about Aristotle; and we want to learn about Aristotle because we want to get a degree, perhaps; and we want to get a degree because . . . and so on. Now, most of the things that we do involve know-how. We need to learn how to read, and, indeed, how to read Aristotle; know-how is needed for making a ship, or a CD. These various bodies of knowledge are structured, just as our reasons for individual actions are. Practical sciences such as marine engineering or electronics are presupposed by the science of commerce (which needs ships) or the music industry (which needs CDs), and these in turn have their own aims. His point is that these second-level aims explain why the first-level aims are important to us. He then raises this question: is there some highest-level practical science to which all the others are subordinate? If there is, its end will be the highest of all ends, and to understand it would be to understand how everything else fits together, and why in the end we do anything at all.

His answer (in I, 2) is that there is indeed a plausible candidate for the position of highest-level practical science – politics. To see why he says this, we need to grasp two points. The first concerns the way in which Aristotle thinks of the science of politics. The word 'politics' does not have for him the somewhat ambiguous overtones it might have for us, where to be a politician might suggest being adept at wheeling and dealing, manipulating the levers of power, and so on. Nor does he mean what we might mean by 'political science', which is a *theoretical* study of how political institutions work and interact. Like Plato, Aristotle had a notion of politics which was at once more idealistic and more practical. The science of politics consists in knowing how to organize the community for the best.[3] 'Politics' is all-embracing, involving all the many ways in which we should interact with one another in a community. The people whose task it is to organize the community are the ones who in the end decide what is to be

---

[3] 'Community', since it is important to remember that at this period the political unit was a comparatively small city – a *polis* – and such empires as there had been in Greece were nevertheless thought of as alliances of individual cities, even if there were a dominant partner (as Athens had once been, and Macedon was to become.)

taught and to whom, how money is to be spent, what laws are to be enacted, what plays and festivals to be celebrated, which types of behaviour to be encouraged, and which not. Plato took it for granted, and Aristotle would not have disputed, that all these practical decisions have as their ultimate purpose the well-being of the citizens, as individuals and as a community. If we could understand how to achieve that goal, then, says Aristotle, we could see how each action of each individual might be good for that person and might also contribute to a flourishing community. Ethics and politics are alike concerned with what is most important to us; ethics looking at it from the point of view of the individual, and politics from the point of view of the community as a whole. The *Ethics*, then, will attempt to answer questions about what each of us should do by showing how the answers can be found; and answers can be found by considering what it is that is ultimately important to us.

Aristotle's Preface (2): Realistic expectations

Will the study of ethics tell us exactly what we should do in every situation in which we find ourselves? Certainly not, says Aristotle. Only someone who had no knowledge of the subject would expect that kind of detailed clarity.

> The discussion will be quite sufficient if it attains to as much clarity as the subject allows. Detailed accuracy is not to be looked for equally in all discussions any more than in the various things we can make.
>
> (I, 3, 1094b11–12)

In talking about what we should do, we must not expect the precision that we might expect in, say, mathematics, or in the physical sciences. Only the ill-informed would expect the same degree of rigour. Once again, Aristotle is here making an introductory remark, for which he will give his detailed reasons later (partly in Book II, and partly in Book VI). Now, it might not strike us as too surprising to say that ethics (or politics) is not an exact science in the way in which physics or astronomy are. We might be inclined to say that moral principles are very different from scientific laws. At least ideally, scientific laws have no exceptions, whereas moral principles, such as 'You should not tell a lie' surely have all kinds of exceptions. Someone might even wish to argue that, whereas the truths of physics should be accepted by anyone, different individuals or cultures need not accept the same ethical principles at all. Despite what he has just said about unreasonable expectations in ethics, Aristotle would nevertheless at this point urge caution until we see how the inquiry into ethics turns out. Ethics and politics are indeed different from physics. Aristotle admits that in contrast with the natural world 'noble and just actions, which are the subject matter of politics, differ and vary so much that it might appear as if they depend simply upon human convention rather than nature' (1094b14–16). So it might seem. But, as we shall see, Aristotle does not in fact endorse that conclusion. While ethics and politics may be inexact by comparison with the physical sciences, it does not follow that there are no natural limits to what should be regarded as morally or politically admirable, or that ethics cannot in any sense be regarded as a scientific discipline. We shall have to wait and see.

Aristotle's Preface (3): Suitable students

As we saw, Aristotle's aim in writing the *Ethics* is not just to teach people theory, it is to help people to become good. While in a way that seems fair enough (though perhaps the emphasis is not one which would always be found in moral philosophy lectures nowadays!), one might be forgiven for thinking that there is nevertheless something of a paradox here. If, by Aristotle's own account, attending a course on moral philosophy will not guarantee that the students will end up being morally good, then why should reading Aristotle's *Ethics* or listening to his lectures be any more effective? It's not enough for him simply to *say* that his aim is not just theoretical but practical. How is that supposed to work out?

Aristotle would take the point. No more than a contemporary lecturer in moral philosophy would Aristotle have thought it his business to provide the kind of good moral training one might look for from parents or schools. Such training has to start in early childhood, so that the young person acquires habits of good behaviour. Still, someone who has been well brought up will typically come to wonder *why* they have been trained to behave in this way rather than that. Indeed they might well question whether their upbringing has been along the right lines at all. Doubtless there were rebellious adolescents in Athens too. Rather than getting hold of them at once, however, Aristotle would have considered them as still too young to profit from his lectures. The rebellious adolescent simply does not as yet have enough experience of life and its complexities to be able to form mature moral judgements. So Aristotle considered as prerequisites for his course that people should have been well brought up, and, further, that they should already have had some experience of life and of the complex problems which life presents one with. He remarks that:

> While young men become geometricians and mathematicians and very adept at such subjects [we might include being marvellous at dealing with computers], it is commonly believed that a young man does not learn practical wisdom. ... A young man has no experience, for it is length of time that gives experience.
>
> (VI, 8, 1142a11–15)

Here is a forthright description of the kind of student he does *not* want:

> A young man is not a suitable person to take a course on how to run a city, for he is inexperienced in the affairs of life (which are the starting point and subject-matter of the course). Besides, since he tends to be led by his feelings, attending the course will be pointless and unprofitable, since the aim of the course is not knowledge but action. It makes no difference whether he is young in years, or immature in character. The problem is not a matter of time, but a life-style which pursues one kind of thing after another as feelings dictate. To people like this knowledge is no use, any more than it is to people who lack self-control. But for those whose desires and actions are directed in a well-ordered way, it would be very helpful to have knowledge about such topics.
>
> (I, 3, 1095a2–11)

What Aristotle is trying to do, then, is to give his students an explanation of why they should have been brought up as they were, and an account of how an adult is to go about making good decisions. He hopes that what he has to say will have the *practical* effect of crystallizing for them attitudes and ways of thinking which they have as yet not been able to explain or justify for themselves. His lectures were to provide the final stage of a process of moral education; or, to be more exact, they were to give the theoretical backing to a process of moral training which had already been largely completed. In so doing, he aimed to produce morally thoughtful adults who would be good people, and good members of the community.

In the chapters that follow, I shall not adhere strictly to Aristotle's order of exposition (if indeed it is Aristotle's). I shall try to explain the key parts of it first, and then fill in the surroundings later. I would suggest that a good plan to follow would be to read fairly quickly through the sections of the text which are dealt with in each chapter of this book, which are given at the start of each chapter: then read the chapter carefully, following up the references to the text as you go along.

Chapter 3

The fulfilled
life

Relevant texts:
Book I chs 1–8, and Book X, chs 6–9

Problems of interpretation
- Does Aristotle have one consistent account of *eudaimonia*?
- What is the relationship between *theōria* and the moral life?

Critical questions
- Does Aristotle offer a convincing basis for ethics?
- Is his Function Argument sharp enough to be useful?

What makes life worth living? What connection, if any, is there between living a fulfilled life and living as we should – as we *morally* should? These are the questions with which Aristotle starts his *Ethics*. His answers are

disconcertingly brief: what makes life worth living is *eudaimonia*; and to live a life which can be characterized by *eudaimonia* is precisely the aim of morality. At least straight off, this is neither helpful nor obviously true, for two reasons: first, it is not at all obvious what Aristotle means by *eudaimonia*: and secondly, if the answer to that question is something like 'self-fulfilment', might it not seem that Aristotle's morality is unduly self-regarding?

In Book I of the *Ethics*, Aristotle sketches out his approach to *eudaimonia*, and the basis on which he thinks his view rests; and in Book X he offers a more detailed account. It is this more detailed account that can seem either quite bizarre, or slightly strange, or reasonably obvious, depending on how one settles a few key issues of interpretation. In this chapter, then, we shall try to establish at least the main outlines of his view, and to assess the adequacy of the reasons he offers in support of it.

The meanings of *eudaimonia* and *aretē*

One of the first things we have to decide when trying to understand Aristotle is how to understand his technical terms, and hence how to translate what he says into English. Passages that seem to make no sense at all using one translation of the key words can often seem perfectly clear if one translates differently. Here, at the very outset, we need to consider carefully how to translate two words which turn out to be key terms in the *Ethics*. *Eudaimonia* is almost always translated 'happiness', but this translation can easily give a misleading impression. 'Happiness' in English suggests a feeling of one kind or another, perhaps a feeling of contentment, or delight, or pleasure. Aristotle makes it quite clear that he does not have any such feeling in mind at all. At X, 7, 1177a11 he says that *eudaimonia* is achieving one's full potential; and that surely is not simply a matter of feeling, even if to do so would be very satisfying. It is much more closely connected with what one has made of oneself and one's life. Again, at I, 4, 1095a19 he says that at least everyone agrees that happiness is somehow 'living well' or 'doing well'. In this spirit, I propose to translate the noun *eudaimonia* by 'a fulfilled life' or simply 'fulfilment', and the adjective *eudaimōn* as 'fulfilled'. Even this is not quite right, and there are at least some places in which 'living a worthwhile life' might come closer to the emphasis which Aristotle is looking for. One might, for instance, want to say that to lay down one's life for others or in order to defend one's country is supremely worthwhile: but it would be stretching things to describe that action as fulfilling. Still, a translation more or less along these lines is recommended by the fact that it makes more sense of many of Aristotle's questions and arguments, as I hope will become clear in the course of this chapter.[1]

The second word we need to look at is *aretē*. *Aretē* was used to refer to many different qualities. The skill of a craftsman is his *aretē*; being resonant and in tune is the *aretē* of a lyre because it makes it a good example of its kind. So *aretē* is sometimes translated rather vaguely as 'excellence'. Again, for someone to possess an *aretē* is for that person to be good at something, so that the word is often translated 'virtue', not always in a moral sense. We might say of a footballer that he has the virtue of being strong in the air, or of a car that it has the virtue of being cheap to run. To do something *kat' aretēn* ('in accordance with *aretē*'), then, is to do it in such a way that one's skill, or virtue, is expressed in the way it is done. Often the phrase simply means to do something well. In the *Ethics*, Aristotle speaks in particular of two kinds of *aretē*, distinguished by the fact that some belong to one's moral character (for example, courage, or generosity), and others to one's skill at thinking (such as being good at planning, or quick to grasp the point of something).

Different translators adopt different policies when coping with these complexities. Some will try, if it is at all possible, always to use the same English word for the same Greek word, even if it sounds a little strange on occasion, just so that the reader can easily tell which Greek word is involved. Others will use a range of words, depending on the context – 'happiness', or 'fulfilment' or even 'human

---

[1] One has to be careful when appealing to the etymology of Greek words. But, for what it is worth, *eudaimonia* is derived from two words, *eu*, which means 'well', and *daimōn*, a kind of guiding spirit (not necessarily malevolent like an English demon). If one is lucky enough to have one's life guided by a benign spirit, one does well, and is *eudaimōn*. One's *daimōn* might see to it that one is well-born, long-lived, not too afflicted by illness or misfortune, etc. Aristotle does not base his arguments on the existence of any such *daimōn*; but the notions of luck, success, and living well are certainly there in his overall approach.

flourishing' for *eudaimonia*; 'virtue'; 'excellence', 'skill', 'being good at' for *aretē*. I myself will adopt this second policy, but will point out the places where my choice may be especially controversial.

Fulfilled lives?

We have already seen that Aristotle proposes to start by asking why people do anything at all. Answering this question will, he hopes, lead to an ordered chain of 'Why?'-questions which finally ends up with asking, 'Why do we try to run cities as we do?' The answer to that top-level question is, 'To enable the citizens to live fulfilled lives'. There can be no higher end for the statesman to strive for, just as there can be no higher aim for the individual than to live a fulfilled life.

To pursue this inquiry, Aristotle starts, as he so often does, from the *endoxa* – the views held either by people in general or by other philosophers. What do people aim for in life? The answers given to this question in Aristotle's time were not so very different from the answers we might get if we were to ask the same question now. Everyone, he says, is agreed that what they want in life is personal fulfilment – *eudaimonia*. But there, he goes on to say, the agreement ends. When people are asked what *eudaimonia* consists in, some think it consists in pleasure, others in money, others in honours; and Plato thinks it is living in the light of one's knowledge of the Form of the Good. On the other hand, in contrast to all these single-item answers, others might well say that they aim at very many things, and that a fulfilled life cannot be reduced to just one dimension, so to speak.

The 'lives' which Aristotle considers briefly in I, 4 and I, 5 are in effect characterized by the different answers their proponents would give to the question, 'What is a fulfilled life?' The three ways of life mentioned in these chapters had already been discussed often enough by his predecessors, which perhaps explains why Aristotle can be so brief and dismissive here. At any rate, his reasons are as follows:

(1) Money-making can't be what ultimately makes a life fulfilled, since we want money only for the sake of what money can bring.

(2) Pleasures can't be what makes life fulfilling, since a life of pleasure seeking is fit only for brute beasts.

(3) Being well thought of can't be the ultimate explanation either: for people don't just want to be well thought of, they want to be well thought of *because they are good people.*

Aristotle thinks that money is the least plausible candidate for being the ultimate aim in life, since it simply is not valued for its own sake at all. In this respect it is different from pleasure and honours, which are.[2] The argument against pleasure apparently assumes that human fulfilment must be something which is simply unattainable by any animal. Moreover, Aristotle presumably has in mind purely physical pleasures, since he will argue much later on that a fulfilled life *is* also a pleasurable life, indeed the most pleasurable life. His fully explicit view is far from being as dismissive of the claims of pleasure as might be suggested by what he says here. In I, 8, 1099a29–31 he cites an inscription above the entrance to the Temple of Leto the mother of Apollo on the island of Delos:

> Noblest is what is most just, most to be prized is health,
> But sweetest of all is to win one's love.

Aristotle disagrees with the implied split between what is noble, what is best, and what is pleasant, and maintains (for reasons which we shall see later) that a virtuous life is at once the best, the most noble and the most enjoyable. But the pleasures of the fulfilled life are presumably different ones from the pleasures of the typical pleasure seeker. Aristotle must have in mind here something similar to John Stuart Mill's distinction between 'higher' and 'lower' pleasures, and, like Mill, must take it for granted that his audience would know which were which. Well, maybe it is easy enough to distinguish 'higher' from 'lower' pleasures if one takes carefully selected examples like the lager-lout or the beach-bum on the one hand, and, on the other, a woman who takes delight in her family and who has thoroughly enjoyed her career as a barrister. Other examples might not be so simply classified. What about a jockey turned horse-trainer who just loves working with horses? Is that a higher or lower pleasure?

---

[2] 1096a10–12. What about a miser who simply wants to have money just for the sake of counting it over and over? Maybe Aristotle doesn't quite believe such a person could exist, or maybe he thought that the miser wants money for the sense of achievement it gives him.

But perhaps Aristotle has a different kind of argument to distinguish the life of the pleasure seeker from the worthwhile life of the fulfilled person. The pleasure seeker makes an indiscriminate identification between pleasurable experiences and *eudaimonia*; but *eudaimonia* has to be an ultimate explanation of why one lives as one does. So, if asked why something is worth doing, the pleasure seeker's answer will have to be that anything whatever is worth doing provided only that it is enjoyable. Aristotle might wish to suggest, by way of contrast, that if the mother were asked why she had spent so much time and effort on her children and on her clients, she would *not* say that in the end she did it *because* she enjoyed it; she would say that she did it because she could think of nothing more worthwhile. (For the moment, we can leave it as an open question whether Aristotle would think this to be the best answer she could have given: it is enough that it is quite a different answer from the pleasure seeker's.) Enjoyment, even a 'higher' enjoyment, is not the *point*. A fulfilled life, then, is not just a set of actions; it is a set of actions performed by someone who does them because they correctly see the point of doing them.

The life spent in trying to be well thought of can be assessed in a similar way. Aristotle here does not even consider the person who does not care who thinks well of them nor why. He has in mind the person who wants to be well thought of by good people who see his good character. That fact, Aristotle thinks, shows that it is not so much being well thought of which the person values (though he does value that), it is his good character. So, is *eudaimonia* then just the possession of a good character? Surely not *just* that: one might have a good character and spend one's life in sleep, or in an irreversible coma. A fulfilled life must at least involve acting in such a way as to express the good character that one has. In I, 8 Aristotle returns to this view, and shows how it fits with what many people might have said in the first place. A fulfilled life will indeed be enjoyable, and well regarded by good people; but its point consists in the living of it, and doing so precisely because it is worthwhile.[3]

---

[3] In I, 6 Aristotle spends some time in a technical refutation of Plato's view that to explain a good life one needs to hold that there exists a Form of the Good. He argues that such a Form is of no help for ethics; more important are the

This is all very well, but it does not seem to get us very much closer to discovering how to live a fulfilled life. We simply do not know what a fulfilled life is. Indeed, the examples which Aristotle has just considered might suggest that it is a mistake to suppose that fulfilment can be just *one* thing, like pleasure, or reputation, or money. Indeed, is Aristotle not open to a more serious criticism, that his claim that we all have fulfilment as our ultimate aim is plausible only because 'fulfilment' is such a vague term? Because it is a singular term, it misleadingly suggests that there is some one thing which we all aim at. But surely a fulfilled life must be richer than that, more complex, more diversified? And won't fulfilment be different for each individual?

A central problem: 'Dominant' or 'Inclusive'?

For this reason, Aristotle's apparently straightforward proposal that we should ask what it is that we all ultimately aim at is the starting point for a major dispute about the interpretation of Books I and X of the *Ethics*. Which side of the dispute one takes tends to colour one's interpretation of many of the individual passages. A quick first look at the broad outlines of the dispute will help us to see why these passages are so contentious.

The convenient (if not entirely accurate) labels for the two positions are 'dominant' and 'inclusive'.[4] Those who maintain that Aristotle takes a dominant view about *eudaimonia* claim that in the end he believes that there is just *one* ultimate answer to the chain of 'Why do we do X?' questions. There is just one type of activity for the sake of which we do everything else, and which makes one's life worthwhile. By contrast, those who take the inclusive view maintain that there are in fact many answers, all equally ultimate; or, slightly differently, that the ultimate answer is a package of activities, rather than just one single kind of activity. Inclusivist interpreters maintain

various different ways in which goodness is involved in the things we can do. A more detailed discussion can be found in Hardie [1968], ch. IV.

[4] The terminology 'inclusive/exclusive' was introduced by W. F. R. Hardie [1968], ch. 2, p. 23. 'Dominant' is a refinement on 'exclusive'.

not merely that their interpretation better fits the texts, but that it is also a much more sensible view in itself. What reasonable person would ever think that there was ultimately just one supremely worthwhile activity, for the sake of which we did everything else? In their opinion, the dominant view attributes to Aristotle an opinion which is at best implausible, and at worst perhaps downright immoral. Supporters of the dominant view, therefore, have to argue not only that their interpretation better fits the text, but also that we need not attribute to Aristotle a view which is obviously untenable.

Nobody denies that in Aristotle's view we do everything for the sake of a fulfilled, worthwhile life, for which his term is *eudaimonia*. That answer is sufficiently vague to be acceptable to both sides. But the dispute is simply shifted to asking what Aristotle believes such a life consists in – just one activity, or many? A clue, it is sometimes said, is to be found in the way Aristotle uses the phrase 'for the sake of', and on this the differences of opinion start right at the beginning, over a passage in the Preface:

> If there is some point to everything we do, something we want for its own sake and which explains why we do everything else, then obviously this has to be *the* good, the best of all. And there has to be some such point, otherwise everything would be chosen for the sake of something else and we would have an infinite regress, with the result that it would be futile and pointless to want anything at all.
>
> (I, 2, 1094a18–22)

The problem is easy to see. Inclusivist interpreters at once ask why there has to be just *one* ultimate aim which explains everything else that we do? Surely we might want to go for a walk just for its own sake, we might want to learn philosophy just for the sake of it, and wish to have friends just because we value having them, without there being any one further thing for which ultimately we value all of these things? It does not sound very plausible to suggest that everything we do is done for the sake of improving our minds, or making money, or providing for our children, or any other single aim.

So J. L. Ackrill, who did much to popularize this inclusivist approach, argues that *eudaimonia* must consist in a package of worthwhile things and activities, each of which is desired for its own sake. To say that we value each of them 'for the sake of' *eudaimonia* is simply to say that we value each of them *as part of* the all-inclusive package.

Richard Kraut, who takes the other side, argues that when Aristotle speaks of doing X for the sake of Y, he always thinks of X as having a causal influence on Y. Thus, we can say that we make bridles for the sake of horsemanship, since a bridle causally affects the riding of horses, just as horse-riding has a causal effect on, say, winning a battle. Kraut maintains that Aristotle never says that we can do X simply for the sake of some package-deal consisting of $\{X + Y + Z + \ldots\}$ Yet something like that would have to be involved if the inclusivist interpretation was correct. Ackrill's view, says Kraut, involves the strange suggestion that *eudaimonia* might consist in an enormous collection of quite unrelated goods to which there is no overall coherence or rationale. Surely Aristotle could not have intended to say that human fulfilment could consist in anything so shapeless? He certainly would not have accepted that we mow the lawn for the sake of {mowing the lawn and having a cup of tea and watching TV} or any other such unstructured collection.[5]

There is a middle position between these two. When Aristotle says that we do X for the sake of Y, it need not be the case that X (directly or indirectly) *causes* Y; it is sufficient that Y *in some way explains* why we do X. Kraut is to that extent correct, but requires too much when he insists that the explanation be a causal one. It seems to me that Aristotle *would* at least sometimes allow us to say that we do X for the sake of Y when X is a constituent of Y; thus, we might have roast beef for the sake of having a nice meal, and we might have a nice meal for the sake of celebrating an anniversary. The roast beef is not the *cause* of the meal, it is part of the meal: and having the meal does not cause the celebration, it *is* the celebration. Yet our desire to celebrate does explain why we are having the meal. The explanation is tighter than it is in Ackrill's account.

So the passage we have just looked at leaves the inclusive *versus* dominant controversy unresolved either way, as yet. We shall see

[5] See Ackrill [1980], and Kraut[1989], pp. 200–25.

which interpretation better fits the arguments Aristotle uses once he starts the discussion proper. But first, a suggestion.

Perhaps we get such a variety of answers to the question 'What is a fulfilled life?' because the original question is too coarse-grained. There are several different questions which we would do well to separate in our minds:[6]

(1)   What activities does a fulfilled life contain?
(2)   Which of these activities explains why a life is a fulfilled life?
(3)   Which of the activities mentioned in (2) is the most worthwhile?

Obviously, an answer to (1) will mention all kinds of activities, including brushing one's teeth, going shopping, paying bills, catching trains and taking the dog for a walk, as well as what we might think of as 'higher' activities like spending time with one's friends, or enjoying the company of one's family, studying philosophy, or doing voluntary work in the local hospital. Not all of these activities will be sensible answers to (2). Suppose, for the sake of argument, we answer (2) by saying 'spending time with those who are closest to us, and raising money for Oxfam'. In that case, it might still be pertinent to ask (3), which of those do you find is most fulfilling?

Put in Aristotle's terms, fulfilment is the ultimate *telos* – the point – of our activities. Whatever we do is ultimately explained in terms of its contribution to living a fulfilled life. We brush our teeth or visit the doctor in order to safeguard our health, and we safeguard our health because we think it easier to live a fulfilled life if we are healthy than if we are not. And if something in the end makes no difference at all to whether we live a fulfilled life or not, we eventually find ourselves asking 'But what's the point of doing that?'

Activities like the ones I have just mentioned, such as brushing one's teeth, or visiting the doctor, are done as *means* to fulfilment. But 'The reason my life is fulfilled is that I brush my teeth every day' is hardly an appropriate answer to (2): at best it might be a piece of advertising hype for Denticleen. An appropriate answer to (2) will have to be an answer to the question, 'What does fulfilment consist in?' It consists, perhaps, in having good friends and in doing something to

[6] For a more elaborate version of these questions, see Heinaman [1988].

help others, or in something else along similar lines. Aristotle does not offer his own answer as yet. And if there are several answers to (2), we still need to ask whether any one of them is an answer to (3).

So, was Aristotle making an unwarranted assumption when he suggested that there might be one ultimate *telos* towards which all our actions are directed? Critics of the passage just quoted have not been slow to point out that even if there must be *some* ultimate answer to the question 'Why are you doing that?' it certainly does not follow that it must always be the *same* answer. But the ultimate *telos*, for Aristotle, is supposed to be the one explanation for *everything* we do. How does he know that there is just one such *telos*?

The first thing to be said is that at several places in Book I he explicitly leaves it as an open question whether or not there is just one ultimate aim of all our activities. He at least does not start off with the assumption that there is only one answer. He would also accept that if, when someone was asked 'Why are you brushing your teeth?', they were to reply 'Because I want to have a fulfilled life', the reply would indeed seem strange. But he might still argue that the more obvious answers ('to keep them clean', 'to be more comfortable', 'to keep them healthy') could in turn be questioned, and that in the end the person *would* have to say 'But that's what life is ultimately all about, that's what a worthwhile, fulfilled life is like'. So there is in the end just one final explanation, even if it is not the explanation we would start off by giving. Whatever the problem with the passage we have just considered, then, it is not that Aristotle has made some elementary blunder without noticing.

Two further agreed characteristics of *eudaimonia*

At the beginning of I, 7 Aristotle admits that the discussion of these various ways of life was a digression. It does serve, though, to make the point that disagreements about what a fulfilled life amounts to take place within a general agreement that it is a fulfilled life that everyone is aiming for. Aristotle gets back to this area of agreement by pointing out two further features of the fulfilled life which everyone is agreed about: it is *the most complete* end, and it is *sufficient of itself*. By the first, he means that it alone is sought after for its own sake and not for the sake of anything else as well. We don't need, and could not in any case find, any further explanation of why we should wish for a fulfilled life. He then says, in a remark which is important for a correct understanding of this much-controverted chapter, that the same conclusion follows if we consider why we think of a fulfilled life as sufficient of itself. For by that is meant that, if one is fulfilled, then there is nothing more required, and hence no further end which needs to be pursued.

Why do I say that this last remark is so important? Because the point about self-sufficiency has been interpreted quite differently, as part of the inclusive/dominant controversy already mentioned. The key passage reads as follows:

> We define 'sufficient of itself' as that which, taken by itself, makes life worth living, and lacking in nothing. This is what we take *eudaimonia* – fulfilment – to be like. Moreover, we think that fulfilment is what is most worth having, rather than counting it as one good thing among others. Fulfilment, counted as one good thing among others, would be still more worth having if even the least of the others were added to it. For what is added on produces a larger total of good things, and of good things the more the better, always.

(I, 7, 1097b14–20)[7]

Inclusivists ask why Aristotle should say that nothing can be added to *eudaimonia*; and their answer is that nothing can be added to it since it already contains all the other goods. *Eudaimonia* is simply the name we give to the total package. There seem to me to be several reasons why this interpretation will not do. The most important is that his earlier point, that *eudaimonia* is complete, is explicitly put on the same level as what he says here about its being sufficient of itself. Now, in his treatment of 'completeness' Aristotle says nothing about what fulfilment *consists in*; the point is about its status as an end. If the parallel with completeness is to hold, then to say that fulfilment is

[7] No translation can be at once unambiguous and completely uncontroversial, since the precise relationship of each phrase to the others is not totally clear in the Greek. Compare my version here with others you may have available.

not one good thing among others is likewise a remark about its status, rather than about what it consists in. If you are already living a truly fulfilled life, then winning the lottery, or receiving a knighthood, or going on a Caribbean cruise cannot make it any *more* fulfilled.[8] If any of these things improved your life, that would show only that it could not previously have been a truly fulfilled life. So in the passage we are considering, Aristotle did not take himself to be saying anything controversial at all, so far. He was making a perfectly simple point, and that point has nothing to do with what fulfilment does or does not include. It is that a fulfilled life, by definition, is not sought for the sake of anything further – what else could be *its* point? – and it can't be improved upon. That is why Aristotle immediately goes on to say that so far we seem to have laboured an obvious truth about how we use the term 'fulfilled', and it is time to begin to ask what fulfilment consists in. *Now*, and not before, we reach the point where agreement ends, and argument is required.

Background: Aristotle's views on the human soul

To understand Aristotle's answer, we need to know at least the outlines of how Aristotle understands what it is to be a human being.

Plato identified the self with the soul; and he thought of the soul as an immaterial being which pre-existed its association with this particular body, and would survive bodily death. Accordingly, since it is one's self which is ultimately valuable, Platonic ethics required that one should care for one's soul, and that the body should be treated in such a way as not to impede the proper activities of the soul.[9] In his earlier works, Plato identified the soul with reason. He later modified this narrower view, since he came to believe that desires and emotions could be at odds with one's reason (for example, in cases of personal moral struggle), and that such conflicts took place within the soul. Nevertheless, he continued to take it as obvious that it is the pursuit

[8] The examples are chosen to reflect the aims of money, honour and pleasure which he has already discussed.

[9] A passage typical of Plato's middle period is to be found in his *Phaedo* 64c ff.

of true knowledge by the use of reason which is the highest of human aims.[10]

Aristotle's views on the soul are in some respects not unlike Plato's, but in others they are markedly different. His starting point is to be found in his interest in biology. There is a crucial difference between organisms, which are alive, and other things, which are not. Aristotle's general word for what accounts for this difference is *psychē*, soul. Unlike Plato, he is thus quite prepared to talk of all plants and animals as having souls. The feature which characterizes all organisms is just what our word for them suggests – they are internally *organized*; they have an inbuilt natural aim. He does not mean by this that a geranium or even a lion cub consciously sets out to achieve an aim in life, any more than a contemporary biologist, when suggesting that every gene has as its aim to reproduce itself as widely as possible, would intend to attribute to it any kind of conscious striving. Talk about the aim, or *telos*, is rather a way of explaining how it is that the organism typically behaves. Its organizational purposiveness governs all its activities. That is why an organism is radically different from mountains, or atoms, or any other inanimate object.

An individual organism, say, a tree or an animal, is a single thing; but Aristotle held that we have to look at several different aspects of it in order to explain fully what it is and how it works. Thus, we can say what it is made of, and how there is a steady flow of material from the environment into the organism and back to the environment. What an organism is made of will explain how heavy it is, what it can feed upon, and so on. This Aristotle would term a *material* explanation. We need quite a different kind of explanation to account for how it is organized. Plants and animals might all consist of more or less the same things (water, DNA, fat, etc.), but they are put together in very different ways, and they retain this specific structure, this precise type of organization, throughout their lives. Oaks are

---

[10] His later view is to be found in brief in *Republic*, IV, 441–45. Plato later, in IX, 580d–583a discusses three ways of living corresponding to the three parts of the soul, which are not dissimilar to the three 'lives' which we have just met in Aristotle.

constructed differently from geraniums, and differently again from fish or dogs or humans. This self-perpetuating organizational structure goes hand-in-hand with the different ways in which each organism typically functions. An explanation of this type Aristotle calls a *'formal explanation'*. The formal explanation of an organism just is its *psychē*, its soul. A soul is the way the body of an organism is purposively structured.[11] It is not, as Plato thought, a separate thing which inhabits a body. My true self is not a Platonic soul, but is rather this living body, with all its capabilities.[12]

Souls, then, are of different kinds, each of which can be defined in terms of the capabilities which correspond to the different ways in which the bodies of different organisms are organized. All organisms can grow and reproduce: animals can sense, and move and have emotions; humans can do all these, and in addition can think, plan, and choose. To say that plants, animals and humans have different types of soul is simply to say that their respective bodies are so organized as to have very different capabilities. Aristotle then makes the crucial move: the well-being of any organism consists in the integrated exercise of these capabilities. That is its *telos*.

Since Aristotle relates the *telos*, the aim we have in life, to ethics, he must therefore be suggesting that ethics is based on the capabilities of the human soul. We cannot simply decide what we shall count as fulfilment; our nature determines what fulfilment for us must be like. How does he make good this claim?

---

[11] Aristotle speaks of four types of explanation. The general word for 'explanation' here is *aitia*; and the four are 'matter' (*hylē*), 'form' (*eidos* or *morphē*), 'purpose' (*telos*), and 'origin of movement'. In the case of organisms, *eidos* and *telos* coincide.

[12] I have given here only the bare outlines of Aristotle's account. His full-length treatise *On the Soul* (usually referred to by its Latin title *De Anima*) was probably written after the *Ethics*. It may allow that souls can be separated from bodies in a sense which goes beyond what I have suggested here. In any event, as Aristotle himself says, the more technical details of the discussion need not concern us here. (See I, 13, 1102a16–25.)

The Function Argument

The central feature of I, 7 is what has come to be called the 'Function Argument'. Aristotle here outlines the general method for discovering what fulfilment consists in. The argument is based on his metaphysical view of the soul, and proceeds along the lines we have just seen. He thus takes himself to be providing an independently established foundation upon which ethics (and politics) can be based. He hopes in this way to provide a criterion for assessing our generally held beliefs about ethics, some of which will (as in the case of the examples he has already briefly discussed) turn out to be false. More importantly, he hopes that he will also explain *why* many of our generally held moral beliefs are in fact well-founded.

We might discover what fulfilment consists in if we can grasp what is the function of a human being.[13] To inquire about the function of something – for instance, a dialysis machine – is to inquire about what it is supposed to do, what its purpose is. In the case of things like machines, or doctors or musicians, what they are supposed to do is decided by those who designed them, or employ them for a purpose. We use dialysis machines to purify the blood of people suffering from kidney failure; we employ musicians to make music. In the case of organisms, how they are supposed to function is determined by their internal purposive organization. Of course, we may use a geranium to cheer up the living-room; but the function – the *ergon* – of the geranium itself is not to be decorative, but to produce leaves and flowers and seeds; that is what it is naturally organized to do. Things in general can work properly, or not: dialysis machines can purify blood completely, or only partially, or not at all; musicians can play out of tune or without rhythm; geraniums can wilt or fail to flower.

Humans are organisms, and hence they too will have an inbuilt function (*ergon*) and an inbuilt goal (*telos*) which is achieved when they function properly. Humans will live fulfilled lives if they func-

---

[13] The word for 'function' is *ergon*. The ordinary meanings of *ergon* are 'deed', 'job' or 'work'. Here, Aristotle uses it to mean 'how something is supposed to work'.

tion properly. To function properly is to exercise the capacities to be found in the human soul, and to exercise them well.[14] Understanding what these capacities are is the first step to understanding what a fulfilled life for humans must be like.

Aristotle makes an important further step, though. The *ergon* of a human being must involve not merely the good exercise of those capacities which we humans have; he says that it must consist in the exercise of those capacities which are specifically human, the ones which we *don't* share with animals. These capacities belong to our reason (not forgetting the fact that our reason can influence our emotions – for our emotions can be reasonable or unreasonable). The Function Argument claims that human fulfilment consists in performing well those activities of which our soul renders us capable: and, if there is more than one of these, then it will consist in performing well that activity which is the best, that is, the most characteristic of the human *telos*.[15]

Aristotle, so far, has merely sketched out the basis on which he might be able to define human fulfilment precisely. He has not spelt out in detail the conclusions to which following that method will lead. Already, though, there are problems enough with what he says. Here are some of them:

(1) Is it true to say that human beings have an *ergon*?
(2) Even if they do, would such activity have anything to do with living a fulfilled life?
(3) Could fulfilment, so defined, be a proper basis for ethics?

Let us consider these in turn.

---

[14] Aristotle's phrase which I have translated 'well' or 'properly' is *kat' aretēn*.

[15] What I have said is intended to give the gist of I, 7, 1098a16–18, rather than to translate it exactly. An exact translation would be 'The human good consists in the activity of soul in accordance with excellence (or 'virtue', *kat' aretēn*: see the preceding note); and if there are several excellences, then in accordance with the one which is best and closest to the human goal (*telos*).' Aristotle speaks of several excellences, where my paraphrase speaks of several activities each properly performed.

The characteristic activity of humans

An initial reaction to Aristotle's question, 'Can it be the case that everything else has a characteristic activity, and humans have none?' (1097b28–33), might be to say that if he means to ask whether there are any human activities which other organisms cannot perform, then the answer is that there seem to be many characteristically human activities: thinking, playing chess, giving to charity, embezzling money, lying, breaking promises, conducting genetic research. A very mixed bag, one might think. One might, conversely, suggest that acting bravely, caring for one's children, remaining faithful to one spouse, and maybe even thinking are activities which it appears that at least some other animals can perform, and are therefore *not* characteristically human on Aristotle's definition.[16] At the very least, then, his view of what is characteristically human is extremely inexact.

Aristotle, in reply to this, would start by flatly denying that animals can think. The behaviour of non-human animals is instinctive rather than thoughtful, and so is quite different from the actions performed by humans, even if we might use the same words in speaking of both. In so saying, he would be drawing a much sharper distinction than would seem plausible to us nowadays. But even if we (to some extent under the influence of evolutionary theory, of which of course Aristotle knew nothing) would see animal and human behaviour as lying on a continuous spectrum from the less to the more complex, perhaps Aristotle's point is not wholly invalidated. There might still be some activities which, while they have their animal counterparts, are much more complex when performed by humans, as well as some activities which only humans perform. Humans can normally envisage all kinds of alternatives to what they do, and all kinds of subtle variations in how they do what they do. So much of human life involves adaptation and learning to control the environment to make a wider range of choice available. Perhaps Aristotle might settle for that. What he would insist upon is that how humans should function is dependent on their natural characteristics.

[16] A useful and entertaining counter to oversimplification here is Mary Midgley [1980], where many of the continuities between humans and other animals are spelt out, and the connection with ethics discussed.

It is also worth noting that Aristotle's Function Argument depends on characteristics which all humans share. Not merely does it not differentiate between, say, sportsmen and writers, soldiers and doctors, artists and farmers. It does not even differentiate between men and women. This last point is particularly worrisome, since Aristotle's views on women might suggest that they in fact cannot achieve a fulfilled life as Aristotle defines that life – and this is true either on the dominant or the inclusive interpretation. And, more generally, even if it were true that the fulfilled life must be basically, or essentially, similar for all humans, one would surely expect that the wide differences in temperament and natural endowments would have as a consequence that a life which was fulfilling for one person might be considerably different from what would be worthwhile for someone else. I suppose that Aristotle would be willing to admit that his argument allows for considerable individual variations. He might also be forced to admit that he had simply underestimated the capacities which some people possess.

As for my somewhat mischievous inclusion in the list of characteristically human activities such items as embezzlement, or lying, Aristotle's answer is clear enough. He would not deny that these are characteristically human activities; but he would insist that a fulfilled life requires us to exercise our rational capacities *well*. To engage in embezzlement or lying is not to use our human capacities well. But if that's what he would say, clearly further problems arise about what he now means by 'well'. Can't fraud and deception be extremely clever, well planned, and intelligent? More on this in the next section but one.

The characteristically human and the fulfilled life

Is it not strange that, having on biological grounds started from a very all-inclusive account of the capabilities of humans, Aristotle seems prepared to say that only some of these activities are central to human fulfilment? If we are highly complex animals, should not the whole range of capabilities in terms of which the human *psychē* is defined be involved in a fulfilled life?

This is just the argument that the Inclusivists would make. Indeed, they would urge us to reread the Function Argument in order to find in Aristotle's text just such a broad account of a fulfilled life. My version of the last phrase of the Function Argument was: 'performing well that activity which is the best, that is, the most characteristic of the human *telos*'. This, the Inclusivists would argue, is a most misleading rendering. Instead, I should have said something like 'according to the best and *the most perfect virtue*';[17] and 'most perfect', Inclusivists will argue, is here to be taken to mean 'including all the virtues'. (Think of the way in which we might talk of a really good person, meaning not that they had just one virtue, but that they had them all.) In this way, Inclusivists relate this remark back to the discussion of self-sufficiency, where (on their reading of it) fulfilment is not one good among others, because it already includes them all.

It seems to me very difficult to find this meaning in the texts.[18] But if Aristotle does mean what I think he means and concentrates on just one activity, then is this not a strange position for him to hold, given his efforts to base ethics on biology? Are we to suppose that such activities as eating, or having sex, or enjoying music, or just relaxing, simply don't count when we are deciding what a fulfilled life is? Even J. S. Mill never argued that 'lower' pleasures had *no* place in a utilitarian calculation; they just did not count for as much as the 'higher' pleasures.

I think Aristotle might have replied to this that he would never wish to deny that a fulfilled life contains many activities, some of them very mundane, some of them pleasurable in themselves, some of them worth doing for their own sake (though not only for their own sake), and so on. Given our biology, it will doubtless be the case that we should try to keep our bodies in good working order by providing food and warmth and medicines. We will also need to develop our

[17] The trouble lies with just one Greek word, *teleiotatēn*. This is the adjective related to the noun *telos*, an aim, or end; it can mean 'most perfect', 'most complete', or, as I have (somewhat evasively) translated, 'most closely related to the end'.

[18] Notice, for example, the repetition of the conclusion of the Function Argument at I, 8, 1099a29–31, where it is hard to avoid the conclusion that he is talking about a single activity well performed.

emotional lives so that our emotional reactions to life are balanced and appropriate. What he would emphasize is that merely to say this does not answer the different question: 'Which of these activities explains why our life is a fulfilled life, if it is?' If there is more than one answer to this question (and he still just about keeps his options open on this), then we need to know which is the most important answer. At least it is surely clear that we do not live fulfilled lives *because* we are well fed, or warm, or in good health, or *because* we have children, helpful as all of these might be.[19] A study of our human nature should make it clear that, unlike other animals which do well by acting on instinct, human fulfilment must essentially consist in *intelligent* action, to which our other capabilities contribute, either by providing the necessary conditions (such as food, a healthy body, etc.) or by themselves being involved in intelligent actions.[20] He will later go on to explain how it is that our emotions are involved in a particularly intimate way, and what qualities of mind are required if mind-directed actions are to be performed well.

The fulfilled life and the morally admirable

Quite apart from doubts one might have about the stress on reason in Aristotle's account of human fulfilment, there are questions to be raised about his method, and in particular about the way he derives conclusions about ethics from facts about human nature. The first is a very broad question, whether moral conclusions can ever be derived from any purely factual information. Even if Aristotle is correct in his view of human nature and in supposing that a humanly fulfilled life involves acting well according to our natural capacities, does that prove anything about what is *morally* worthwhile? To put it really crudely, is ethics just applied biology? G. E. Moore makes just this criticism of Aristotle: 'His treatment of Ethics is indeed, in the most important points, highly unsystematic and confused, owing to his attempt to base

[19] He discusses the prerequisites for a fulfilled life in I, 8.

[20] There is a similar line of thought in Kant's *Groundwork of the Metaphysic of Morals*, ch. 1, §§395–96.

41

it on the naturalistic fallacy.'[21] The naturalistic fallacy, in Moore's view, is the mistaken attempt to define something in terms of something else. In this case, it would be the attempt to define what is morally worthwhile in terms of biology or psychology. He would have thought that to reduce ethics to something else in this way would be to lose that indefinable quality which is moral value.

Moore thought there was an easy way to see whether someone's argument involved this kind of mistake or not. Contrast these two questions:

> Is a bachelor unmarried?
> Is it morally good to exercise some natural capability?

Moore would have said that the first question cannot be taken seriously – isn't, in his terms, a genuinely open question at all. That is because 'bachelor' is correctly defined in terms of being unmarried. But the second question surely is an open question, to which the answer is not at all obvious. That fact, Moore argues, shows that moral value cannot be defined in terms of our natural capacities. So Aristotle's entire procedure is a crude mistake.

The mistake is Moore's, however. There are plenty of questions to which the answer is not altogether obvious. For example: Is a circle the largest area that can be enclosed by a line of a given length?

Despite the answer to this question not being altogether obvious, it is nevertheless true that a circle could be defined in just that way. So the 'Open Question' argument proves too much. It is still perfectly possible for Aristotle to say that, even if it is not *obvious* that what is morally valuable depends upon our natural capabilities, it is still true that it does.[22]

---

[21] G. E. Moore [1903], p. 176. Moore is far from clear about precisely what the alleged fallacy consists in: see the following note.

[22] Moore sometimes insists (reasonably enough) that the *sense* of any moral term is irreducible to the sense of any non-moral term: but at other times his (highly contentious) counter-claim is that no moral property can be identical to any non-moral property. He probably confused these two positions. That two expressions have different senses does nothing to show that they do not refer to the same thing. The phrase 'The Morning Star' does not have the same sense as the phrase 'The Evening Star', but both of them refer to the same heavenly body, the planet

So, how might Aristotle respond to Moore? Does the phrase 'a fulfilled life' have the same *sense* as 'a life consisting of acting well according to our natural human capacities'? Aristotle would have agreed with Moore that it does not. After all, those who think that a fulfilled life consists in a life spent in the pursuit of pleasure, while mistaken, are not misusing words, or contradicting themselves as they would be if they thought that bachelors could be married. But there is another very different question. Is living a fulfilled life identical with acting well according to our natural human capacities? Aristotle would have said that is exactly what a fulfilled life consists in. His reasons would be (1) that it would be strange if a fulfilled, and therefore morally worthwhile, life had nothing to do with the kind of beings that we are; and (2) that once one sees what is involved in exercising our human capacities well, we can come to see that it is reasonable to identify this with human fulfilment and with what is morally worthwhile, since it explains so much of what people actually believe about ethics. The theory fits the facts, and we have independent grounds based on biology for believing the theory, even if it is not immediately obvious.

Fair enough, I think, but only as a first step. Let us think again about my embezzlement example, and ask what exactly Aristotle means by 'exercising our characteristically human capacities *well*'. Would an extremely skilful, emotionally calm, wonderfully calculating thief not be exercising characteristically human capacities very well indeed? Now of course Aristotle's students (remember, they have all been well brought up) would be scathing about such a suggestion. Aristotle could safely assume that they would never have supposed that the thief's activities were 'performed in accordance with *aretē*' – in accordance with virtue, or excellently.[23] But it is one thing for Aristotle to hope that his Function Argument would broadly lead to conclusions which his audience would generally find reasonable; it is

Venus. For a good account and effective rebuttal of Moore's arguments, see W. K. Frankena [1939].

[23] Sarah Broadie rightly points out that throughout the discussion so far, Aristotle could count on a shared background education in his students. See Broadie [1991] ch. 7 at several points.

quite another to show that the argument is not equally compatible with conclusions which would seem morally outrageous, as in the case of the embezzler or the thief.

Ideally, Aristotle would hope that his Function Argument, appealing to undeniable facts about human nature, would provide an uncontroversial basis for ethics, and hence would also provide an objective standard against which our pre-philosophical moral beliefs could be assessed. He would be quite prepared in the light of the theory as a whole to ask us to believe that some of our moral beliefs were simply mistaken; but he would quite accept that if some theory were to suggest that most of the moral beliefs, or some absolutely central moral beliefs held by both the ordinary person and by the wise, were in fact mistaken, it would be reasonable to reply by saying 'so much the worse for that theory!'. Ideally, then, we can discover a theory of ethics which seems to us reasonable in itself, which explains why we are justified in at least most of the moral beliefs we hold, and perhaps also might explain how we could have come to be mistaken about others.

So, is the highly intelligent and emotionally balanced and wonderfully calculating thief exercising his human capacities well, or not? The question turns out to be ambiguous. If we ask what it is for a human being to function well, the answer will be quite clear if we consider our purely biological functions. No *moral* assumptions need be smuggled into the argument in order to show that pneumonia is a disease, or sterility a malfunction. Even at this level, though, not every-thing is uncontroversial. Is homosexual orientation a malfunction or just a variation? In the field of mental health and emotional balance, things are still less clear-cut. Are the highs and lows which go with what is sometimes called an 'artistic temperament' somehow unbal-anced? Is a dislike of members of another race an emotional malfunction? The reason for this uncertainty is surely that humans are doubly complex. Our genetic programming is complex and can issue in wide varieties of capabilities: and in addition, as Aristotle himself recognizes, our emotional responses are in large measure learnt, and can be learnt in various different ways. Human beings are at this level malleable as well as being variously genetically programmed. The same goes for the exercise of our minds. We can turn them to all kinds of activities, from crossword puzzles to theft, from football to philosophy, and a multitude of things in between. Could we not *learn* to be fulfilled by a life devoted to any of a wide variety of ends – being a concert pianist, a successful con artist, a champion weight-lifter, or a social worker or a philosopher? Is there any morally neutral way of showing that any one of these lives is 'lower' or 'higher' than another, given that all of them require careful thought and planning? What exactly is written into the notion of a human being functioning well, and why? To answer this question, we need to see how Aristotle proposes to treat the virtues, and to ask how he knows which ways of acting are virtuous and which not. We shall discuss these issues in the next chapter.

Meanwhile, though, it is important to note that, even in Aristotle's own view, the Function Argument leaves the question of the fulfilled life, if not wide open, at least answered only in broad outline (I, 7, 1098a20–24). In particular, it has not conclusively settled the debate between the inclusive and the dominant view of what it is that explains why a life is fulfilled, even if it has given some strong hints that there will turn out to be just one most worthwhile end.

Theōria and being a good citizen

It is in Book X, chapters 7 and 8, that Aristotle finally draws the conclusions to which he believes the Function Argument leads. The trouble is that once again he at least seems to give two very different answers, and commentators have been much exercised in trying to give a coherent interpretation. X, 7 seems to say that human fulfilment consists in the exercise of our highest and most distinctively human capacity, our capacity for rational thought. On the other hand, X, 8 seems to envisage a very different view, that human fulfilment consists in the many-faceted activities which go into the life of a good public-spirited citizen. Since the first of these two interpretations is in line with the 'dominant' interpretation of I, 7, while the second, involving as it does a large variety of virtuous activities, is one version of the 'inclusive' interpretation, these two chapters reopen the controversy, this time in an acute form.

First, we need to understand *theōria*, which is introduced as the exercise of our highest human capacity.[24] *Theōria*, Aristotle says, is the activity which is most characteristic of the gods, or of God. It consists in the intellectual grasp of the most noble objects: and these, in the best Platonic tradition, are those which are changeless and perfect. Precisely what Aristotle intends to include is not clear: certainly, scientific knowledge of God's own nature and of the natures of the heavenly bodies; an understanding of the first principles of metaphysics and of what follows from these. All these are unchanging – whether the unchangeable reality of the Prime Mover, or the unchanging truths of metaphysics. Less certainly, he may intend also to include in *theōria* the unchanging principles of physics and mathematics (VI, 7, 1141a16–20, 1141b2–8). Vaguely, but uncontroversially, *theōria* is the active consideration of the ultimate explanation of everything that there is; seeing how it all fits together, and ultimately grasping why the cosmos is the way it is.[25]

The conclusion of the Function Argument was that human fulfilment consists in the exercise of that capacity which distinguishes humans from other animals – our minds. And if there is more than one way of using our minds well, then fulfilment consists in the best way of using our minds well. As we shall see in the following chapters of this book, Aristotle distinguishes between two broad ranges of topic to which we can turn our minds: theoretical issues, and practical issues. Most of the Books which follow are devoted to exploring how we are to think well about what we should do – just the practical conclusion one would expect if ethics is to be the first step towards politics.

---

[24] In what follows, I am much indebted to Sarah Broadie [1991], ch. 7, especially pp. 398–433. Her account seems to me to be the most rounded and balanced interpretation of the many difficult texts, even if (as always!) not everyone would accept it in every detail. See also Kenny [1992], ch. 8, for an account with a very different emphasis.

[25] Aristotle says that it is not the *seeking* of such an understanding, but the active consideration of the understanding that one has achieved (1177a27). I prefer 'active consideration' to the common translation 'contemplation', which, as Sarah Broadie says [1991], p. 401, has the unfortunate connotations of a 'locked gaze'.

It therefore comes as something of a rude shock when Aristotle, at the start of X, 7 gives a brisk recapitulation of the Function Argument, and concludes that the best use of our minds is *theōria*. He has already said that *theōria* is 'useless' (1141b7), and he repeats that remark here. *Theōria* has no practical value (1177b1–4).

In X, 7, Aristotle, nothing daunted, proceeds to justify this surprising conclusion by arguing that this theoretical use of our minds is the exercise of what is most divine in us. Why most divine? Because Aristotle's picture of God is of a being which is pure Thought (X, 8 1178b21–22, and see *Metaphysics* XII, 9). Part of the justification of this astonishing position consists in the almost Platonic assertion that each of us just *is* our mind. To add to the puzzlement, Aristotle makes these remarks just after he has pointed out that a life devoted entirely to *theōria* would be the life of a God, too high for humans (1177b26–29). That's exactly what one would have expected him to say, since on his usual view humans are *thinking bodies*, rather than disembodied minds, or even embodied minds. Trying to live a life like that of God would surely not be at all appropriate for us. Yet that, Aristotle clearly states, is just what we should endeavour to do 'as far as is possible'. Is that last phrase intended to put strict limits on the godlike life, or not? If Aristotle is serious, and really means that the most fulfilled and fulfilling life for humans is to engage in scientific thought to the greatest possible extent, then surely his view is very strange. Even in Athens in his day, such a life would have been a realistic possibility only for very few even of those who were full citizens. Can one really hold up as an ideal of human living a way of life which only a small elite minority have any chance of achieving? And in any case, deeply satisfying as the life of a totally single-minded theoretical physicist, or a theologian, or a mathematician might be, is it credible – and especially is it credible given Aristotle's views of the soul – to suggest that such a one-sided life is the ideal?

On the other hand, in X, 8 he begins by talking about 'a life lived in accordance with the other *aretē*'. I think this last phrase must refer to *phronēsis* (practical wisdom), the highest skill or virtue of the mind when we turn to thinking about practical matters. Of this kind of life, Aristotle says that it is fulfilled in a second kind of way.[26] He points out, as well he might, that to conduct one's practical living well is just what one might hope a 'composite being' (what I have termed a 'thinking body') would do (1178a20), and precisely not the kind of thing one would expect God to be bothered with (1178b7–22). X, 9 continues in similar vein, showing how ethics leads into politics, and commending the serious study of various constitutions as a preliminary to seeing how best one should run a city. This view would, I suppose, be much more acceptable to our way of thinking than the one which emphasized *theōria* in such an exaggerated way.

How are these two very different versions of what makes for a fulfilled life to be reconciled? Does Aristotle think the fulfilled human being is one who spends as much time as possible in considering the wonders of theology and philosophy, leaving the ivory tower only because, like anyone else, they have a need for companions and to earn a living? At its worst, could one conclude from his argument that one should take all possible means, moral or immoral, to ensure that one has as much time for *theōria* as possible? (It has recently been said that this is more or less what Einstein did, treating his wife and other members of his family disgracefully in the process!) Or is his ideally fulfilled human being someone who not merely lives a morally admirable life, but contributes to running a city in such a way that a morally admirable life is fostered in all the citizens?

Maybe a complete harmonization of everything that Aristotle says is not possible. But any acceptable interpretation must surely come to terms with the fact that the emphasis of the *Ethics* falls upon the many, often complex, issues with which any adult will be faced when living in a community with others: issues of responsibility, praise and blame: of justice, educational policy, practical decision making, the conduct of our friendships and other relationships. The treatment of *theōria* occupies just one chapter, together with some passing references elsewhere. It seems to me difficult to reconcile these facts with the interpretation which has Aristotle urging us to spend as much time

---

[26] Some translations give the impression that such a life could be said to be fulfilled only in a second-class way. Aristotle's Greek can, but just possibly need not, bear this interpretation.

as possible in considering the truths of physics, metaphysics and theology.

I offer just one rather simple suggestion, which does not solve all the problems of the text, but might point in the right direction. In X, 9, from 1181a12 to the end, Aristotle criticizes teachers of politics who rely entirely on experience with no theoretical background; and the *Ethics* concludes by advocating the study of various political systems as a preliminary to deciding which is the best. This study is, I think, to be understood as a *theoretical* study, which can then be the basis for practical judgements about what should be done. The principles of politics are known by theoretical reason, while the application of those principles requires practical wisdom. Politics as a science requires both experience and theoretical backing.

As with politics, so too with individual ethics. We have already seen that Aristotle's *Ethics* depends on a theoretical account of human nature, which in turn depends upon a grasp of biology and, doubtless of physics as well. These are theoretical sciences, which nevertheless provide both the context for, and the basis of, ethics and politics. In the last analysis, Aristotle believes that the deepest theoretical study of physics and biology and psychology will eventually lead to metaphysics and God. Now of course one *can* make good practical decisions without a detailed knowledge of any, let alone all, of these theoretical matters. But our very human nature, best adapted as it is to practical living, itself impels us to grasp the theoretical underpinnings which situate the moral life in an intelligent grasp of the nature of the cosmos as a whole. Human practical living cannot be divorced from thoughtful action: and the very nature of thinking eventually leads us to considerations which are theoretical, not practical, and yet which provide the basis for even our most practical decisions. As I shall suggest when we come to consider in detail what Aristotle says about practical wisdom, the principles which we use in our moral decision making are theoretical, even though the use to which those principles are put is practical.

The most fulfilling life will then be a practical life lived well in the light of a grasp of what it all means and how it is that such a life makes ultimate sense. Human beings are to that crucial, even if limited, extent naturally inclined to share something of the understanding which belongs properly to God.[27] We differ from other animals (at least as Aristotle conceives of them) in that while other animals may flourish and be content, they cannot, he says, be *fulfilled* (1178b24–32). We humans can. For a human being to be fulfilled without qualification it is not enough to conduct one's life well: it is necessary to be able at times to stand back, reflectively, and *understand* oneself, one's life, and the world into which that life fits. One needs to be able to answer the question 'What is it all about?'

Could someone live a whole life in a morally admirable way while remaining completely unreflective about why such a life was admirable, and how it fitted into the scheme of things as a whole? I think Aristotle would say that although one can make some decisions well without any deeper understanding, one cannot consistently do so over the course of a whole life. And even if one could, Aristotle would at least have thought such a life-style would be far from completely fulfilling, because failing to capitalize on that capacity for insight which we share with God.

If this interpretation is along the right lines, then neither the 'dominant' nor the 'inclusive' view is quite right. The dominant view, which identifies *eudaimonia* with *theōria*, has to explain how it is that everything else is done for the sake of *theōria*. This can at a pinch be done, but at least to me the efforts to do so seem somewhat forced.[28] The Inclusivist position in most of its versions fails to explain the special place given to *theōria*; but it is correct in that it does give due weight to the fact that the *Ethics* is largely devoted to aspects of the practical moral life. In contrast to both these views, the position for which I have argued above would suggest that both *theōria* and the life of a morally admirable member of the community are explained by the fact that a fulfilled life involves using our minds on both levels, so far as is possible, and explains why we value using our minds well to think about both practical and theoretical questions. We do so precisely because it is humanly fulfilling to do so. It thus fits in with

[27] The first sentence of Aristotle's *Metaphysics* is 'All human beings by nature desire to know.'

[28] For a good version of such an attempt, see Kraut [1989], ch. 2.

the Function Argument, while still showing how it is that *theōria* grows out of and completes the moral life of the good citizen. To live a fulfilled life absolutely requires us to see our life, with all its varied activities, in a particular light, to see that it has made sense. It is this vision of ourselves which is distinctively human, and which illuminates all the other things we do.

Chapter 4

Moral virtues and moral training

Relevant texts:
Book II, Book X, ch. 9

Problems of interpretation
- How does Aristotle think virtues, emotions and choices are related to one another?
- What is the point of the 'Doctrine of the Mean'?

Critical issues
- Is Aristotle's view of moral training tantamount to indoctrination?
- How do we know which are virtues and which vices?

We have seen that it is Aristotle's view that a fulfilled life is a life lived *kat' aretēn* – in accordance with virtue. It is a life in which our human capacities, and in particular our *specifically* human capacities, are put

53

to their best use. To fill out this sketch, we need to take a closer look at what Aristotle has to say about virtues. He groups them into two classes, virtues of character (often called moral virtues), and virtues of the mind (often called intellectual virtues). Moral virtues are the subject of the present chapter, and intellectual virtues will be treated in the following one.

The definition of moral virtue

The quickest way to get to grips with Aristotle's views on moral virtues is to consider his formal definition:

> So, a [moral] virtue is a habitual disposition connected with choice, lying in a mean relative to us, a mean which is determined by reason, by which the person of practical wisdom would determine it.

> (II, 6, 1106b36–1107a2)

'A habitual disposition'

Dispositions are properties of things which give rise to relatively fixed patterns of behaviour. So, brittleness is a dispositional property of many kinds of glass, sensitivity to light is a dispositional property of film, and many species of animal are by disposition inclined to fight to protect their young. Having these dispositions influences the way in which things behave: glass shatters when struck sharply, film changes its surface chemistry in response to light, animals attack anything which they perceive as a threat to their young. Some, but not all, dispositions are habits, as Aristotle uses the term in the *Ethics*. As he explains in II, 1, some of our dispositions are produced automatically in the course of the way in which human nature normally develops. Thus our dispositional tendencies to grow, to digest food, to have sensations, to have desires and emotions, to think thoughts, are all natural dispositions whose development can be altered only by interfering with the natural processes by which they are formed in the womb.

A *habitual* disposition, which Aristotle calls a *hexis*, also has a basis in our nature, in that we are naturally capable of developing such a habit. But although we are by nature capable of acquiring such habits we do not develop them automatically. The development of a *hexis* comes about only by some form of training; and since training can either be good or bad, we can develop either good or bad habits. Good habits perfect our nature, and bad habits fail to do so. But even the development of bad habits does not violate our nature in the way in which, for instance, a bad diet or illness during pregnancy can damage the natural dispositions of a child.[1]

Habitual dispositions are either *aretai* ('virtues') or *technai* ('skills'). We can be trained to develop the skills proper to pianists, or footballers, or potters or carpenters (and either well-trained or badly trained); and we can be trained to possess moral virtues.[2] That the meanings of the words for skills and for virtues to a large extent overlapped in ordinary Greek might explain why the Greeks found it difficult to say exactly how virtues and skills differed. So we might wonder whether Aristotle's moral virtues are just social and interpersonal skills. Are they no more than some ancient Greek version of knowing how to make friends and influence people?

Not quite. Aristotle tries to differentiate between virtues and skills in II, 4, 1105a17–b5. We judge whether or not someone possesses a skill by looking at the quality of the product of the skill. So, one might look at a carving and see how delicate it is, or at a building and see how well designed it is, or at a wound and see how well the stitches have been put in. Except in the rare cases in which something might happen by a lucky accident rather than by design (which Aristotle mentions briefly at 1105a17–25), the excellence of the product is sufficient for us to say that the agent acted skilfully. Not so, he argues, in the case of virtues. Simply looking at the 'product' isn't enough. If we are to conclude that someone acted virtuously, we need to see not only what she did or said; we need to know how she saw what she was doing or saying. Kind words and gentle gestures

[1] See II, 1, 1103a14–25.

[2] Aristotle spells out the ways in which skills and virtues are similar in II, 1, 1103b6–25.

towards an old person, even if they pleased the person to whom they were addressed, might stem from a desire to control rather than to be genuinely kind. The action would then be a highly skilful piece of manipulation which altogether fails to be virtuous. Aristotle here calls upon a distinction he later draws between productions and actions.[3] An action, in Aristotle's technical sense, is defined in terms of how the agent sees what they are doing. Skills are assessed in terms of the product: actions are assessed in more complex ways, as we shall shortly see.

The most important characteristic of the moral virtues is that they involve a particular pattern of emotional response to situations. In II, 5 Aristotle gives an argument for this conclusion:

(1) There are just three conditions to be found in the soul: feelings, dispositions and habits.
(2) Virtues are neither of the first two:
     (a) we are not described as good or bad simply because of how we feel;
     (b) nor because we possess the dispositions which enable us to have feelings.
(3) Therefore, virtues are habits.

The steps in this argument need some defence and some explanation. If the argument is to be valid, then the list given in (1) must be complete. Evidently it is not, for there are many other conditions to be found in the soul – for example, thoughts, or memories, or images, not to mention the skills we might have learned. Aristotle must therefore be making some unspoken assumptions here. He takes it for granted that the virtues and vices we have in mind – such things as courage, or being even-tempered, or jealousy, or bitterness – are all linked to our feelings and emotions. Accepting that common view enables him to narrow down the field of inquiry. While this is a reasonable enough assumption to start with, it might need to be amended, or at any rate stretched a bit, to deal with such virtues as generosity and justice, which on the face of it do not seem to involve feelings or emotions, or at least do not involve them in quite the same way.

[3] See VI, 4 and 5.

Aristotle further assumes that we can make favourable or unfavourable moral assessments of people's character in terms of the virtues and vices that they possess. We praise people for being generous, or brave, or honest, and criticize them for being jealous, or spiteful, or ill-tempered. This assumption is, I think, uncontroversial. He then goes on to argue that nobody is assessed morally simply because they are *able* to have feelings and emotions. Such abilities are ours by nature, and moral assessment on these grounds makes no more sense than it would to make moral judgements on someone because they have 20/20 vision, or because they have an excellent digestive system. Virtues, then, are not just any kind of natural dispositions.[4]

Are moral virtues then actual feelings? The same argument applies here too. We do not make moral assessments of people's characters simply because they have this or that feeling; it depends on when they have it, and why they have it. Moreover, we do not call someone ill-tempered if they lose their temper only very rarely or only when under extreme provocation. To criticize someone for being ill-tempered is to say something about a regular pattern of feeling-response which they exhibit. Virtues and vices, then, are *habitual* dispositions to respond to situations by having appropriate or inappropriate feelings.[5]

[4] Aristotle is talking about normal human beings. He recognizes that there are abnormalities arising from deformities or madness; his examples include the dispositions to enjoy cannibalism, eating foetuses ripped from pregnant women, having sex with children, or eating coal. He admits that some of these propensities might be the result of custom; but where they arise from nature or illness they do not count as vices, presumably because they do not involve any exercise of rationality at all. See VII, 5, 1148b15–1149a3. To take a modern example, if a psychopath is simply incapable of feeling any of the range of emotions connected with morality, then he is not vicious; rather he is severely handicapped, emotionally dysfunctional. Here modern terminology and the Function Argument agree.

[5] A word on the use of 'feeling' in this argument. Aristotle's term is *pathos* (plural *pathē*) which is even broader than 'feeling' is in English. The term *pathos* is used of just about anything which can happen to someone, or be done to them. Hence it can be used of such things as a bruise, or a wound, or an illness, which certainly could not be described as 'feelings' in English. These instances of *pathē* do not concern us here.

The feelings which are relevant to virtue and vice are those, Aristotle tells us, which are concerned with pleasures and pains.[6] And he uses 'pleasures and pains' in a broad sense, to refer to any experiences which we might welcome or seek to avoid.

Many of the feelings Aristotle has in mind here are emotions, as the beginning of II, 5 makes clear. It is worth pausing a moment to clarify what emotions are. Unlike other types of feeling, emotions are essentially cognitive states, which is to say, a state involving some kind of beliefs. I feel fear, for instance, because I experience something as likely to cause pain, or harm, or to be in some other way threatening.[7] So fear differs from hunger, or tiredness, for example, in that it involves an assessment of how the world is. Fear involves the belief that the situation is somehow dangerous. If I can change my 'perception' of the situation by convincing myself that there is no danger involved, or much less danger than I thought, then I might (of course, I might not) thereby change the degree of fear which I feel.[8] Emotions, then, are to some extent subject to rational guidance. In most cases Aristotle thinks of moral virtues as involving emotions. To be precise, he defines moral virtue in terms of a habitual disposition to have a certain pattern of emotional response.

This is not the whole story, however. As well as including some *pathē* which are emotions, the list at the beginning of II, 5 includes desire. Desires, as I have just mentioned, are such states as hunger, or thirst, or tiredness, or sexual desire, which we would not normally think of as emotions, since they do not involve an assessment of the world in quite the same way. Which desires has Aristotle in mind here? A clue can be found in the discussion of the virtue of modera-

[6] See, for example, 1104b9, 1152b1, 1172a22.

[7] In putting the matter in this way, I am not necessarily accepting that in emotions there are two clearly separate components, a belief (or 'perception' in a broad sense), and an accompanying feeling. It may be better to say that to have an emotion is an immediately affective-cognitive response to a situation in which the belief is not an explicit, separate, element which then causes the feeling. I speak as I do in the text only for the sake of analytical clarity.

[8] There are other ways of changing how I feel which do not involve changing my beliefs about danger. See the section on moral training, p. 70.

tion[9] in III, 10–11. Moderation, he says, 'is a mean with regard to pleasures', by which, as he explains, he here means bodily pleasures, and of these, primarily those stemming from taste and touch. The virtue of moderation is a balanced set of desires especially in connection with eating and sex. Aristotle makes some amusing comments about gourmets, wine-tasters, cooks, massage, and perhaps even aromatherapy, in the course of which he attempts to identify the kinds of behaviour we might call over-indulgent.[10]

Now, in contrast to emotions, it does not seem plausible to say that other feelings are similarly subject to rational control. Toothache, or the hunger I feel if I have not eaten for many hours, are not feelings which I can argue myself out of, even if I can minimize them in other ways, say, by pain-killers, or appetite suppressants, or by trying to distract myself. So can they be controlled?

Aristotle makes the following statements in expanding his view of the virtue of moderation:

(1) Moderation and overindulgence are concerned with the kinds of pleasures which other animals share, which is why they appear characteristic of slaves and beasts. (1118a23–25)

(2) People are called 'addicts'[11] of whatever it is because they enjoy what they shouldn't, or they enjoy it more than most people, or enjoy it in the wrong way. The overindulgent go beyond the limit in all three ways. (1118b22–25)

(3) The person of moderation strikes a balance over these things, neither enjoying those things which the overindulgent enjoy most (but rather disliking them), nor, in general, enjoying what he should not, nor anything to excess. Nor, if these things are not to be had, does he feel disproportionate pangs or cravings – not more than he should, nor when he shouldn't, nor in any other inappropriate way. (1119a12–20)

---

[9] The Greek word is *sōphrosunē*, which is often translated 'temperance'.

[10] 1117b27–1118b27.

[11] I intend 'addicts' here in a colloquial rather then a technical sense; as we might talk of people being chocoholics, and workaholics. The Greek word simply means 'lovers of whatever it is', and is a similarly artificial construction.

There are several things worth noticing about these texts. In the first one, Aristotle appeals to just the same test as he did in the Function Argument. People lacking in moderation in effect behave as though they were animals, and hence fail to function as humans should. But here, the criticism is all the sharper by being put in terms of *bodily* pleasures, contrary at least to the more integrated account of the body–soul relationship which he eventually developed. This emphasis gives a distorted picture even of such pleasures as eating (as if they were purely physical) and even more of sex, as if enjoying sex were wholly independent of the quality of the personal relationship involved.

There are two distinct lines of criticism discernible in (2) and (3). Consider the following example. A glutton who has eaten well at the buffet supper suddenly notices another dish which he has not sampled. So he goes and piles his plate yet again, and then wolfs it down. We might criticize him for still feeling inclined to eat more; and, on different grounds, for the way in which he seems to enjoy simply shovelling the food down, rather than appreciating it. The person of moderation would, the suggestion is, fail in neither of these two ways. So even when he is dealing with desires rather than emotions, Aristotle still takes a very similar line. Desires, like emotions, can be unbalanced in different ways; moreover, he thinks that we can learn to shape our desires and enjoyments, just as we can learn to have a more mature and balanced set of emotional responses. But if this is so (and we shall discuss whether it is later in this chapter), at least in the case of desires it cannot be done in the way in which it can often be done in the case of emotions. I might cope with a feeling of nervousness before giving a speech by deliberately remembering that I have often coped well enough in the past; and by reshaping my thoughts in this way I might cause myself to feel less nervous. Emotions have a cognitive aspect, and can sometimes and to some extent be changed by altering my beliefs. But this is not true of the glutton's desire for food, or indeed the normal person's hunger. I will not feel less hungry by reminding myself that I have to stick to a diet. Nor, I imagine, will the glutton feel less inclined to shovel down his food by being told that he is failing to appreciate an old and very subtle Provençal recipe. So the question which we must consider presently is this: how can desires (as distinct from emotions) be shaped so that we feel inclined for something only when we should, in the way that we should, and to the degree that we should? And is there a parallel way of shaping our emotions when the direct approach by trying to think ourselves into feeling differently fails, and I still feel nervous despite remembering that I managed well enough in the past?

Before answering these questions, we must first consider the notion of a 'mean' which has already appeared in the texts we have just been looking at.

'Lying in a mean relative to us'

In II, 6, Aristotle develops his account of the way in which the emotions are involved in moral virtue. The habitual disposition to respond emotionally will be a virtue only if the pattern of emotional responses is *appropriate*. Obviously enough, what is appropriate will depend upon circumstances. Aristotle gives as an illustrative parallel the amount and kind of diet required by a professional wrestler and by an ordinary individual. Once again, we can perhaps see the influence of his biology on his approach to ethics. Similarly, what is highly dangerous for a novice at mountaineering might not be so very dangerous for an experienced climber; what is a very generous gift from a person of limited means may not be a generous gift from someone who is much better off. It would be appropriate to be extremely angry at someone who caused an accident by driving when drunk; but less appropriate to be angry at a child who clumsily knocked over a valuable antique vase.

Plainly, then, when Aristotle speaks of moral virtues as 'lying in a mean', he is *not* saying that the virtuous person is one who is by character disposed to have only moderate emotional responses. The appropriate emotional response may be very low key, or moderate, or very intense, depending on the situation. As so often, the straightforward biological example is the easiest to be clear about. Desiring more, or less, food than one's body needs is an inappropriate response, because there is a clear enough way of determining what would be harmful. More complex examples, especially those where emotions are involved, are less easy to determine. But even here, at least in a rough and ready way, we can perhaps think of cases in which people are harmed by their own excessive anger, or by being too passive and not angry enough. 'Rough and ready', because the notion of harm here is itself very imprecise.

'Lying in a mean' is therefore not a *criterion* for discovering what the appropriate response is; indeed, to say that a virtuous response must be an appropriate response is tautologous. Aristotle is sometimes criticized on just these grounds, as if he were offering 'lying in the mean' as a test for virtuous responses, and the test turns out to be useless. The criticism is surely unfair. He does not intend to offer a criterion at this point. As we shall see presently, his criterion for a virtuous response is quite a different one.

Why, then, does Aristotle speak of a 'mean' at all? I think the answer is fairly obvious, and relatively uncontroversial. We often speak of emotional responses as instances either of over- or under-reacting; and very often (though, as Aristotle points out, not in every case) we will have two sets of words to denote the vices characterised by habitual over- or under-reacting. Note, once more, that to say that an appropriate response is neither an over- nor an under-reaction does not offer us any test for which is which. But it is still true that we have cowardice and rashness to contrast with bravery (1107b1–4), profligacy and meanness to contrast with generosity (1107b8–14), and so on.[12] Aristotle also notes that there are some emotional responses which are by definition inappropriate, such as feelings of spitefulness, shamelessness and envy. One cannot have just the right degree of spite-fulness or envy. In these cases, there just is no 'mean', just as there are some types of action which are by definition always wrong, such as adultery, theft or murder. The basis for the 'doctrine of the mean' is the fact that, in Aristotle's Greek as in contemporary English, words for virtues and vices commonly come in triplets, even if they do not do so in every case. This linguistic fact embodies the judgements which we – the ordinary people and the wise alike – make about people's responses to situations; and Aristotle believes that these judgements are always to be taken seriously.

In most cases, then, the appropriate response patterns can be contrasted both with over- and under-reacting. To say that virtues lie

[12] Several other examples are given in II, 7.

in the mean says no more than that appropriate patterns of response will come somewhere between over- and under-reacting.[13] The same is to be said about desires, as we have already seen. The person with the virtue of moderation does not desire when he should not, nor more than he should, nor in a way that he should not. But 'should' and 'should not' can be defined only relatively to individuals in each set of circumstances.

'A mean which is determined by reason'

The word translated 'reason' here is *logos*. Sometimes *logos* can be translated as 'rule'; but we have already seen that Aristotle does not believe that any rules can be given which will determine what is appropriate in each individual case. At most, one can offer some generalizations which might hold more often than not. So, there are not many cases in which the appropriate response is to feel very angry indeed, nor many cases of need in which sympathy is totally out of place. But such generalizations are just that, generalizations, rather than rules.[14] As Aristotle puts it:

> But [hitting the mean] is no doubt difficult, especially in partic-
> ular cases. It is not easy to determine in what way one should
> be angry, with whom, on what grounds, and for how long. Even
> we ourselves are liable sometimes to praise those who fail to be
> angry enough by describing them as gentle, and to praise people
> who are difficult by saying that they are assertive. But someone
> who is only slightly out of line in either direction is not blamed;
> only someone who is way out of line is blamed, for they don't
> escape notice. But how far and to what extent someone should
> be blamed is not easy to define in a rule, any more than any
> thing else which is perceptible. [Blaming in such cases] depends

[13] Good discussions of the Doctrine of the Mean are to be found in L. A. Kosman [1980], and J. O. Urmson [1973].

[14] Hardie [1968] in chapter VII, 'Virtue Is a Mean' conducts an excellent demo-lition of views which seek to make the Doctrine of the Mean more complex and ambitious than the text warrants. It remains true, though, that it is not entirely clear what is the best way to translate *logos* here.

> upon particular circumstances, and judgement [about them] depends on perception.
>
> (II, 9, 1109b14–23)

The word which I have translated 'rule' in the third last line of this text is, once again, *logos*. Aristotle tries to distinguish between formulating rules about anger, moderation, or any virtue or vice, and using our reason in a quite different way which is akin to simply perceiving. At the beginning of Book II he has already made the same point:

> Let us agree at the outset that every statement about conduct has to be in outline rather than in detail. As we said at the beginning, the type of statements we make should reflect the nature of the subject. There is nothing fixed about conduct or about what would be helpful for us, any more than there is about health. This applies to our general statements, and statements about particular cases are even less exact. They do not fall under any art or precept. In every case it is the people concerned who have to see what the situation demands, just as they do in questions about medicine or navigation.
>
> (II, 2 1103b34–1104a10)

'By which the person of practical wisdom would determine it'

Here, and not before, we have Aristotle's standard for determining which responses are appropriate, and hence for deciding which habitual dispositions are virtues and which are not. Appropriate responses are the ones which are in accord with the judgement of a particular type of person – the person of practical wisdom. Moreover, virtues are to be defined in terms of a *judgement*. This is a very important claim. The implication is that for an emotional response to be virtuous it must be in accord with what reason judges to be the true demands of the situation, since reason aims at truth. Feelings, then, are not simply to be accepted as given. They are subject to rational assessment and ideally to rational control. The standard by which virtuous and vicious dispositions are distinguished from one another is a rational standard.

The examples of virtues and vices which he gives here in Book II are taken from the morality of ordinary Athenians, from just that background to which he assumes that his students belong. As he points out at the beginning of II, 7, his general account should illuminate the individual examples of virtues and vices which his audience would recognize.

> However we must not just say this in general terms without applying it to individual cases. When we are speaking about actions, what is said in general will apply more broadly, but what is said about specific instances will be truer, since actions are concerned with individual cases, and what we say must harmonize with these. Examples can be taken from the diagram.
>
> $(1107a28–33)^{15}$

So Aristotle at least takes his general account – by which I take it he means the view that virtue is to be found in the mean – to be one which would be endorsed by the person of practical wisdom. He also thinks it is confirmed by being seen to be applicable to particular cases. What does he have in mind? There are two possibilities.

The mention of 'the diagram' suggests that the particular cases are all examples of triplets consisting of one virtue-term and two contrasting vice-terms. That in turn suggests that by 'particular cases' he means particular instances of virtue-terms. This interpretation fits well with a remark he makes at 1108a9–19, where, in a discussion of virtues and vices connected with our social dealings with one another, he tries to produce examples of the triplets which the theory of the mean would lead us to expect. He admits that we do not in fact have words for all the instances of extremes, or for all the means, but says that we should try to find words if at all possible, 'to make things clear and easy to follow'. Exactly how is finding words for nameless states supposed to help? Here is one suggestion. The theory that virtue is in

---

[15] At 1107a33 Aristotle mentions a 'diagram'. We do not have in the *Nico-machaean Ethics* any clear statement about what such a diagram might have contained. But there is an example of the kind of thing he has in mind in the *Eudemian Ethics* at 1220b23–1221a14. This can most easily be found in Woods [1992], p. 17. It consists of a list of virtues and the corresponding pairs of contrasting vices.

a mean between extremes will be better confirmed the more cases we can find which fit the theory. We should not be put off simply because we don't have a *word* for whatever it is. So we think it is a virtue in someone to be open, and something of a fault to be reserved; but we don't have a word (or at least I cannot readily think of one) for the opposite failing. Perhaps 'gushing' or even 'intrusive'? What Aristotle thinks is important, though, is that in every case we can discern and if possible name the patterns of emotional over- and under-reaction, since this will confirm his thesis that virtues consist in appropriate patterns of emotional response.

Another possible interpretation depends upon taking 'actions are concerned with individual cases' more literally, to mean not just different types of case, but individual instances. On this reading, Aristotle would be asking us to think of individual pieces of good or bad behaviour, and to see whether we could classify it as involving an emotional over- or under-reaction, or as involving an appropriate emotional response. To the extent that we can do this, we will once again confirm Aristotle's general account of what virtues and vices are.

I do not think we need to choose between these two accounts. They are different, but I think Aristotle would accept them both. A successful theory should fit with at least many of our pre-theoretical beliefs; and if these beliefs include both the beliefs enshrined in our everyday moral vocabulary, and in the beliefs we have about individual pieces of behaviour, then the confirmation will be all the stronger for that.

Does Aristotle assume that the person of practical wisdom would simply endorse conventional Athenian morality, so that such a person could be recognized simply by seeing who was generally regarded as living a good life? Not necessarily. What such a person would endorse is Aristotle's claim that the account of virtue as 'lying in a mean' fits well with the individual virtues and vices with which his audience is familiar. But it remains true that when Aristotle develops this point by showing how it applies in several individual instances, he does not attempt to say precisely where generosity shades into wastefulness in the one direction or meanness in the other. He is content to point out that one can go wrong in either direction. What the person of practical wisdom does is to get the balance right every time. Nothing Aristotle has so far said takes sides on the precise extent to which the judgements of such a person would agree with where most Athenians would draw the lines.

Of course, to say this much does not help at all to explain how the person of practical wisdom arrives at these correct decisions. Consideration of that topic comes later, in Book VI. But already we would do well to remember Aristotle's remarks towards the end of I, 7 about the impossibility of being exact in ethics. He himself reminds us of just this point at II, 2, 1103b26–1104a11. He offers to give us some help; but not to give us rules which will produce solutions for practical decisions automatically.

'Concerned with choice'[16]

This phrase is vague, as it is in the Greek. There are three possible ways in which it might be taken:

(1)   Virtues are patterns of emotional response which facilitate choice.
(2)   Virtues are patterns of emotional response which issue in choices.
(3)   Virtues are habitual patterns of choosing or acting.

The first fits in well enough with the (rather oversimplified) picture which has emerged from the discussion so far. The picture is like this. The virtuous character is one with balanced emotional dispositions. Such a person will respond emotionally to situations in just the appropriate way; she will be just as angry as the case demands, just as afraid as the danger threatening suggests she should be; she will feel inclined to be generous just when to be so would not be wasteful, and so on. In responding in this way, she makes it easy for herself to choose to act rightly, since she will feel inclined to do just that.[17]

---

[16] I will give here the usual translation, 'choice', since it is not misleading in this context. For reasons why it is not entirely accurate, see the section on 'Moral Conclusions' in Chapter 6, p. 129.

[17] The case with courage is more complicated, since one reasonably should have the highest degree of fear when one is in danger of death; yet some people might have to risk death in order to do their duty. On this, see the last section of Chapter 9 in this volume.

Should she decide to act, she will not have to exercise self-control, or fight with herself in order to do the right thing. More strongly still, in responding as she does she is responding to, and hence alerting herself to, features of the situation which are morally important, and to that extent is guiding her choice. Virtues are not morally neutral dispositions: they consist in the ability to have an affective grasp of what is morally important in a situation, and an affective estimate of how important that something is.[18]

(2) is stronger than (1), in that it suggests that one's emotional response makes the corresponding choice inevitable. It might be argued that it is Aristotle's view that choice is determined by the desires and emotions one has at the time, and not simply facilitated by those desires or emotions. We must postpone this discussion to Chapter 6.

But something needs to be said now about the third possible understanding of how a virtue functions. Both in (1) and in (2) virtues are defined in terms of what we habitually feel; in (3) virtues are defined in terms of how we habitually behave. Here are two examples to illustrate the difference. Suppose there are two novice parachutists about to make their first jump, in ideal conditions and with every safety precaution in place. Mr A feels exhilarated, and jumps when told to without a moment's hesitation: B feels extremely nervous, though he realizes that his fears are quite disproportionate; still, he steels himself, grits his teeth and jumps. I think many people in such a case would be inclined to say that B exhibited courage, whereas A did not. On the other hand, suppose that A and B are faced with someone collecting for some good cause. A cheerfully donates a reasonable sum; B feels very disinclined to give away his money; but realizes that perhaps he should give something: so, grudgingly, matches A's donation. In this case, it seems to me we might think A a generous person, while B is mean. So, in the bravery example, we tend to measure courage by actions rather than feelings: but we usually do precisely the reverse in the case of generosity.

I have so far presented Aristotle's treatment of moral virtues in terms of a habitual disposition to have appropriate *feelings*. On that

[18] See again the cautionary remarks in note 7, p. 58.

showing, he holds either (1) or (2). But at least in some places Aristotle seems to include more, and in particular seems to include not merely feelings, but also choices. As part of his argument to show that virtues are not simply feelings, he says:

> A further argument: we become angry, or afraid, without choosing to; but moral virtues are choices, or [rather] are not without choice.
>
> (II, 5, 1106a2–4)

and he also remarks that:

> Moral virtue is a habit related to choice and choice is deliberated desire.
>
> (VI, 2, 1139a22–23)

The suggestion might be that a virtue just is a *habit of choosing*, because it is what one wants to do after thinking things out, rather than a spontaneous affective response as I have been arguing. If one takes this line, then one might find confirmation in remarks such as:

> Moral virtue has to do with feelings and actions . . .
>
> (II, 6, 1106b24–25)

Moreover, the examples of virtues he gives both at this point in Book II and later on in Book IV are examples of actions, rather than emotional responses. These texts might suggest that he believes that virtues are inseparable from choosing to behave virtuously. Indeed, the first text at least appears to say that virtues just are choices.

Nevertheless, this reading does, I think, press the texts too far. Of course Aristotle would suppose that a person whose character was virtuous would typically express their character in appropriate behaviour. This is surely right, since the choices we make usually (though not on every occasion) do express the characters we have, for better or for worse. But immediately after saying that virtues are choices, he immediately goes on to say 'or involve choice'. This surely reads like a deliberate correction of the earlier and less accurate statement, as my translation, inserting the word 'rather' after the 'or', attempts to suggest. And to say that virtues 'have to do with actions' need say no more than that virtuous dispositions will normally express themselves in action. Similarly, to say that choices are deliberated desires is not to identify choices with virtues, or even with the spontaneous affective response in which virtues express themselves. As we shall see in Chapter 5, even the spontaneous responses of the good person might not be quite the same as what they, upon reflection, want to do.

True, it might further be argued that in Aristotle's view virtuous dispositions *necessarily* issue in action. After all, Aristotle compares a virtuous character to a 'second nature'; and we repeat his phrase when we say that a way of behaving has become second nature to someone. Aristotle would think it impossible for someone to have a virtuous disposition which did not usually find expression in action. Despite all that, though, it still seems to me that he *defines* virtue in terms of emotional response rather than in terms of the actions to which such emotional responses typically lead. To grit one's teeth and jump despite one's nervousness is indeed, he would say, to exercise self-control; but it is not a display of courage, for the courageous person would not feel frightened in a situation where fear was groundless. Similarly, giving a donation is a generous action only if one feels inclined to be generous, and one typically feels so inclined in appropriate circumstances.

Moral training

Aristotle expects the students in his course already to have had the kind of moral upbringing and sufficient experience of life which will enable them to profit from what they will hear. How tough a requirement is this meant to be? Does he mean that the students must already have a fully-formed adult moral judgement, so that all that they now need is the theoretical background to what they are successfully doing already? Or is it enough that they have already acquired the habits of emotional balance, and need only to learn the intellectual skills upon which a mature adult moral judgement depends?

Unfortunately, neither of these interpretations can easily be reconciled with the texts. Aristotle repeatedly stresses that the purpose of his course is practical, not theoretical, for instance at II, 2, 1103b26–29:

Our present inquiry (unlike our others) is not aimed at theoretical knowledge. We are not conducting our inquiry in order to know the definition of virtue, but in order to become good, otherwise it would not benefit us at all.

So his course is more than an account of the theory which underpins good moral behaviour. Something practical is still lacking in his students.

The second alternative is more plausible, that students who already have virtuous characters are to be taught how to think about moral decisions. This at least would be to give them something practical. But this, too, fails as an account of Aristotle's requirement, for what might at first sight seem a strange reason. Aristotle does not believe that it is possible to be truly virtuous unless one has already acquired the ability to *think* correctly about moral decisions:

[Moral] virtue is not simply a habit in accordance with right reason, but a habit which exists [only] alongside right reason ... Socrates thought that virtues were instances of thinking, on the grounds that they were instances of knowledge; whereas we think they exist [only] alongside thinking. From what we have said it follows that it is not possible for someone to be fully virtuous without practical wisdom, nor to have practical wisdom without moral virtue.

(VI, 13, 1144b26–32)

So, while Aristotle is indeed modifying Plato's view that virtue is knowledge, yet he is also denying, as Plato would, that someone can be virtuous unless he has an adult moral *judgement*. The students, we are to believe, cannot be fully virtuous if they still need help with developing such judgement; yet they cannot have such a judgement unless and until they become fully virtuous. Mature moral judgement and a morally admirable character are interdependent, and he would have us believe that one cannot have stable patterns of appropriate moral responses unless one also is good at making correct moral decisions. We shall have to examine this apparently paradoxical contention more in detail later. For the moment, we can begin by asking what exactly does he expect his students to have before they start, and what is it that they still have to get out of their course?

What they already have

In II, 1 Aristotle explains how we can train our emotional responses so that they are more appropriate to the situations in which we find ourselves. We do so by engaging in appropriate actions, no matter how we might at first feel about doing them. For instance, someone who feels nervous about walking along a reasonably safe mountain ridge or about jumping out of a plane into empty space just has to grit their teeth and do it, like the novice parachutist in my example. As both Aristotle and the ruthless paratrooper sergeant might say, after they've done it repeatedly they will come to feel confident, so they just have to get on with it. Similar conditioning can alter other forms of inappropriate response.

> In a word, habits are born of similar activities. So we have to engage in behaviour of the relevant kinds, since the habits formed will follow upon the various ways we behave. It is no trivial matter, then, that we form habits of one kind or another right from childhood; on the contrary, it is very important, indeed all-important.

> (II, 1, 1103b21–25)[19]

Perhaps that last phrase is a slight exaggeration. For Aristotle does not simply have in mind a process of thoughtless conditioning. In the final chapter of the *Ethics* (X, 9) he returns to the theme of moral training, and gives a relatively complex account of what is involved. He mentions parental guidance and instruction; the framework of legal and social expectations in which children are brought up; the threat of punishment, the force of argument, and the sense of shame. Not all these elements in a moral education will be equally effective with everyone, not all will be needed on every occasion, and not one of them is sufficient of itself.

In particular, it is clear that Aristotle envisages instruction, for he mentions that children have a natural inclination to listen to and obey

---

[19] What is here said about emotions applies equally to desires; see II, 3, 1104b11–16.

their parents (1180b5–7). We are to suppose, I think, that parents will say to their children such things as 'That's being selfish', or 'It was very good of you to share your toys like that'. Parents will praise them to others, 'David was very brave at the dentist's this afternoon', so that the child can proudly say 'I didn't cry even when it hurt', and so on. The children not merely become used to injections so that they eventually are not afraid of them, they come to see not being afraid in those circumstances as something in which they can take proper pride. Doubtless, the examples will change as the child grows and encounters more complex difficulties, say with the emotions involved in personal relationships. And where parental guidance is lacking or insufficient, there is at least the climate of public opinion, and a set of legal sanctions which express what the community regards as admirable or disgraceful. Aristotle also believes that the child has to make choices – whether or not to do what he is told, to take advice, to listen to what is explained to him.[20] In short, moral training is not merely a quasi-Pavlovian conditioning of knee-jerk responses; it involves the young also in learning to use the concepts of morality with increasing sophistication, to esteem morally admirable behaviour, and to feel shame when they fail to live up to the standards proposed to them. Their more nuanced moral vocabulary goes hand in hand with more discriminating affective responses to situations, and together these add up to a gradually improving ability to make good moral judgements.

An important and somewhat difficult passage from the end of I, 7 gives a more general explanation of what is going on here. Aristotle has just explained that precise conclusions are not to be looked for in ethics in the way that they are in the natural sciences. He goes on:

> We should not ask for the explanation in the same way in every case. Sometimes it is sufficient to have satisfactorily established that something is the case – with starting points, for example. That something is the case is basic, and is a starting point. Now some starting points are seen by induction, others by

[20] See, for instance, III, 5, and especially 1114b16–25, and 1114b31–1115a3.

perception, others by some kind of habituation, and others in other ways.

(I, 7, 1098a34–b4)[21]

A very similar point is made in connection with the discussion in I, 4 about where a course in politics should begin. Aristotle suggests that we should start from what we already know:

> That is why someone who is going to profit from attending a course on what is noble and just – in short a course on politics – needs to have been well brought up. The starting point is what is the case; and if that is sufficiently clear [to him] there is no need for the explanation as well. The person who has been well trained either already has or can easily get hold of the starting points.[22]

(I, 4, 1095b4–8)

We start with what we know to be true, and then we look for explanations, which will not be difficult to find. We cannot, and hence should not, ask for explanations of everything, or we will have a vicious regress. At some point we simply have to grasp that basic truths just are basic.

Consider, then, how we might do this 'by induction', as he puts it. The child or young person is told by his parents that this action is brave, and that is foolhardy, and that is cowardly. If he is being well-instructed, he can take these parental statements as true; what they say is in fact the case. So the child can start from there to build up, inductively, his knowledge of what courage is. He will do the same with other parts of the vocabulary of ethics – virtue terms such as 'generous'

---

[21] The word here translated 'starting point' is *archē*; literally it means 'a beginning' or 'an origin', and can have the technical sense of 'a first principle'.

[22] There is an apparent difference between these two remarks, in that the first one takes what is the case as absolutely basic, whereas the second envisages going behind what is the case in order to discover why it is so. That is because Aristotle sometimes uses 'starting point' to refer to where we actually start from – what we already know – and sometimes to refer to what is in the end fundamental to the process of explanation.

and 'unfair', and also more general moral terms such as 'noble', 'admirable' and 'shameful'. In so doing, he will be putting together the evidence on the basis of which he might finally know what courage is. He cannot *prove*, by appeal to something more basic, that this is what courage is. The definition of courage is itself one of the first principles of ethics, which has simply to be seen by grasping what all the courageous actions have in common. This knowledge of what courage is will then function as a starting point in his subsequent moral deliberations, as well as providing the explanation for the particular truths about individual actions taught him by his parents and teachers.

Aristotle also says that some first principles (or starting points) are grasped by 'habituation'. As Burnyeat rightly points out, if habituation is to result in a grasp of first principles, it must be more than merely a process of conditioning involving feelings and desires. It must involve what he terms a 'cognitive slant'.[23] I think that what Aristotle has in mind is that, as I have already suggested, emotions are *not* simply 'feelings' in some vague sense of that vague term; they involve a grasp of a situation as having a certain quality – for instance, as being an instance of danger, or of betrayal, or an instance of being insulted. So the young person's understanding of morally admirable behaviour is gained in part through a growing grasp of the use of moral terms. But it is important to see that the person also learns through the gradual development of appropriate emotional responses through which situations are interpreted. There is all the difference in the world between the way in which one's limb might respond to a blow by pain, and the way in which someone might respond to an insult by feeling angry, or to a hug with a feeling of reassurance. Trained habits of emotional response are *interpretations* of what is going on, not just blind reactions, and, like any interpretation, they can be accurate, quite mistaken, or anywhere between the two. The point about moral training is that we gradually learn to respond emotionally with ever greater accuracy.

[23] Miles Burnyeat, 'Aristotle on Learning to be Good', in Rorty [1980], 69–92. The reference is on p. 73.

What they still need

Why, then, are the young people who are so trained and so equipped not yet in the full sense virtuous? As we have already seen, the short answer is that they do not as yet have practical wisdom; practical wisdom and the fullness of virtue go hand in hand. Each presupposes the presence of the other.

Details of this will be discussed in the next chapter. But perhaps the following suggestion might point to a way in which the near-virtues of Aristotle's students might still be incomplete. We are to suppose that the young people have appropriately moderate desires, and are emotionally balanced in their responses to situations. But it is natural also to suppose that the situations with which they have so far been faced have been comparatively simple. We might still wonder how they will react to the more complex situations which are commonplace in adult life. Perhaps with conflicting emotions, corresponding to the conflicting morally significant features of the situation. What they do not, and as yet cannot, confidently and habitually do is arrive at a decision with which they are emotionally comfortable, and which, in consequence, they are unambiguously motivated to carry out. It may be, then, that the ability to resolve emotional conflicts and respond upon reflection to complex adult situations with an unequivocal emotional commitment and a correspondingly clear judgement is what Aristotle's students still lack, however admirable their early upbringing has been.

There is some textual support for this suggestion. Aristotle contrasts moral virtues with natural virtues (such as intelligence, or an equable temperament), and asks whether one can have one moral virtue without the others:

In this way, we can refute the dialectical argument that the [moral] virtues are quite separate from one another. The same person, it might be argued, is not by nature equally disposed to all the virtues, so he might already have acquired one without having acquired the others. This is possible in the case of the natural virtues, but not in the case of the [moral] ones on the basis of which he is described as a good person without

qualification. For with the presence of the single virtue of practical reason all the virtues are present.

(VI, 13, 1144b32–1145a2)

This is more of an assertion than an argument, it must be said.
It is true that all the moral virtues are defined in terms of how the
person of practical wisdom would judge. So there is one standard for
assessing them all. But that in itself does nothing to show that one
cannot have one moral virtue without having all the others. Might one
not be brave without being generous or loyal?

It will help to recall that to be brave in Aristotle's sense is to feel
inclined to incur danger precisely when that is what one should do;
suppose, then, that one's comrade is lying wounded on the battlefield,
under fire. Other things being equal, it might be foolhardy to leave
one's cover under fire; but if that is the only way of saving one's
comrade, then perhaps what would otherwise be foolhardy becomes
an act of bravery. So only the person who feels loyalty to his comrade
will feel inclined to run the risks involved in trying to rescue him.
Bravery – the appropriate emotional response to danger – is in part
defined in terms of the appropriate emotion of loyalty, and conversely.
Admittedly, to construct conflict-situations so as to illustrate the connections between all the moral virtues would take quite an effort of
imagination; but I think that it is precisely the possibility of such conflicting claims which leads Aristotle to say that one cannot have one
moral virtue without having them all. So perhaps while the students
have sufficient experience of life to understand examples like these,
they do not as yet understand how to think about them, and still do
not respond appropriately. The habits acquired through their early
training are, as it were, the right raw material for forming an adult
emotional response, but they are as yet no more than that. The students
are well brought up, interested in doing what is right, but they are
still liable to be confused. It is only by learning how to *think*
morally even in such difficult circumstances that they will find that they
also can *respond* in the proper way. In the end, I think that Aristotle
does not believe that there are absolutely irresolvable moral conflicts
– dilemmas to which there is no morally acceptable answer. But only
the morally experienced person who has a thoroughly integrated

pattern of emotional response and who possesses practical wisdom will be able to see how complex moral difficulties are to be resolved.

Indoctrination?

The very comprehensiveness of Aristotle's belief that one cannot have one moral virtue without having them all, and that moral judgement and the possession of the moral virtues go hand in hand, leaves him particularly open to the charge that his view of moral training amounts to nothing less than indoctrination. That he can say that our early training is 'very important, *indeed all-important*' (1103b25) reinforces this impression.

Indoctrination is something we would regard as unjustifiable and therefore to be avoided. So how are we to distinguish indoctrination from proper training and education? Attempts are sometimes made to distinguish between them by saying that in true education the students are allowed to make up their own minds about things, whereas no such liberty is possible when they are indoctrinated. Plainly, this explanation simply will not do. Nobody thinks children are being indoctrinated in any unwelcome sense if they are told that the planets revolve round the sun, or that the Battle of Hastings took place in 1066, or if young people are brought up to believe that rape is wrong. We might indeed, if we are impractical enough, wish that the full reasons for each of these beliefs were communicated as well as the beliefs themselves: but we would not claim that a proper attitude to education requires that they be asked to make up their own minds on these issues.

I think there are two related points here. The first concerns the difference between issues where truth is involved and issues where truth is not involved at all. There would be no justification for insisting that children or students should approve of this, or disapprove of that, if there is no issue of truth involved. Some things just are a matter of personal preference, and in general people's preferences ought to be respected. Now of course it has been argued that moral principles, too, express preferences rather than truths, and that it is therefore wrong, other things being equal, to insist that people adopt a particular set of ethical attitudes rather than some other, or to attempt to ensure their compliance in a way which suggests there is no other possible option.[24] But this point has no bearing on Aristotle. It is clear enough that Aristotle does hold that there are true and false beliefs in ethics, and would defend himself vigorously against the accusation that his view of moral training sought to impose a particular set of preferences without any justification. Justification is exactly what he seeks to provide. It is, Aristotle would claim, in the end indefensible to suppose that we are free to decide what is morally valuable, or morally right or wrong. The facts of life, the constraints of our nature will eventually catch up with us.

A second, quite different, view of indoctrination is that it arises at the point at which someone sets out to teach as *uncontroversially* true beliefs which are broadly regarded as open to reasonable dispute. So the accusation against Aristotle's view of moral training might be that, precisely because he thinks that people's emotional responses can be conditioned, and that those responses will subsequently have a profound effect on their moral judgements, his view of the importance of being schooled in virtues early in life just is indoctrination. The child or very young person can, of course, up to a point choose whether to listen to their parents or educators or not. But it is quite unrealistic to suppose that they have any sufficient basis for assessing the moral stance within which they are being brought up; and by the time they might have been able to assess it, their moral judgements have already been irretrievably slanted.

Much of the force of this type of criticism depends upon precisely what is to be regarded as controversial in ethics and what is not. The accusation can be rebutted only by a detailed study, issue by issue. But the general line of Aristotle's reply must surely be to try to establish three points:

(1)   The Function Argument, read in the context of any reasonable view of human nature and human emotions, will suffice to establish in general terms that courage, temperance, fairness,

---

[24] There is a further question about precisely how someone who does not believe that ethical utterances express truths can argue against indoctrination. They can, obviously, disapprove of it, refuse to do it themselves, try to dissuade would-be indoctrinators; what they cannot consistently do is claim that the indoctrinator makes some kind of *mistake*.

truthfulness, generosity, and friendship are virtues, emotional dispositions which uncontroversially are worth developing.

(2) There are surely some uncontroversially true moral beliefs which any normal human could be expected to accept, and can see as securely based on human nature.

(3) He himself has frequently reiterated that ethics and politics are not exact sciences. The result of his training will not be an imposed uniformity of moral view which takes no account of the circumstances of individual cases; rather it will be an informed judgement emotionally sensitive to the various complex features which have to be taken into account.

Would these claims, if true, be a sufficient defence against the charge of indoctrination? It seems to me that they would. It might be objected that even if it is the case that there must be some – perhaps very general – moral beliefs which are uncontroversially true, any given society is always liable to suppose that most of its own moral beliefs fall into this category. Indeed, this temptation might be all the more plausible if a society has little contact with any group which has a very different morality. So Aristotle and his all too like-minded and homogeneous pupils will indeed take it for granted that the main lines of their moral beliefs are surely beyond serious questioning; and so will see no reason to object to inculcating those beliefs in the young. Even when a society is well aware that there are other groups which do not share their moral beliefs (and the Athenians of Aristotle's day were certainly aware of that), they will still all too easily be inclined to dismiss these alien beliefs and practices as clearly mistaken.

I think Aristotle's best line of reply to this difficulty is to say that *any* way of educating the young is, like it or not, inevitably going to inculcate *some* morally significant beliefs and traits of character. The idea that one can maintain a complete moral neutrality in the upbringing of the young is simply an illusion, and a potentially dangerous one at that. But if the moral code in which the young are educated includes teaching the distinction between what is basic and what is less obvious in ethics, and includes the outlines of a method of assessing moral beliefs, one can justifiably claim that no alternative training can be shown to be less indoctrinatory. Aristotle might justifiably claim that in stressing the role of time and experience and balance, he has made it quite clear that in the complexities of ethics one cannot leap to conclusions.

Chapter 5

Practical wisdom

Relevant text: Book VI

Problems of interpretation
- How is practical wisdom different from other intellectual skills?
- How are theory and practice connected?
- Is practical wisdom concerned only with means, not with ends?
- How is practical wisdom related to moral virtue?

Critical issues
- Is Aristotle vulnerable to Humean or Kantian criticisms?
- Is his account simply circular?
- Does he do more than accept the moral assumptions of his society?

The discussion of emotions and other feelings was needed for two reasons: in so far as *eudaimonia* requires the exercise of our natural capacities *kat' aretēn* ('in accordance with virtue'), we needed to form some conception of what it is to be functioning well on the level of emotions and desires. As I have already suggested, and as will appear more clearly in the present chapter, Aristotle suggests that a balanced emotional sensitivity is an important element which makes for good moral decision making. But he certainly does not think that moral decision making is simply an emotional response to situations. Moral decisions involve choices, made for reasons; and to speak of choice and reason is to speak of the exercise of an *intellectual* capacity. Aristotle believes that we can train ourselves in good moral decision making, just as we can train ourselves to have appropriate emotional responses to situations. So he has to examine what the intellectual ability to make good decisions, and hence good moral decisions, consists in. And, having done that, he then has to try to present an integrated account of how the intellectual and the emotional relate to one another in good moral decision making.

Overview of the issues

What Aristotle has to say about practical wisdom has occasioned more discussion and more controversy than almost any other part of the *Ethics*. So I shall start by trying to give a general survey of what is going on in this part of the book – with the warning that any attempt to put it neatly and clearly will inevitably result in oversimplification.

To possess practical wisdom, in Aristotle's view, is to be good at thinking about what one should do. He is careful to make it clear that he has a very particular use of 'should' in mind. He is not speaking about occasions when we might say of a footballer that he should have passed sooner than he did, or of a cook that she should not have used such a hot oven, or of a doctor that she should have noticed that the patient was somewhat confused. In contrast to these occasions when we use 'should' almost in a technical sense, Aristotle has in mind something which comes close to a moral use; as he puts it, to have practical wisdom is to be good at thinking about how to live a fulfilled and worthwhile life as a whole.

The very way in which I have described practical wisdom, in terms of being good at a particular kind of thinking, will easily suggest that practical wisdom is a type of intellectual skill, perhaps like being good at crossword puzzles, or good at mathematics. Aristotle is in some ways quite struck by the possible similarities here, even though his explicit view is that practical wisdom is definitely not a skill. It will be recalled that he had a very similar problem in separating moral virtues from skills. Why is being good at moral decision making not a matter of possessing what might, in the jargon phrase, be described as the appropriate life-skills? One set of problems, then, arises from trying to sort out exactly what the similarities and differences are, and precisely how moral thinking differs from other types of intellectual pursuit.

This set of problems is linked to another. One way of characterizing a skill is in terms of what the skill aims at producing. To possess the skill is to be good at producing the end-product: to be a good sculptor is to be good at making statues and so on, and to be good at solving crosswords is to be able to produce the correct solution. By their fruits you shall know them. The test for whether someone is skilled or not is whether they can take the right steps or means to the end which the skill aims at. So one chooses suitable stone, prepares one's tools, and starts chipping away, now here, now there, doing whatever is required to produce an impressive statue. If practical wisdom is like that, then being good at moral thinking consists in knowing how to take the best means to achieve one's goals in life.

It is just here that the major difficulties in interpreting Aristotle's intentions start. Sometimes he does seem to suggest that practical wisdom never thinks about ends but only about the means to achieve ends which are taken as already fixed; but on other occasions he equally seems to suggest that practical wisdom involves thinking about the ends, too. Indeed one would surely have thought that any sensible account of practical wisdom – being good at thinking morally – would involve thinking about what one's goals in life should be, and not just about how to achieve goals which are taken as given. One might even think that the most fundamental difficulty in trying to live morally lies in knowing what it is that one is aiming at: if we could get that clear, it might seem comparatively easy to work out the practical details of how to achieve it.

So what is it to be good at thinking morally? One answer, perhaps not very plausible, would be that being good at thinking morally consists in having a good grasp of a set of moral principles – to know that stealing is wrong, or that one ought to be generous to those in need, and so on. But then, do not such principles have to be applied to individual situations? So is it perhaps more important to know what to do at any given instant, rather than to have an abstract grasp of moral principles? But perhaps both kinds of ability are required: we could hope both to have the right principles and to know how to apply them by seeing what is the right thing to do here and now. Aristotle seems to say something along these lines. To help the reader, he gives some examples of how the good practical thinker might think. But the examples, often described as 'practical syllogisms', are less clear than one might wish, as are the explanatory comments Aristotle makes about them. So we need to try to get clear about these, too.

Finally, we have already seen that Aristotle defines the moral virtues in terms of the choices made by the person who has practical wisdom. In this section of the *Ethics* he elaborates on this connection from the other end, as it were. What positive contribution do the moral virtues make to one's ability to think well about how to live a morally admirable life? Or, to put the question more concretely, exactly what does emotional balance have to do with moral judgement?

These, then, are some of the issues with which Aristotle deals in Book VI. The account of practical wisdom lies at the very heart of his position, and differences of interpretation here have repercussions on one's interpretation of almost everything else which he says. But quite apart from the problems of getting the interpretation of the text right, there is the question whether Aristotle gives a realistic picture of how we do in fact think about moral issues, and whether he manages to defend that picture satisfactorily.

So much for an outline of the issues. Aristotle makes a start by distinguishing intellectual virtues from the moral virtues we have already considered, and by focusing on two key intellectual virtues.

Practical wisdom and theoretical ability

In contrast to the moral virtues, Aristotle considers two virtues which we can come to possess precisely as thinking beings, and which are distinguished by the subject-matter we think about. The ability to think well about scientific subjects he calls *sophia*; the habit of being good at thinking about practical matters he calls *phronēsis*.[1] It is this latter, 'practical wisdom' as the usual translation goes, which concerns us now. The person who has practical wisdom has a good moral judgement.

The differences between scientific and practical thinking are sketched out in VI, 1. In the case of the sciences, says Aristotle, we think about things which either happen inevitably, or inevitably remain the way they are: for example, the changes in the heavens, or the nature of God, or the principles of metaphysics, or medical science. The aim of theoretical thinking is to arrive at a correct understanding of *why* things are as they are. By contrast, practical thinking is concerned with what we can do to change things, and why we might decide to act in one way rather than another. So we must ask, what does it take to be good at thinking about what to do? Aristotle's most general answer to this is that it takes *orthos logos*. This phrase could be translated as 'right reason', or 'correct thinking'. Either way, though, it might not seem particularly helpful to be told that in order to be good at practical thinking one needs to have correct thinking. As Aristotle himself puts it:

> While this statement is true, it is not at all clear. In all the other areas which are objects of knowledge, one can no doubt say that we must do neither too much nor too little, but just the intermediate amount which correct thinking requires. But to be told only that would leave one none the wiser. For example, what medicines should we apply to our body? It would be no help to be told to apply those ones which medical science prescribes, in

[1] At least, this is how he finally speaks of them, at the end of VI, 11, 1143b14–17, and in VI, 12. Earlier, he gives a list of five such virtues, perhaps taken from Plato. He probably thinks they can be grouped under the two main headings with which he ends up.

the way in which the physician would apply them. Just so, it is not enough just to make this correct statement about the habitual dispositions of the soul; we must go on to determine what the nature and the limits of correct thinking are.

(VI, 1, 1138b25–34)

Sometimes, the word I have translated as 'limits' is translated 'definition'. But the reader who searches through the rest of Book VI will certainly not find a *definition* of *orthos logos*. What Aristotle tries to do is to build up gradually a picture of the factors which contribute to thinking well about practical matters, by showing how practical thinking is related to theoretical thinking, to the practical skill of a craftsman, and to the moral virtues.

Is practical wisdom like other practical skills?

Though practical wisdom obviously involves some kind of practical know-how, Aristotle is intent upon distinguishing it from other practical skills. His first move is to repeat the distinction we have already noticed between what he calls 'acting' (*praxis*) and 'producing' (*poiēsis*). At first sight the similarities between performing an action and making something are more obvious than the differences. In both cases, the agent does something which need not have been done: both involve thought and care; being good at how one lives and being good at making things are both skills which can be learnt, and which have to be learnt through practice and experience. So we might think to construct the following parallel, taking the practical skill of the physician as an illustration of a craft, and taking our cue from Aristotle's own example:

(a) Physicians aim at producing healthy patients.
(b) In order to do so, physicians must know what being healthy involves.
(c) Physicians must also learn what medicines to prescribe, and in what quantities – neither too much nor too little.

(A) Every person aims at producing fulfilment.
(B) In order to do so, people must know what fulfilment involves.

(C) People must also learn what actions will produce fulfilment, and those actions, as we have seen, must be virtuous, 'lying in the mean'.

Aristotle can see some force in the parallels here, but he also thinks they should not be exaggerated. So, in IV, 4, he first tries to undermine the parallel between (c) and (C). Health is indeed the product of the art of medicine, just as a house is the product of architecture, or a statue of sculpture. But *eudaimonia* is not the *product* of the actions of a good person. Fulfilment in life is not something over and above someone's actions which those actions produce.[2] Fulfilment consists in doing what one does just because one sees those actions as noble and worthwhile. Again, whether someone is good at architecture, or sculpture, or medicine is determined by the kind of houses, or statues, or patients they can produce; whereas being good at living a fulfilled life just is being able to live such a life, and living it is not a process one undertakes for the sake of something else which is produced as a result. The point of the good life just is the living of it.

It is important not to misunderstand Aristotle's view here. When he says that acting morally is not *producing* something, he is not taking sides on the modern question whether the consequences of our actions should make a difference to what we should do. He is neither asserting nor denying that the goodness of a generous action depends upon the benefits it brings to others. He is not taking sides on whether breaking promises is wrong because of its bad consequences for our social relationships, or whether the action of promise-breaking is wrong in itself. One reason for this is that Aristotle does not use the term 'action' in the way that it is used in the debate between modern consequentialists and their deontologist critics. Aristotle has nothing comparable to Bentham's definition of an action as a 'mere bodily movement', from which it would indeed follow that the value of an action must depend upon the consequences which that action produces, as Bentham says.

---

[2] This is another example of a place where translating *eudaimonia* as 'happiness', and going on to think of happiness as a special kind of feeling, might mislead us into thinking that *eudaimonia* is what good actions produce.

Instead, Aristotle defines an action in terms of how the agent describes or sees their behaviour at the time, and draws no particular line between an action and its consequences.[3] Which of the many 'consequences' (as Bentham would see them) the Aristotelian agent takes into account will depend upon the features of each situation. The good person knows what to have in mind when acting, and why to have precisely those considerations and no others in mind.

Unlike consequentialists, then, Aristotle does not regard an action as trying to bring something about, so that its moral worth would depend upon its successfully producing the required result. What is morally important, he says, is whether or not the agent can see what he is doing as making sense from the point of view of a fulfilled life. This in turn depends upon an integrated understanding of the function of a human being; so it ties in with what we have already seen about the emotional response of the virtuous person: for that response, too, involves an affective reading of the situation in an appropriate way. On this more later.

Whatever other similarities there might be between practical wisdom and an intellectual skill, then, (A) will now have to be revised in order to avoid seeing a fulfilled life as a *product* of what one does. Given that alteration, is there nevertheless a parallel between (a) and (A)? Again, one might think that there is, since Aristotle says that everything we do, we do for the sake of living worthwhile and fulfilled lives, just as everything a doctor does, he does for the sake of restoring his patients to health. Moreover, just as there are incompetent doctors who cannot recognize when someone is healthy or not, so there are incompetent people who just fail to see what a worthwhile and fulfilled life is like – they think it consists in wealth, or honours, or pleasure. One might still argue, though, that the *aims* are still parallel. Doctors aim at health, just as people aim at fulfilled lives.

But is this accurate? Think of the doctors in the Nazi concentration camps. Surely it can be argued that they were experts at the art of medicine, precisely using their medical skills to carry out the most horrendous experiments. A misused skill is still a skill. But plainly,

---

[3] This will need some qualification to deal with negligence. But it will do for the purposes of the point being made here.

Aristotle at least here assumes that a doctor, *by definition*, aims at making patients healthy. In that case, he would have to have said that the Nazis in the concentration camps were not *doctors*, whatever else they were. If that is so, then the parallel between (a) and (A) breaks down again; for Aristotle does not think that it is a mere matter of verbal definition that people aim at living fulfilled lives: they do so by natural necessity. As we shall see, even when people culpably fail to live up to their moral ideals, they do so only by somehow disguising from themselves that this is what they are doing. So there is a reason to suppose that crafts/skills and practical wisdom are not the same, which is linked to the distinction Aristotle makes between producing and acting. Skills can be misused, at will, to produce poor, shoddy, and at times morally grotesque results: practical wisdom cannot.

Now let us consider whether (b) is parallel to (B). What does a doctor have to know about health? Ideally, he needs to know a great deal about physiology and biology, hormones and the properties of the blood and the like. Most of this is information which doctors such as Aristotle's father could not possibly have had. In practice, though, even without such knowledge people can in a rough and ready way distinguish between the sick and the healthy, and Aristotle's father could certainly have done that. Even quite untrained people with no knowledge of medical theory have discovered folk-remedies, and while doctors can often propose remedies more accurately to the extent that they have understood the exact nature of illnesses, they can and do use remedies which work in ways which are still not understood. The truth of (b) therefore certainly does not require that doctors have a perfect grasp of what it is for humans to be healthy.

If (b) were parallel to (B), the implication would be that we can all at least roughly identify instances of people living fulfilled lives, and so gradually build up some understanding of *why* their lives are fulfilled, despite the fact that what they do may on the surface seem to be very different in each individual case. This in turn might suggest that, to the extent that we have learnt why their lives are fulfilled, we would have built up a *theoretical* understanding, parallel to medical science. But even this theoretical understanding of ethics will be in very general terms, perhaps much more so than in medicine, for the very good reason that human fulfilment is not like the smooth running

of machines, or even the well-being of other organisms. Human fulfilment is much more variable, because of the complexity and flexibility
of our distinctively human capacities. Nonetheless the conclusion, if
the parallel holds, would be that we can live more or less fulfilled
lives even if we have no very accurate understanding of what a fulfilled
life involves.

So, is (b) parallel to (B)? Perhaps we should first ask whether
Aristotle thinks that (B) is true. Do we need to have a grasp of what
fulfilment is before we can live a fulfilled life? The argument so far
in the *Ethics* suggests that the answer to this question is 'in a way yes,
and in a way no', for much the same reasons as explain the qualifications we need to read into (b). We know that *eudaimonia* consists in
living a life according to the moral virtues, and that we are by nature
inclined towards the kinds of reflection in which *theōria* consists.
Eudaimonia consists in making ultimate sense of the morally admirable life. That's it, in a nutshell. But even if we agree with all that,
do we know what counts as living according to the moral virtues?
Recall that the moral virtues are defined in terms of what the person
of practical wisdom would see to be right. So far, however, we have
no independent account of what such a person would decide, or why,
or how. Until we do, we do not know what such a person's life is like.
Moreover, what is there to *know* about such a life? Aristotle has already
made it clear that it cannot be exactly described, since different people
will have to behave variously in different circumstances. There is no
blueprint for living well, and in that sense no clear-cut definition of
what living well consists in. What Aristotle will offer here in Book VI
to illuminate his conception of practical wisdom is much more like a
general account of what goes to make up a skill.

But to be more exact, we perhaps need to distinguish, both in
medicine and in morality, between whatever theoretical understanding
we might reach and our ability to use that understanding in practice.[4]
Moral science in Aristotle's view is much less exact than, say, medicine; but so far as the application of theory to practice is concerned
the parallel seems to be quite close.

[4] For this distinction see X, 9 generally, and in particular 1180b13–28. Medicine
is a good example of something which includes both a science and a skill.

Finally, we may look at (c) and (C). Once again, (C) would have to be rephrased to avoid the term 'produce', so the parallel with (c) is at best very inexact. Medicines do cause health, whereas virtuous actions do not cause fulfilment. Fulfilment is not a state of affairs, nor is it a feeling such as pain, or pleasure, or contentment. It is a way of living a particular kind of life thoughtfully. The thought that goes into fulfilled living is not like the thought that goes into the choice of treatment for a patient, or of materials for a house or a ship. In these cases, what one has to think about is causal effectiveness – will this drug work, will this beam be strong enough to withstand the stress, and so on. In the case of a good life, one has to think specifically of the quality of what one is doing, and only secondarily, on occasions, of the causal effectiveness of what one is doing. For example, the person who volunteers to visit prisoners presumably wishes to encourage them, and to help them in all kinds of ways. He will therefore have to think about the most effective ways of doing so, and will quite rightly be disappointed if he cannot always find what it would be helpful to say or do. But, in Aristotle's view, more important *morally* is how he regards the entire enterprise, and what, for him, is the point of it all. He tries to think what would be really helpful because that is a fine and noble thing to do.

So, an initial look at practical wisdom suggests that it is unlike other skills, in that we cannot simply decide to misuse it, both because by definition it consists in doing what is morally admirable, and because by nature we are all of necessity oriented towards what we can present to ourselves as living a fulfilled life. That being said, practical wisdom does resemble other skills, in that it is backed by a theoretical understanding, but essentially consists in the ability to apply such an understanding in individual situations.

Having distinguished practical wisdom from both craft/skill and from theoretical wisdom, Aristotle then remarks:

> It is commonly thought that it is characteristic of the man of practical wisdom to be able to deliberate well about the things which are good and helpful for himself, not in some restricted way (good for his health, or his strength) but about living well in general.

> (VI, 5, 1140a25–28)

This common-sense view is one which he himself is willing to endorse:

> It remains, then, that it is a true and thoughtful habit concerning actions regarding those things which are good and bad for human beings.

$$\text{(VI, 5, 1140b4--6)}$$

The key element in this account is the claim that practical wisdom has to do with what is the specifically human good; and that alone serves to distinguish it from all the other practical skills. They are concerned with a good product; practical wisdom is concerned with good actions, whose goodness is intrinsic to the actions themselves. It enables someone to arrive at the true answers to questions about what they have to do.

Practical wisdom: about means or about ends?

So far so good. But it is at this point that it becomes really difficult to interpret what Aristotle says. The difficulty is that he seems to say quite incompatible things in different places. There are two problems which need immediate attention: how to sort out what Aristotle says about 'particulars' and 'universals'; and what does he mean when he speaks about practical wisdom as the capacity to deliberate?

Some preliminaries about terminology, and how logicians use 'universal' and 'particular'. Let's consider again the kind of example I have already used:

> Physicians aim at producing healthy patients.
> Removing Annabel's appendix would restore her to health.
> So, I should have Annabel's appendix removed.

Here we have what Aristotle calls a practical syllogism – a set of premises leading to a conclusion about what one should do. The first premise of this argument is universal: and by that is meant, it talks about kinds or types of thing, rather than about any individual: physicians, rather than Doctor Crippen or Doctor Smith next door; healthy patients rather than Annabel or Algernon. 'Physician', 'patient', and 'healthy patient' are all universal expressions. Notice, especially, that although 'healthy patient' is a more specific, restricted, term than the more general term 'patient', it is still universal. In contrast, the second premise and the conclusion are both particular statements, talking about particular individuals of the kinds mentioned in the universal first premises. I, Annabel, and Annabel's appendix are particular, individual, things.

So, there are two related problems we need to think about. The first is about the practical syllogisms we have already looked at. The first premise is universal, and the second premise is particular. Which of these is the focus for practical wisdom? The second problem ties in with the first: for the first premise can be regarded as setting out the aim of an action, whereas the second premise is concerned with how that aim is to be achieved in practice. So, putting the two together, the question is whether practical wisdom, focusing on the particular, is concerned only with means to an end? Or is it also concerned with establishing in universal terms the end at which our actions should aim?

'Particulars' and 'Universals'

The following text illustrates the problem:

> The person who is without qualification good at deliberating is the person who can aim with rational calculation at the best for man of the things which can be achieved by action. Practical wisdom is not only about universals: it must also recognize particulars, since it is concerned with actions, and actions are concerned with particulars. That is why some people who lack knowledge are more practical than others who have knowledge, especially if they have experience. For if someone knew that light meats are easily digested and healthy, but did not know which kinds of meat are light, he would not produce health as effectively as the person who knows that poultry meat is healthy. Practical wisdom is about actions, so it must have both types of knowledge, especially the second.
>
> (VI, 7, 1141b12–22)

The first sentence makes the point we have already seen. Being good at deliberation 'without qualification' picks up the contrast with being good at deliberating about some specific field such as medicine, or architecture. Practical wisdom is concerned with what is morally good and noble, and hence with living a worthwhile and fulfilled life as a whole. The illustration about light meats is somewhat disconcerting at first, since it seems to be concerned with health and diet, rather than with what is good without qualification. But Aristotle is simply trying to illustrate a point which holds good of anything practical, not just ethics: to know what should be done is in the end more important than to know *why* it should be done. The experienced housewife knows that poultry is good for health, though she may not know why it is. Somewhere here there is surely some version of the contrast between theoretical knowledge and the ability to apply that knowledge in practice which we have already mentioned.

But the details are still difficult to sort out. If the chicken example is supposed to be some kind of parallel to illustrate the nature of moral deliberation, how is the moral parallel supposed to run? There is unfortunately more than one possibility:

Here is one version of how it might run:

	Light meats are healthy	Being kind is virtuous
	Poultry meats are light	Encouraging people is being kind
So	Poultry meats are healthy	Encouraging people is virtuous

Someone might know that light meats are healthy, but not know that poultry meats are light; and hence will not reliably choose to eat poultry even when they are trying to eat a healthy diet. The moral parallel is then supposed to be that someone may know that one should be kind to people, but not know which types of behaving are ways of being kind. Such a person will not reliably succeed in being kind on practice. Much better in practice, we are to suppose, is the person who knows that it is good to encourage people without knowing why this might be so.

One problem with this interpretation is that it is not too easy to see how someone could know that it was good to encourage people and still not know why this is so (e.g. because it is an act of kindness); and there is a further possible difficulty, in that the second premise in each case is said by Aristotle to be *particular*; but both the second premises in this reconstruction are universal, because they speak about *kinds* of meat, or *types* of action, rather than individual instances of those types.[5]

So perhaps we should try again:

Light meats are healthy	Being kind is virtuous
This piece of chicken is light	Saying 'Well done!' here and now is being kind
This piece of chicken is healthy	Saying 'Well done!' here and now is virtuous

Here, what the person knows is a particular – something about *this* piece of chicken on the plate, or about saying precisely *these* words here and now. But we are still to suppose that the person as it were instinctively knows that they should say 'Well done!' but might not know that to do so would be an act of kindness, which again seems less than likely. The basic trouble stems from the fact that in the chicken case, the middle term of the argument, 'light meat', is quite a technical expression, and refers to a feature which it is easy to imagine someone not knowing. A still more convincing example might depend on some notion such as 'polyunsaturated'. But 'kind', which is the middle term in the moral parallel, seems entirely unproblematic, so the moral parallels are too 'easy' to be convincing.

So perhaps we might try a more difficult moral example while keeping the same overall structure. There are occasions on which, as the saying goes, one needs to be cruel to be kind. Suppose, then, that a budding author asks for an opinion on the manuscript of a novel, and that it really is not at all good. We would have the following parallel:

Light meats are healthy	Being kind is virtuous
This piece of chicken is light	Saying 'This will never sell' now is being kind
This piece of chicken is healthy	Saying 'This will never sell' now is virtuous

[5] This is not perhaps a very serious difficulty: Aristotle does not always distinguish between the relationship between sub-classes and the class to which they belong, and that between a class and the individual members of that class; just as we might think of chicken as a *particular* kind of meat.

It is perhaps a bit easier to imagine someone knowing what they should say, without seeing that to do so might be an act of kindness. They lack the experience to understand that on occasions this might be so. Maybe they think that to say anything else would be dishonest, and that's why one should be honest here; it's got nothing to do with kindness, in their mind; it's a matter of honesty. This fits in well with the contrast between theoretical knowledge and knowing how to apply that knowledge in practice. Even without experience – or at any rate without much experience – a person will probably manage to get the easy cases right. Obviously one says 'Well done!' when someone has just won a race, or made a good speech. It is the difficult cases in which it may not be obvious what precise words are required in order to be kind here and now, or whether kindness is important in this case. Only the person of experience can be relied upon to get it right. Upon reflection, one can see that there are many instances of this kind of problem – involving such notions as 'unreasonable request', or 'unfair dismissal' or 'due care and attention'. One can have a general idea what such terms mean, and hence of instances which would clearly fall under them, while still remaining quite uncertain in many other cases.

But there is still a problem. The parallel with the exercise of the craft of medicine takes us only so far. Eating chicken will produce health, whether or not one understands why it does so. But if my arguments in the previous chapter are correct, saying 'This will never sell' is not a virtuous action unless the agent understands it as such; and that remains true even if, being well brought up, the agent spontaneously feels that this is what should be said. An appropriate emotional response is a necessary, but not a sufficient condition for moral virtue in its full sense. The agent needs practical wisdom, which involves understanding. An action is not virtuous because it is in one way or another effective, but because it is seen by the agent in a particular way. We need to inquire further about what this 'seeing' involves:

> We say that people who do just actions are not thereby just; not, for instance, if they obey what is laid down by the law either unwillingly or through ignorance rather than for the sake of doing so (even though they do what they should, i.e. all that the just

man should do.) So it appears that in order to be good one has to act in a certain state [of mind], I mean by choosing and doing so for the sake of the actions concerned.

(VI, 12, 1144a13–19)

The chicken example is not entirely clear, but it, too, contains some hints about what the person of practical wisdom 'sees' or 'recognizes'. Thus: 'Practical wisdom is not only about universals: it must also recognize particulars, since it is concerned with actions, and actions are concerned with particulars.' Aristotle elaborates on this remark in VI, 8. He first points out that though the young may well be good at geometry or mathematics they are not usually thought to possess practical wisdom, because they lack experience with 'particulars'. By this he must mean the multitude of individual situations which a person with experience will have faced and learned from (1142a11–18). He then gives an illustration, which is just like the health example we have already seen (1142a20–23) before continuing with a passage which, once again, has proved very difficult to interpret:

That practical wisdom is not scientific knowledge is clear: it concerns the ultimate [particular], as we have said; for what has to be done is [particular].[6] So practical wisdom is contrasted with insight (*nous*), which is concerned with definitions for which no argument can be given, whereas practical wisdom is concerned with the ultimate [particular] of which we have not scientific knowledge but perception. This is not the perception of the qualities which are proper to each of our senses, but the kind of perception by which we see that this particular figure is a triangle; for it will stop here, too. This is closer to ordinary perception than practical wisdom is, though it is a different kind of perception.

(1142a23–30)

[6] Aristotle simply says 'the ultimate'; the context suggests that he means a particular; and he uses 'ultimate' precisely because there is nothing more basic which is presupposed.

Here is one reasonable reading of this much-discussed passage. Aristotle intends to make the following points:

(1) Practical wisdom is not like scientific knowledge, which is of universal principles.

(2) The definitions of things (for instance, of eclipses, or lions, or substances) are arrived at by looking at many instances, and grasping what is essential to all of them. One simply spots the connection, rather than arguing for it, or deducing it logically.[7] *Nous* is Aristotle's term for the ability to do this.

(3) Practical wisdom sees an individual action as an action of a particular kind, just as we can simply see that a figure is a triangle.

(4) Seeing that something is a triangle is not simply a perception (as would be seeing the lines, or seeing something red, or feeling warm). It involves a 'seeing as', which is an act of classification. Once again, there is no need for proof or argument; one simply notices what it is.[8]

(5) Seeing something as a triangle is nevertheless more like seeing lines than it is like the moral perception in which practical wisdom consists.

This interpretation has the merit of explaining why Aristotle should say that practical wisdom is not concerned only with universals but also with particulars. I take it that what the person 'sees' is that to say 'This will never sell' would in these circumstances be an act of kindness. (In different circumstances, to say the same words would perhaps be unhelpfully discouraging; while to say 'This is a good start!' in the present circumstances would be untrue.) *Phronēsis*

[7] Another kind of example might be this: what is the next member of the series JFMAMJJ? One cannot produce an argument or proof which will solve this problem. One just has to spot the link which defines the series as a whole.

[8] There is a difference of opinions among commentators about (3) and (4). Some see in this passage a reference back to III, 5, 1112b20–24, and argue that what the person sees is that a triangle is the simplest (in that sense 'ultimate') plane figure from which to start in producing a geometrical construction. On this issue, see the section below on 'means and ends'.

is concerned not just with the universal, which I take to be 'To be kind is virtuous'. It also involves the ability to discern in this particular instance whether saying 'This will never sell' would be an act of kindness or an unsympathetic lack of encouragement to a nervous beginner. The ability to discern in this way requires not merely an understanding of what kindness is, but also the experience to use that understanding correctly. More precisely still, a correct grasp of what kindness is just is the flip side of knowing *both* that now is a time for kindness, *and* what it would be kind to say here and now. I take it that Aristotle's students, being well brought up, would have some overall grasp of what kindness is, and would feel inclined to be kind in a general way. What they lack is the experience to know how to do that in every case, and in which cases kindness is what is called for. To that extent, they lack an *accurate* grasp of the universal as well.

This also fits well enough with some remarks in VI, 11. Aristotle is here explaining how some commonly recognized natural intellectual abilities[9] contribute to the acquired intellectual virtue of practical wisdom. All these abilities, he says, deal with particulars. He then goes on, in yet another difficult text, to explain why these abilities have to do with particulars. The reason is that they are all concerned with doing something. But this text needs a good deal of teasing out if we are to make sense of it:

> Everything which is done is a particular, that is to say an ultimate. So the person of practical wisdom needs to recognize particulars, just as understanding and judgement too are concerned with things which are done, and so with ultimates. Now insight (*nous*) is concerned with ultimates in both directions: it is insight rather than argument which gives us both the initial definitions and ultimates as well; in scientific proofs it provides the unchanging definitions from which they

[9] He outlines these in chapters 9 and 10, and in the first part of 11. They include being able to make good guesses; reasoning ability, planning ability, being quick on the uptake, and being considerate. Here again, as so often, he is showing how his own views can explain the ordinary terms which his readers would be familiar with.

start; and in practical matters it provides a grasp of the particular which could be otherwise, and is given by the minor premise. These [particular insights] are the origins of the end one has in view, since universals are derived from particulars. Of these particulars, then, we must have a perception, and that is insight.

(VI, 12, 1143a32–b5)

Once again, by 'ultimates' he means something which is to be taken as basic, beyond which one cannot go by finding some yet more fundamental argument or ground. Insight, as we have seen, is required in the sciences to see the essential connections between the at first sight very diverse particular things one is studying. Here Aristotle uses the same term, *nous*, for the special kind of perception which is required to see the 'minor premise', such as, 'To say *this, now*, would be an act of kindness'. What is new about this passage is that he explicitly says that in practical matters we build up our notion of the end to aim at – kindness, for example – by grasping instances of it. 'Universals are derived from particulars.' He also contrasts theoretical definitions with the universals we use in practical matters. Unlike the unchanging essences from which scientific explanations start, practical universals such as kindness, courage, or temperance are flexible and inexact, since their instances escape precise codification. It is not possible to give rules for kindness which will automatically sort out what would be an act of kindness in every situation.

The key points, then, are these:

(1) Practical wisdom involves a combination of understanding and experience.
(2) It consists in the ability to read individual situations aright.
(3) In so doing, one is drawing on previous experience (which has helped to build up an understanding of the demands of truthfulness, kindness, courage, etc.).
(4) One is also continually enhancing that understanding in the light of each particular situation with which one is confronted.

Deliberation, means and ends[10]

The account I have just given strongly suggests that practical wisdom, in dealing with particular choices which have to be made, 'reads' situations in universal terms, and in so doing often refines our understanding of the sense of the universal itself. Perhaps, then, a similar account will turn out to explain Aristotle's remarks about means and ends. In deciding what means have to be employed, one clarifies one's understanding of the end at which one should be aiming. So one cannot deliberate about means without wondering about ends as well. Or so I shall try to argue. We shall see.

To many commentators it appears clear enough that Aristotle restricts the scope of practical wisdom to means. Aristotle makes this quite explicit at least in most of the clear texts on the point. These commentators will point out that the examples like those we have already seen (for instance, how to produce health, or how to navigate a ship, or to build a good house) all assume that the major premise of a practical argument is simply given: doctors aim at health, navigators at a safe arrival at the desired destination, architects at a weatherproof and convenient building. What needs deliberation is how to act in such a way that the desired outcome results. If these examples illustrate anything about deliberation, and hence about moral deliberation, they show clearly enough that the problems about which we deliberate are problems about means, not about the ends to be achieved.

The alternative view, to which I subscribe, denies this. Defenders of this view hope to show that the texts are not so clear as the friends of the first view would have us believe; we would also argue that it would be strange indeed if Aristotle thought that morally serious people never had to think about what their actions aimed at, or wonder whether they were aiming at the right things in life. After all, Aristotle does say that practical wisdom is to be applied not only to the personal lives of individuals, but is also the virtue of politicians who have to think about the good of the community as a whole (VI, 8). Surely politicians routinely have to consider what they should be aiming at, and Aristotle clearly thinks they do.

---

[10] Aristotle's term for 'deliberation' is *bouleusis*.

The case for the 'means only' view goes like this. Aristotle says that it is typical of the person of practical wisdom to deliberate well about what is good and helpful for himself, and about what will be conducive to the good life in general (VI, 5, 1140a24–28). To see what he is getting at, we need to start by getting clear about what he means by 'to deliberate'.[11] At the very end of III, 2, Aristotle makes two suggestions: (1) that whereas it is ends that we wish for, what we choose is the means to those ends (1111b26–29); and (2) choice has to do with deliberation (1112a15–16). In the next chapter, III, 3, he does some ground-clearing. We do not deliberate about what it is impossible to change – the universe, geometrical facts, the weather or the movements of the stars. We deliberate only about what it is in our power to affect. Then (and it is argued, crucially) he says that we do not deliberate about ends, but about the means to those ends (1112b11–12: see also 1113b2–4), and goes on to give the usual examples; orators, doctors, statesmen, bakers. In each case, the end is given, but ways and means are open to discussion and choice.

These passages from Book III, it is argued, must surely be taken seriously when we come to read what he says here in Book VI (as is suggested already at the end of VI, 1), especially given the fact that very similar examples occur here too. So we find texts like this:

> What affirmation and negation are to thinking, so pursuit and avoidance are to desire. Now moral virtue is a habitual state connected with choice, and choice is a deliberated desire. Hence both the thinking must be true and the desire right if the choice is to be good, so that reason affirms just what desire pursues.
>
> (VI, 2, 1139a21–26)

[11] Aristotle repeatedly speaks as if every good action must be the result of deliberation. But he can hardly have failed to recall that we are frequently in a position to know what we should do without needing to ponder over it at all. He does once say that to be able to deliberate quickly is better than having to take a long time about it (1142b26–28). Perhaps the general explanation is that he tends to concentrate on more difficult decisions as being more problematic; perhaps, too, he is intent on exhibiting the logic of all our decisions, rather than describing a single psychological process by which they are made in every case.

The suggestion is that we should read this as saying that it is our desires which determine what our ends will be; deliberation then works out how this end is to be achieved; and choice is just this combination of desire and deliberation. So when, in deliberating, we come to see how we can actually go about achieving what we desire, we then choose to do it.

I would quite agree that we do not, in Aristotle's view, deliberate about whether or not to aim at a fulfilled life. That desire is implanted in us by nature, and is therefore not something about which we have a choice (1111b28–30). At most, then, we might have to think about what a fulfilled life would be like. Proponents of the 'means only' view correctly see this; but they then go on to apply the analogy of a craft-skill too literally, concluding that we deliberate only about the means to the predetermined end. I have already suggested above that the parallel is far from exact. In particular, good actions are not means to produce a fulfilled life. If they were, they would produce such a life no matter how the agent regarded them. This Aristotle clearly denies, as we have seen.

The key point is that *phronēsis* is the ability to find some action in particular circumstances which the agent can see as the virtuous thing to do. The discussion (in I, 5) of the claims that a fulfilled life might consist in the pursuit of wealth, honour or pleasure surely suggests that these claims, and Aristotle's counter-claim, are topics about which we might have to reflect and discuss. We do not deliberate about trying to be fulfilled, but we do have to think about what fulfilment might be like. If what I have said earlier in this section is right, we still have to build up our picture of a fulfilled life gradually and bit by bit, by exercising practical wisdom in particular decisions. It is not the case that we have a blueprint specifying precisely what needs to be achieved, so that all we have to do is to find out means to achieve it. Our early moral training in virtue is a necessary, but not a sufficient condition of seeing what has to be done in the complex situations of adult life. We come to understand the end – what a fulfilled life involves – better precisely by deliberating about what to do, situation by situation. Where the moral life is concerned, to deliberate about particular actions is also to deliberate about what a fulfilled and worthwhile life involves. It is therefore to become the kind of person who sees life in a particular way, and sees one's decisions as fitting into that vision of a life. This blend of practical living and *theōria* is the activity of a particular kind of agent – a morally admirable person; it has little or nothing to do with ends and means to an end.

Practical wisdom and moral virtue

In VI, 5, Aristotle remarks that temperance (and doubtless the other moral virtues as well) preserves practical wisdom, since it preserves our beliefs about what is to be done. He points out that while a lack of virtue does not upset our beliefs about geometry, it does distort our perceptions of what has to be done and why. We are doubtless all familiar with instances in which our emotional imbalance has made it impossible for us to have a perceptive judgement about what has to be done; we are too involved, too close to the situation to be able to rely on our judgement. What, precisely is this 'judgement', then? Aristotle gives us one possible way to answer this question, by examining the contrast between the practical deliberations of the good man and those of someone who is merely clever. He thus takes into account the kind of example I gave earlier about the Nazi doctors:

> Now, if the aim is noble, cleverness is praiseworthy; if it is base, then cleverness is just unscrupulousness. So we describe both people of practical wisdom and those who are unscrupulous as clever. But practical wisdom is not just cleverness, though it does require cleverness. It is a habitual state which is developed in the eye of the soul only in the presence of moral virtue, as we have already said and is clear enough. For instances of reasoning about practical matters have as their starting point 'Since the end is of such and such a kind' (whatever – anything will do as an example). But the end is not clear except to a good person. Wickedness distorts [our judgement] and leads to our being deceived about the starting points of action. Obviously, then, one cannot be a person of practical wisdom without being a good person.
>
> (VI, 12, 1144a26–b1)

At first sight, what this passage seems to say is that practical wisdom just is cleverness when the person also happens to be virtuous. If someone is virtuous, then their aims will be good; and their cleverness will be admirable since it is employed for good ends. This interpretation would fit exactly with the view about ends and means which suggests that we deliberate only about means, but that the ends are not themselves something with which practical wisdom is concerned. Commentators who take this line will then cite in its favour a text which is apparently equally clear and unambiguous:

> Again, the function of a human being is achieved in accordance with practical wisdom and moral virtue. Virtue makes the end right, and practical wisdom those things which are for the end.
>
> (VI, 12, 1144a6–9)

Let us look at this second text first. It is one of the replies to a series of objections, all of which are directed to showing that neither theoretical wisdom nor practical wisdom are of any *use*. Just as we do not have to learn to be doctors in order to look after our health, since it is enough just to do as doctors tell us, so we do not need practical wisdom in order to be good, we just act out our virtuous inclinations, if we are good; and if we are not, mere knowledge (whether theoretical or practical) won't make us good. Aristotle replies that theoretical knowledge does not *produce* a fulfilled life. Rather it is the point of a fulfilled life, which explains why that life is fulfilled. Similarly, practical wisdom does not *produce* good actions, but explains why they are good. Then follows the second of the texts I have just cited. So it must be intended to argue against the objection that practical *knowledge* is useless, and to rebut the suggestion that spontaneously virtuous inclinations are enough to ensure that we act well. I have already suggested that even our most perfectly virtuous inclinations may be too coarse-grained until shaped by a judgement of precisely how they are to fit the particular situation. We may feel inclined to be kind and generous, but until we have understood how to do that here and now, the virtuous inclination is not sharp enough. Yet, once we have *understood* what generosity and kindness require now, it is the action which exactly embodies that understanding which now becomes the content of our virtuous inclination.

Now what the first text makes clear is that if we lack moral virtue, we will be *deceived* about the ends of actions, which will not be *clear* to us. These are surely errors in understanding; it is our judgement about these ends which emotional imbalance distorts. Performing a good and noble action requires us to understand what we are doing in the right way; what we are doing is (for instance) saying 'That will never sell' *as an act of kindness.* It is not enough that we say so because (having been well trained in virtue) we feel inclined to say so, any more than it is enough that we say so because we have been advised by a good person to say so. What moral virtues do is help us to *judge* correctly about what to do and why, just as lack of moral virtue impairs our judgement. To that extent, they ensure that what we aim at will be something that is worth pursuing, in contrast to the intemperate person or someone who lacks moral virtue, and whose *intellectual* horizon is limited by what he can perceive as desirable.

The key to Aristotle's whole position here is his claim that our emotions affect our *understanding* of how we should behave. This is how I would propose to interpret the second text. It does not follow from this that the person of practical wisdom simply follows the end set by his desires: (1) because as we shall see presently, it may not be that our desires point in just one direction; (2) because *exactly* what we desire is something we still have to 'see', by using our undistorted understanding. The action upon which we decide is *to do A as an instance of what is virtuous, fine and noble.* Choice both specifies what we want, and is motivated by the desire thus specified. In the process of deciding, we may, and often will, refine our grasp of what a virtue – say kindness – requires of us.

To sum up, then, we may cite a final text, this time from VI, 9:

> If what is characteristic of people of practical wisdom is to have deliberated well, deliberating well must be correctness concerning what is related to the end of which practical wisdom has a correct grasp.

$$(1142b31–33)^{12}$$

[12] It is just possible to translate the Greek in such a way that what practical wisdom correctly grasps is what is related to the end, rather than the end itself. But this reading is a less natural one; and, if I am right in what I have so far said, there is no need to abandon the more natural reading I have given in the text.

The moral virtues, being states of appropriate emotional balance, respond to features of the situations in which we find ourselves. In so doing, they alert us to the existence of those features and so offer us starting points for choices. Our choices are motivated by our virtuous inclinations, indeed; but what is of central importance is that they express our refined understanding of what to do and why. It is in only so choosing that we can make coherent sense of ourselves and our lives.

The unity of the virtues

One final look at a remark of Aristotle's we have already seen will complete the picture:

> In this way, we can refute the dialectical argument that the [moral] virtues are quite separate from one another. The same person, it might be argued, is not by nature equally disposed to all the virtues, so he might already have acquired one without having acquired the others. This *is* possible in the case of the natural virtues, but not in the case of the ones on the basis of which he is described as a good person without qualification. For with the presence of the single virtue of practical reason all the virtues are present.
>
> (VI, 13, 1144b32–1145a2)

Aristotle agrees that someone might be naturally good at mathematics without being good at athletics, for instance. It is this fact that makes people think that the same must be true of moral virtues as well. But he denies that someone can have the virtue of courage unless he is also honest, or honest unless he is also kind. At first sight this seems a very surprising thing to say, since we surely would often be quite happy to say that someone had a good character in many respects, without being willing to say that they had a good character in all respects.

But this 'dialectical argument'[13] seriously underestimates the

---

[13] Here, as often, 'dialectical' means 'based on what is commonly said'. Once again, Aristotle tries to start from, and sympathetically understand, what is commonly said while still, as here, being willing to disagree with it.

subtlety of Aristotle's views about what a good character has to be like. I think the easiest way to see this is to take not the comparatively simple instances of moral decision making which we have looked at so far, but somewhat more complex ones. I offer two examples:

(1) A beaten army is retreating in disarray towards a river, behind which they hope to make a stand. A small group of soldiers is asked to hold the road against the advancing enemy long enough for their companions to make their escape by boat across the river. The chances of the rearguard surviving are very slight.

Let us assume that the soldiers are 'good without qualification'. What, then, is their emotional response supposed to be, when faced with their desperate assignment? On the one hand, they should rightly be afraid and inclined to run away, since the situation truly is extremely life-threatening for them. Courage, Aristotle would say, leads some-one to feel afraid when fear is appropriate. On the other hand, the soldiers will also feel inclined to stay and fight, since it is a noble thing for them to sacrifice themselves to save their companions. In all normal circumstances, to stay and fight would simply be fool-hardy (which is why the rest of the army is quite properly retreating); but in these circumstances, it is not foolhardy, but generous and noble. Frightened as they will feel, they will on balance feel more inclined to stay, since they have correctly seen that the situation calls for self-sacrifice. Having seen that, their fear is itself modified by their concern for their companions. What counts as appropriate fear is dependent upon what counts as a reasonable sacrifice to ask of them. The appropriate response depends on more than one aspect of the situation. Courage here is courage rather than foolhardiness only because of the demands of generosity. Generosity is reasonable only when it does not require foolhardiness. One cannot have one without the other.

(2) I was once invited by some first-year undergraduates to their house for dinner. They had made enormous efforts to be welcoming, though clearly they were a bit nervous at the prospect of entertaining their teacher, perhaps unsure if they could carry it off properly. The main course of the meal was a quiche. As it turned out, a far from perfect quiche. The cook asked me how I liked it. I said I thought it was lovely.

I have often found that when people are asked about this example, they react in two sharply different ways. Some say that I simply lied, where I ought to have told the truth or at the very least found some more diplomatic way of expressing gratitude without actually lying. Others quite agree that I said exactly what I should have said in the circumstances, rather than undermine a young person's self-confidence and behaving quite ungracefully into the bargain. It has even been suggested that I ought to have considered future guests who might have the same unfortunate experience unless I made it unambiguously clear that culinary improvements were required. Several virtues are invoked in this discussion: truthfulness, kindness, gratitude, concern for the common good. As it seemed, and seems, to me, I did the right thing. Moreover, it does not seem to me that what I did is properly described as lying, or even as lying in a good cause. It seems to me that one lies only when truthfulness is at stake, whereas in this case truthfulness simply was not the issue at all. Similarly, it seems to me that concern for future guests was simply irrelevant in the circumstances. It was clearly, I judged, a time for kindness and gratitude.[14]

Notice several things about this example. The first has to do with understanding and, specifically, with practical wisdom. Each of the virtues which were invoked in the discussion can be accurately understood only to the extent that one has accurately understood all the others. At least as I saw the situation (rightly or wrongly), I simply was not worried about telling an untruth, and hence would not accept that description of what I did. I simply was not being untruthful, any more than I was lacking in compassion for future guests. As some others read my situation, I was being untruthful though, because I was misled by my kind impulses, I failed to see what I said as an instance of lying. Either way, which was the appropriate emotional response will affect one's view not just of one virtue, but of several. This is exactly Aristotle's point. Secondly, notice that I might not

[14] I might point out that those who think that what I did was wrong, because it was a lie, are mostly younger than those who think that what I said was what I should have said. Naturally, I take this to bear out Aristotle's point about considerable experience of life being required for practical wisdom!

have succeeded in saying something kind and encouraging despite my intentions. 'Very nice' might have sounded distinctly unenthusiastic. If I had said that, I would have failed in my choice of 'what is for the end' in failing to grasp the particular correctly. Finally, wanting to say what I did and seeing it as the act of kindness which the situation demanded, are closely interwoven aspects of my action. It could be described equally in terms of what I wanted, and what I judged to be right. The moral virtue and the intellectual virtue go hand in hand.

Is Aristotle's account defensible?

Aristotle builds both emotional response and intellectual judgement into his account of what it is to act morally. He is therefore in principle open to attack from two different directions: from those who think that he overplays the role of intellect: and from those who think that he should not have allowed emotions to be involved at all in the making of moral judgements. His view can be seen either as a well-balanced account of a process which is complex, or as an ill-advised attempt to combine incompatibles.

We might take Hume as an example of someone who would welcome Aristotle's emphasis on the emotions, but object to the central role he gives to practical *reason*. In Hume's view, reason is purely *theoretical*. The only knowledge that reason can provide is knowledge of the relationships between our ideas. But no such theoretical knowledge of the relationships between ideas will tell us about the real world; and there is no way in which such theoretical knowledge can explain why we should connect specifically moral concepts such as 'virtue' or 'vice' with any of the other ideas which we form as a result of our experience. 'Morality', says Hume, 'is more felt than judg'd of.' And again, '. . . when you pronounce any action or character to be vicious, you mean nothing but that from the constitution of your own nature you have a feeling or sentiment of blame from the contemplation of it.'[15] Hume points out that 'Morals excite passions, and produce or prevent actions. Reason of itself is utterly impotent in this particular. The rules of morality, therefore, are not conclusions of our

[15] *Treatise*, 470 and 468: see also 463.

reason.'[16] In consequence, the function of reason in ethics is primarily to work out how to bring about the states of affairs which we desire: as he puts it, 'Reason is, and ought only to be the slave of the passions, and can never pretend to any other office than to serve and obey them.'[17]

As we have just seen, Aristotle has been interpreted in a way which is very similar to this Humean approach. Virtues, which are emotional responses to situations, determine our aims, and the role of practical reason is to calculate the best means to achieve those aims. A remark of Aristotle's, that 'Reason itself, however, moves nothing, but only that reason which aims at an end and is practical' (1039a35–36) might at least at first sight have struck Hume as perfectly correct. I have already argued that this way of reading Aristotle is mistaken. So how would he have replied to Hume? He might first of all have pointed out that Hume is much too optimistic in thinking that we are 'from the constitution of our own nature' disposed to respond appropriately to virtue and vice. Appropriate responses are not part of our nature, they have to be carefully trained. In any case, we have to be able to *judge* which are the appropriate responses which we should try to foster. Second, while Aristotle would agree that moral choices need to be motivated, and not simply thought about, he would deny that we can never act against our inclinations. In the early years of our training, we often do have to act contrary to our inclinations, doing as the generous person might do while, as yet, not feeling generous in the doing of it. If that is so, then it cannot simply be the case that desires which we already have prior to choosing automatically set the aims which we seek to achieve in acting.

To this Hume might reply that this kind of self-control simply shows that we have a desire to do the right thing which is stronger than our inclination to do something else. Aristotle's reply to this would be more complex, and part of it will have to be examined when we consider his account of 'weakness of will'. But we have already seen some of the essential points he might make. The good person

[16] *Treatise*, 457.

[17] *Treatise*, 414.

chooses, and therefore wants, to do some particular action by seeing that it is what should be done. Untrained feelings can distort our moral insights; but even the virtuous feelings of the good person are further shaped and given a more refined focus by the intellectual grasp of a particular action as fine and noble.

Most fundamentally of all, Aristotle would insist that practical wisdom involves both *true* judgement and *correct* desire. That actions possess the moral qualities they do is independent of our beliefs or our feelings about those actions. If Hume were to query the propriety of using a term such as 'correct' to describe a desire, on the grounds that only judgements can be correct or mistaken, Aristotle would reply that the correctness of a desire can be defined in terms of its corresponding to the true judgement of the person of practical reason.

This line of reply would be the basis of Aristotle's rebuttal of the criticisms from the opposite direction, that he allowed too great a role to feelings and inclinations in ethics. A Kantian philosopher, equally anti-Humean, might urge that Aristotle's position does not go far enough.[18] Once one has recognized that our feelings and emotions can distort our rational judgements in practical matters, as Aristotle of course does, must one not admit that *any* input from the side of our feelings into the process of judging what one should do is suspect? Indeed the point could be put rather more sharply. Of course, Aristotle defines moral virtues in terms of the judgement of the person of practical reason, so it might seem that he does not leave moral judgements vulnerable to morally unacceptable feelings or emotions. This would be fine if only Aristotle gave us an independent criterion for the correctness of moral judgements. But he does not, and explicitly refuses to do so. The person of practical wisdom simply 'sees' what the situation requires by way of action. There is no argument or proof on which this judgement is based, and hence no prior test by which we could identify the person of practical reason. It is only by seeing such a person at work that we can know which responses are virtuous, and which choices are correct. So how, on Aristotle's account, are we to tell any of these things? If he is to escape the charge of leaving too much room to the emotions, he owed

[18] Just how close this position might be to Kant's own is a matter of some dispute.

it to us to provide a much clearer criterion for what is to count as good judgement in ethics.

Aristotle has, I think, three possible lines of reply, maybe none of them entirely satisfactory. (1) He can say that in the Function Argument he has already given at least the outline of a theoretical basis for discovering what a fulfilled human life must be like. He has shown how his account disposes of at least some of the obvious competitors (wealth, honours, pleasure), as well as fitting in well enough with many of our pre-reflective beliefs about ethics. (2) He might point out that, just as we can by and large recognize people who are in good health without ourselves having to be skilled in medicine, so we can, again by and large, recognize examples of people living fulfilled lives, without the necessity of having a complete theoretical account of fulfil-ment ready to hand. (3) We do not, and cannot, start to think about ethics with a completely blank page, so to speak. We come to reflect about ethics as heirs of a tradition, already educated in that tradition from childhood. Traditions by definition have endured; and to endure they must at least for the most part work well for people. This is not to say that, as economic or technological circumstances change, tradi-tional ways of behaving might not have to alter to meet the demands of a new social environment. But it is to say that we can reasonably assume that our starting points are, for the most part, defensible. And we must remember that ethics is not an exact science.

Aristotle is not principally concerned with the epistemological questions about proof and justification in ethics in the form in which they are the focus of many moral philosophers today. So far as concerns his account of individual moral judgements, he is open to the charge often brought against ethical intuitionists, that they refuse to provide proof or argument just when we would most like to have it. I think his reply to this would have to go as follows. It is only partly true that no backing can be provided for what the person of practical wisdom simply 'sees' has to be done on each occasion. But although it is true that there is no *proof* that he or she has got it right, they can still *explain* why they acted as they did. They can invoke one or other of the virtues, and thereby invite us to see the situation as they saw it, in the hope that we too will agree that they read the situation aright.

But if he takes that line he does lay himself open to the charge that he does little more than provide a rationalization for the culture of his time, without attempting any kind of fundamental assessment of its strengths and weaknesses. I shall return to this issue in the final chapter of this book. On the other hand, Aristotle does attempt to show that a satisfactory morality must have its roots in a theory of how human beings are by nature constituted; he does present what is surely a realistic and subtly nuanced picture of the way in which people are trained and the way in which adults make moral decisions; and he does offer explanations of why some people lead unfulfilled lives. He might say that it is in principle impossible to do more than that.[19]

---

[19] On Aristotle's defences against moral scepticism, see Irwin [1988], ch. 16.

Chapter 6

Responsibility

Relevant texts: Book III, chs 1–5

Problems of interpretation
- Does Aristotle have a consistent account of willingness?
- Does he contrast compulsive behaviour with behaviour for which one is accountable?
- Does he think children are accountable?

Critical issues
- Are we responsible for our upbringing and character?
- Does Aristotle provide good arguments for Libertarianism?

It was obvious to the Greeks as it is to us that ethics has to be concerned with both private and legal responsibility. Yet although questions of responsibility confront us every day of our lives, it is not as easy as it at

117

first sight appears to determine what constitutes being responsible, or to say who is responsible for what, and why. Aristotle, probably thinking in the first instance of the terminology used in the Athenian courts, says that the key to responsibility, praiseworthiness and blame-worthiness is whether or not someone can be said to act *hekōn*. So he sets out to analyse how this term is used, in order to see under what conditions we are justified in praising or blaming someone either for their character, or for what they do. He hopes that this inquiry will be useful both to add to our understanding of virtues, and to help legis-lators who have to deal with honours and punishments.

Once again, it is tricky to find a good English equivalent for *hekōn*. In Greek there are in fact two pairs of words used in this context: *hekousion* and *akousion*, which are used of actions, and the corresponding words *hekōn* and *akōn* which are used of persons. If, as is often done, *hekousion* is translated 'voluntary', the opposite would have to be 'involuntary'; but it is not right to say that the storm-tossed captain jettisons the cargo involuntarily, though Aristotle says that he does so *akōn*. (One might sneeze involuntarily, and that's quite different from the case of the captain.) I shall therefore mostly use 'willingly' and 'unwillingly', so as to have a neat pair of opposites in English.[1]

As we will discover, Aristotle's account is on the face of it quite simple: but upon closer examination, it is less simple than it looks. I propose to outline the simple version, and then to discuss those remarks which make it more complicated.

'Acting willingly': sorting out common opinions

The simple theory starts once again from what is commonly believed (1109b35), and goes like this. There are just two ways of denying that something was done willingly:

(1) By showing that what was done was done under compulsion.
(2) By showing that what was done was done because of ignorance.

---

[1] For the niceties of English usage in such discussions, see the amusing and perceptive article by J. L. Austin [1956].

In all likelihood, these two types of exculpation reflect the two types of plea which might be accepted in the Athenian courts at the time. Aristotle is being true to his announced intention of helping to clarify the issues for the sake of legislators and juries. At any rate he sets out to comment upon and where necessary to tidy up each of these commonly accepted conditions.

Compulsion

Aristotle starts off with what looks like a definition, which once again might be well taken from contemporary legal practice: something is compelled if its origin comes from outside the agent, who contributes nothing.[2] His examples include sailors being blown off course by a storm; and someone being overpowered and forced to go somewhere (1110a1–4, 1110b2–3). Such events simply are not *actions* at all, as Aristotle defines actions, since they are not to be explained by desires or choices of the agent, nor do they express anything about the agent's character. The cause of what happens comes from outside, and the agent contributes nothing.

Aristotle refuses to allow this type of defence to be stretched too far. Defendants in court tried on occasion to claim that they were overcome by attacks of blind rage as though swept away by a storm, and characters in some of Euripides's tragedies sought to excuse their actions by saying that the Goddess of Love had carried them away with irresistible force.[3] Aristotle will have nothing of this. He refuses to accept that in general someone can escape blame by saying that they were overcome by anger or desire (1110b9–17). The cause of the action is within the agent, he insists. Since desires are involved in *all* actions, acting under the influence of a desire cannot of itself show that one was being forced to act. Moreover, is anyone really going to say that *good* actions, too, are done unwillingly when someone feels

[2] Since I shall argue in the next paragraph but one that this definition is quite misleading, it would certainly be convenient if it could be shown that it is an accepted legal view, but *not* Aristotle's own. He takes it as an accepted starting point, but his own examples effectively undermine its usefulness.

[3] Illustrative texts are cited by Gauthier and Jolif [1970], Vol. II, 2, pp.177–78.

inclined to do them, or will they invoke this theory only when they need an excuse? For these reasons he regards the claim, if it is made quite in general, as simply ridiculous.[4]

However, he is willing to admit at least some exceptions: 'In some cases, though there is no question of praise, we do exonerate[5] someone who does what they should not, when human nature is strained beyond anyone's capacity to endure' (1110a23–26). An example might be Winston in George Orwell's *1984*, who has a phobia of rats. He betrays his girlfriend when he is locked in a cage with a pack of rats that attack him.[6] Aristotle himself gives a different kind of example in VII, 5. He is talking about madness, and about what he describes as cases of 'brutishness': a woman who ate human foetuses, tribes who devour one another's children, a madman who sacrificed and ate his mother. He denies that in such cases it is right to speak of moral weakness. By implication therefore he denies that such behaviour is willingly engaged upon. For this reason, I have translated him as saying that in such cases we exonerate and pity people, rather than saying that we excuse them. Aristotle takes the same line, by implication, in VII, 7, where we forgive people's behaviour if they resisted overpowering desires as much as could be expected (1150b8–16).[7] Perhaps another example is to be found in his remarks about reckless soldiers driven by sheer passion to rush at the enemy. They are not brave, Aristotle says; because 'driven

---

[4] He also makes remarks about the behaviour of children (1111a26), to which we shall return later.

[5] The Greek word *sungnōmē* can mean 'an excuse', 'pity', 'forgiveness' or 'exoneration'. Perhaps here there are overtones both of exoneration and of pity.

[6] T. H. Irwin takes a different view of this and of several other passages, I think on the grounds that Aristotle also says that even terrible threats must sometimes be resisted. I do not see that this undermines the previous sentence in which Aristotle clearly says that some threats are such that nobody could withstand them. See Irwin [1980], and on this passage particularly his comment in note 40. See also Sorabji [1980] ch. 16, which also differs in several details from the interpretation I have given in this section.

[7] The clear example is not being able to contain one's laughter; the other examples involve allusions to incidents in plays whose details are not entirely clear, but have to do with finally not being able to resist crying with pain upon being bitten by a snake, or weeping at the rape of one's daughter.

by pain and anger they rush into danger without foreseeing any of the perils: in that sense even donkeys would be brave when they are hungry!' (III, 8, 1116b33–36). The contrast between being driven and acting with foresight, which explains why such crazed soldiers are not brave, may be similar to that drawn between passions which can be resisted and those which cannot.

Reasonable as Aristotle's approach to these examples is, we should notice that cases of what we would term psychological compulsion at least do not obviously fit the definition of being compelled with which Aristotle started, that 'the origin comes from outside the person, who contributes nothing'. For the desires and fears clearly come from within the persons concerned. We shall have to see later whether he can further explain the grounds on which such behaviour can be regarded as compulsive, beyond asserting that in such cases human nature is strained beyond its limits. In particular, can he perhaps argue that these types of behaviour, too, are not *actions* in the proper sense, any more than being blown off course, or frog-marched, are actions?[8] Simply discussing whether the cause is within the agent or not is of no help at all so far as this problem is concerned. This might reinforce the impression that the distinction is not Aristotle's own, but one which he uses as a starting point since it reflected the common terminology of the courts.

Aristotle goes on to discuss more complex cases, where someone acts under threat – meeting a tyrant's demands in order to save his wife and family, or jettisoning cargo in a storm to save a ship from foundering. He says:

> Nobody simply jettisons cargo willingly, though any sensible person does so to ensure the safety of himself and his companions. So actions like this are mixed, but are more closely comparable to actions done willingly, since at the time of acting they are chosen and the aim of the action accords with the

[8] The issue is further confused by the fact that he does use the Greek verb *prattein* which corresponds to *praxis*, his normal word for an action in the strict sense. I presume that he here uses the word in a non-technical sense. We too can speak of a sleepwalker, for instance, 'doing' something without implying that they performed an action in the proper sense.

situation, and we should use the terms 'willingly' or 'unwillingly' depending upon what someone does at the time. So the person acts willingly. The origin of the movement of the bodily parts in such actions is within the agent, and those actions whose origin is within the agent are things he can either do or not do. Such actions, then, are done willingly, even though when described without qualification they might be said to be done unwillingly, since nobody would choose any such thing for its own sake.

(III, 1, 1110a9–19)

The key to this passage depends upon the view which contemporary philosophers might express by saying that actions are performed under a description. The captain's action is not, given the circumstances of the storm, properly described as simply and without qualification 'jettisoning his cargo'; no reputable captain would simply do that. What he did was more complex: he jettisoned his cargo to save the lives of those on board; and *that* action was, we are to suppose, entirely justifiable. Once again, it is central to Aristotle's view that an agent sees himself as behaving in a particular way for reasons, and that this has to be taken into account when asking what that agent did.[9] That's just what the captain would argue at a public inquiry later on. His defence against any criticism would consist in showing that it is mistaken to say that he just jettisoned the cargo; what he did was a more complex action, jettisoning cargo as the only way to save lives. If he successfully establishes that point, then his defence succeeds. Indeed, if that is what he willingly did, he is not merely not blameworthy, he is to be praised. His action is not *excusable* in the circumstances; it is entirely justifiable and needs no excusing. He did what he did with mixed feelings, however, since we might assume that, being a reputable captain, he regretted the necessity of losing the cargo.

Threat, therefore, functions quite differently from madness, brutishness, or external force. These last undermine the presumption

---

[9] I think it is closer to Aristotle's view to say that simply jettisoning cargo, and jettisoning cargo when the ship is in danger of foundering are two different actions, rather than two ways of looking at or describing one and the same action.

that the person performed an *action*, in the strict sense, at all: things just happen to them. Threat, in contrast, will not incline us to deny that the person acted, but it will often lead us to revise our view about *which* action the person willingly performed, and how that action is accurately to be described. There is, then, an ambiguity in the way in which, both in English and in Greek, someone might be said to be compelled. To behave *compulsively* is not to perform an action at all; but the captain who *was compelled* to jettison the cargo did not behave compulsively, he chose the best course of action in the circumstances. Hence Aristotle in this passage makes it clear that it was, in the circumstances, up to him to jettison or not to jettison; but compulsive behaviour is not in the person's power in that way at all.

Aristotle then goes on to point out that sometimes even dire threats should be resisted, and that people are to be praised for resisting them, even though in different circumstances people might well be criticized for taking enormous risks for no really worthy purpose. Here again, as so often, it is not easy to draw any hard and fast line about what it is worth doing at what cost. He concludes with the remark we have already seen, that when some threat is too much for human nature to withstand, the person deserves to be exonerated, neither praised nor blamed. I think the reason for withholding both praise and blame is that, in cases like the unfortunate Winston, it was not in his power to do other than he did.[10]

Ignorance

We might expect that ignorance, too, will force us to focus on which action the agent can properly be said to be doing. For plainly the agent is aware of the action as he sees it, and that is the action which Aristotle thinks the agent performs. Equally plainly, the agent who acts in ignorance is unaware of the way in which his behaviour would be seen by someone who knew the full facts of the situation. It is simplest to start with those cases where the agent, once he has found out the full facts, regrets what was done. Aristotle gives several examples; passing on knowledge which one did not know was confidential; mistaking a

---

[10] There is what I take to be a parallel text in the *Eudemian Ethics*, 1224a25–26.

sharpened spear for a practice spear with a button on it; giving someone medicine with fatal results, showing someone a loaded military catapult which goes off and injures someone (III, 1, 1111a10–13).[11] Aristotle says two things about these actions: they are not performed willingly (III, 1, 1110b18): and, if the agent subsequently regrets what happened, they can be said to be performed unwillingly (1111a19–21).

Which actions? Clearly, revealing a secret, hurting someone with a spear in practice, killing one's patient, launching a missile at someone. The agent did not perform any of those actions willingly, since he did not perform *those* actions, so described, at all. As he saw it, he was performing quite different actions, and actions are to be defined in terms of the agent's desires and thoughts at the time of acting.

There is a slight problem, though. Aristotle uses the phrase 'not willingly' to describe the action as performed at the time, and 'unwillingly' to describe it in the light of the agent's subsequent reaction to what happened. The first claim is easy to defend. One can neither be willingly nor unwillingly doing something which one is not doing at all, and what one is doing depends on what one believes (1110b20). Moreover, as we have seen, the terms 'willingly' and 'unwillingly' are to be used of actions which the agent performed at the time. The second claim is rather more difficult, since Aristotle here does use 'unwillingly' in the light of hindsight, despite what he has said about these terms being applied to the action as done at the time. Perhaps his thought is that at the time the agent would have been unwilling to behave as he did had he but known. So what if the agent does *not* regret what happened once he finds out? Aristotle is still not willing to say, even with hindsight, that the agent acted willingly. Why does he not treat this case in exactly the same way as he deals with the case of the person who later regrets what happened, and hence say that the unrepentant agent can be said to have acted willingly?

---

[11] It is clear enough that he is thinking of cases where no negligence is involved. So an unsuspected allergy to a drug might do in the medical example. I am not sure how to explain the catapult example, since whether a catapult is loaded or not is usually obvious. Perhaps the release mechanism was abnormally sensitive? He may well have been referring to a well-known legal case, the facts of which would have been clear.

Maybe (and to some extent this must be conjectural) he is once again thinking about the legal implications of what he is saying. Athenian courts would hold someone accountable only if they could properly be said to have acted willingly. Aristotle, then, agrees that the captain could rightly be held accountable for jettisoning the cargo during the storm, since he did so willingly. To avoid being blamed, he would therefore have to show that it was the only way open to him of saving the ship and the lives of those on board. If he could not show that, he would rightly be held liable for damages to the owner of the cargo. Equally, Aristotle does not believe that someone should be held accountable for what they did when they had no way of knowing the full facts; he therefore refuses to regard any such action as willingly performed, since that action was not performed at all. The agent can properly say 'But *that*'s not what I was doing!' This remains true, even if the agent is, with hindsight, pleased at the way things worked out. Still, one does want to make some distinction between the regretful agent and the agent with no subsequent regrets, morally speaking if not legally. That is what Aristotle does, by saying that the regretful agent acted unwillingly, while leaving the agent with no regrets to live with the purely legal let-out that he did not act willingly at the time. The characters of the regretful and the delighted agents are quite different.[12]

In the examples of ignorance which we have so far seen, Aristotle assumes that the agent is not himself responsible for being ignorant or, in modern terminology, that there is no question of negligence or recklessness.[13] Of course, this is not always so. Aristotle deals with other cases by distinguishing things done *because of* ignorance

---

[12] In his *Rhetoric*, I, 13, 1373b25–1374a15, Aristotle insists that someone is accountable only for what was willingly done: and gives several examples of instances in which the accused will admit what happened, but will refuse to admit the prosecution's description of what he did.

[13] Aristotle gives more examples in V, 8, where he explicitly discusses negligence as contrasted with misadventure. The ways in which he uses 'willing' and 'unwilling' in that chapter differ from what is said here in Book III. The differences are in part to be accounted for by the more narrowly legal context of the discussion in V, 8. It must also be remembered that Book V may well originally

(the ones we have already considered) from things done *in* ignorance. The implication is that the ignorance in these latter cases is to be explained by something else – drunkenness, or rage, or wickedness – and hence that what was done was done because of drunkenness, etc., rather than simply because of ignorance.

> There is a difference between acting because of ignorance, and acting in ignorance. Someone who is drunk or in a rage is usually thought to act as they do not because of their ignorance, but because of one of the states just mentioned, even though they act in ignorance and not knowingly. Everyone who is vicious is ignorant of what they ought to do and what they ought to avoid, and because of this failing they become unjust and in general bad. 'Unwilling' is not commonly used of someone who does not know what is good for them.
>
> Ignorance of this kind in choosing does not make someone act unwillingly, but rather viciously. It is not ignorance of the universal which makes someone act unwillingly (people are blamed for ignorance of that kind), but ignorance of the particulars with which action is concerned and in which actions consist. Such cases [deserve] pity and exoneration, since someone who is ignorant of these things acts unwillingly.
>
> (III, 1, 1110b24–1111a1)

The first of these paragraphs is clear enough, except for the reference to viciousness, which is taken up in the second paragraph. A simple example will illustrate the kind of thing Aristotle has in mind. The tragic hero Oedipus killed a man, not knowing that it was his father; and married the dead man's wife, not knowing that she was his mother. So, Aristotle might be saying, he deserves pity and exoneration, since he did not willingly kill his father or marry his mother (and his subsequent personal disintegration showed that his action should be regarded not merely as not willingly done but as unwillingly done). But what if he had seen nothing specially wrong with

have been part of the *Eudemian Ethics*, and hence might not be expected to be in every way consistent with the rest of the *Nicomachaean Ethics*. For a handy summary of the differences, see Sorabji [1980], ch. 17, especially pp. 283–84.

killing his father, or marrying his mother, and had knowingly done so? For that, Aristotle says, he would have been blameworthy, for in that case his actions would have been an expression of wickedness.

That failure to grasp a moral universal is always an indication of wickedness is a very uncompromising doctrine. Does Aristotle make out a good case for it? Once again, it helps to remember the legal context of much of this discussion in Book III. Not normally to allow ignorance of the law as a defence in court was public policy both in Athens in the time of Aristotle, and in most legal jurisdictions since. It is at least an intelligible policy, in that one does not wish to provide an incentive to citizens not to know the demands of the law. Even so, and especially in the case of complicated laws, it is not at all obvious that to be ignorant of the law is always the consequence of a negligent failure to find out.[14] Nor is it so clear that ignorance of moral principle should be put on a par with ignorance of the law of the land.

In any case, the distinction between ignorance of the universal and ignorance of the particulars is by no means as sharp as Aristotle here makes out. We have already seen that the person of practical wisdom sees a particular action as an instance of, say, kindness, and in so doing develops his understanding of what kindness requires. Suppose that someone simply fails to see that what he says is unkind. On the one hand, this would seem to be ignorance of the particular, since it concerns an individual action: but on the other hand, it can be seen also as a failure to understand (fully) what kindness is, and hence to be ignorance of the universal. So how is this different from the Oedipus example? Well, not to know that someone is your father does not suggest any defect in your *moral* perceptiveness, nor do the examples of ignorance of the particular which Aristotle gives (whether a catapult is loaded, etc.) If we exclude negligence, the mistake is a mistake purely of fact. So for a start the distinction he really needed was one between ignorance of the moral quality of an action and ignorance of

---

[14] And indeed it is not infrequently the case that what the law actually is at a given moment remains obscure even to lawyers unless and until a court determines the matter.

some non-moral feature of that action, rather than between universal and particulars.

Even so, the distinction is not always simple to draw. Some opponents of abortion, for instance, would argue that it is a matter of fact that a foetus is a human person, which is why at least many abortions should be seen as murders; others might argue that to say that a foetus is a human person is already a moral judgement rather than a factual one. Even if, for the sake of argument, one concedes that a mistake of some kind is involved, is it a moral mistake or a factual mistake? And what kind of mistake did Aristotle himself make in believing that slaves should not be members of the political community because they are incapable of human fulfilment or choice? Is this ignorance of fact or of moral principle? Surely of both?[15] So even if we can say that ignorance is an excuse provided that it does not depend on a lack of moral perceptiveness, which may be what Aristotle really wishes to say, it is not entirely clear in every case whether the ignorance is of this kind or not. Lack of perceptiveness may be precisely why one missed the salient facts of the case.

To sum up, so far. Aristotle holds the following principles:

(1)   One can be praised, blamed, or held legally accountable, only for what can in the full sense be said to be one's actions.

(2)   Behaviour caused by external forces is not properly described as someone's action.

(3)   Neither is behaviour which is properly described as compulsive.

(4)   Which action someone performs depends primarily on what the person at the time saw themselves as doing.

(5)   However, failure to see what one is doing can itself be a moral failure: in which case it is blameworthy, as are the actions involving such failure.

(6)   Actions for which one can be praised or blamed, or held legally accountable, are done willingly.

(7)   In such cases, the origin of the action can be said to be within the agent, and he is able to perform that action or not.

---

[15] *Politics*, III, 9, 1280a31–34. T. H. Irwin [1988], §249, suggests that Aristotle's political prejudices might have reinforced his factually incorrect beliefs.

In putting things this way round, I have in effect suggested that the otherwise obscure phrases 'the origin is in the agent', or 'it is up to him', are legal phrases. What Aristotle makes of them and how he suggests they should best be taken becomes clear in the light of his discussion of the various examples. They are not and should not be read as clear metaphysical statements which govern how the examples have to be read. Digestion, for example, is something whose origins are in me; but it does not count as an action, nor does compulsive behaviour. Aristotle assumes as a starting point a general grasp of which kinds of behaviour are subject to moral assessment or legal dispute, and he uses some well-known literary or legal examples as illustrations. He sets out to clarify and to some extent correct commonly held views about the conditions under which blame can be shown to be unjustifiable.

Moral conclusions: the best index of character

Not everything is quite such plain sailing, however. Aristotle goes on to discuss what I have decided to call 'moral conclusions' for want of a better translation. What does he mean by 'moral conclusions'? We can perhaps think of ourselves wondering what is to be done for the best in a difficult situation. We might have reached a view on what needs to be done, even though the chance to do anything won't present itself for another couple of days. Of course, it is possible that I might be prevented by circumstances outside my control from acting in the way I now think best. It is also possible that when the time comes, I can't face doing it, and decide to take an easy way out. A moral conclusion, then, is different both from an action, and from a decision, even though, in most normal circumstances, one might expect that one's decisions would in fact be in line with what one has concluded should be done.[16]

---

[16] The Greek word is *prohairesis*, most usually translated as 'choice'. Neither 'choice' nor 'decision' is entirely satisfactory as a translation, since Aristotle makes it clear that a person can do something contrary to their *prohairesis*, whereas it is more than a little odd to say that someone can act contrary to what they have chosen or decided. Moreover, he says that prohairesis can be a better

What is difficult in his discussion of moral conclusions is that so far Aristotle has given us the impression that an action's being done willingly is a sufficient condition for praise or blame and for legal accountability. But this turns out not to be quite right. He claims that there are several kinds of actions which are done willingly, which do not involve moral conclusions: e.g. the behaviour of animals and children, and things we do spontaneously without reflection. The suggestion is that these willing activities are *not* proper objects of praise or blame.

The first of these might appear problematic. For we do praise or blame animals for what they spontaneously do, and indeed for their characters – horses can be bad-tempered, dogs faithful and on occasions brave. Cannot dolphins be caring? Aristotle would say that praise in such cases is merely a favourable assessment, rather than a favourable *moral* assessment.[17] The same goes for children, whom we praise for having sunny dispositions. (By 'children' I think Aristotle here means infants, or at any rate children who are too young to be considered even minimally responsible for what they do.) There is now an apparent conflict in what Aristotle says:

(1) One can be praised or blamed or held accountable for any actions which are done willingly.
(2) Children and animals act willingly.
(3) Children and animals cannot (at least in the full sense) be praised or blamed or held accountable.

The contradiction could be avoided if (2) were rejected, most reasonably on the grounds that the behaviour of animals and infants cannot properly be described as *actions*; whereas is it only *actions* performed willingly which, according to (1) can be morally praised or blamed. As for saying that the behaviour of children, though willingly

clue to someone's character than their actions (1111b6), on the grounds that external circumstances can often prevent someone expressing their moral conclusions in practice (see also X, 8, 1178a23–b4). There is no neat English equivalent that I have been able to find which quite fits all the cases.

[17] Aristotle mentions praising athletes for their strength or running ability (I, 12, 1101b16–18), which clearly is not a moral assessment.

performed, does not amount to action, this might in turn be defended by saying that animals and children do not *assess* what they are going to do, and therefore do not, properly speaking, *reach any conclusion* about what to do. Willingness is thus a necessary, but not a sufficient, condition for moral praise or blame. The person needs to have reached some conclusion about what to do.

What, then, does Aristotle think moral conclusions involve? His account (III, 2), after excluding various inadequate versions, concludes that moral conclusions have the following characteristics:

(1)   They are about things which it is in our power to bring about (1111b20–29).
(2)   They are concerned with the achievement of our aims (1111b27).
(3)   They involve belief (1111a11–13).
(4)   They involve deliberation (1111a15–17).

My present concern is with the claim in (4), that moral conclusions must involve deliberation.[18] If this is so, what are we then to make of those actions which adults do unreflectingly, and hence without deliberating? Are these not to count as involving moral conclusions at all, and hence not as actions in the full sense? The text at 1111b10 seems to suggest that they are not – Aristotle lumps them together with the unreflecting behaviour of children. This would exclude such behaviour, even in adults, from moral assessment altogether. On the other hand, at 1117a17–20 he explicitly praises people who seem all the more brave because they act bravely when they are confronted with a sudden danger and there is no time to think things out or to reflect.

Maybe Aristotle has two rather different contrasts in mind. There are some things which we simply spontaneously do – for instance, shift position in a chair, or rub one's eyes, or hum a tune while waiting for a bus. We do these things spontaneously and willingly. It would be wrong to think of these as like reflex behaviour such as sneezing or closing one's eyes when some dust blows into them. Reflex behaviour

---

[18] Deliberation has already been discussed in Chapter 5; see the section on 'Deliberation, means and ends', together with note 11.

is done neither willingly nor unwillingly; but spontaneous behaviour is done willingly even if unthinkingly. Such behaviour is not subject to moral assessment (unless, which is a different point, the person *should* have thought about what they were doing – perhaps humming or fidgeting was a source of irritation to others).

But a different contrast can also be drawn, between the simply spontaneous and unthinking, and the thoughtful but instant response. The fact that someone does not go through a process of working out what is to be done does not make it any less true that they act as they do because of their beliefs about what is in their power and what will achieve their aims. Suppose a woman sees a child teetering on the edge of a pond as if it will very likely fall in. She immediately moves over and grabs hold of it. This is quite unlike the way in which one might instinctively take one's hand away from a hot surface one has just touched, or blink if something comes close to one's eye. Those responses are reflexes, which do not involve beliefs either about what one wishes to do, or how to do it. It is also different from shifting one's position in a chair, or humming a tune, which are not reflexes, but things we just do unthinkingly. The woman's response to the child is knowingly goal-directed, and might well express her experience of how to grab hold of the child without frightening it into just the fall she is seeking to avoid. As we might say, what she did was calculated to best secure the child's safety; and we can say that without suggesting that at the time she went through a *process* of calculation. She could later explain just why she reached for the child rather than speaking to it, or reached for it in just that particular manner. I think that is all Aristotle requires in order for what she did to count as involving a moral conclusion, and hence as an action in the full sense.[19] What he says is that animals and children cannot act thoughtfully in this kind of way and that even some of the willing behaviour of adults is not thoughtful either, but simply spontaneous.

Perhaps, though, there is no need to draw either line quite as sharply as he gives the impression of doing. Even quite young children can thoughtfully do some things, even if we cannot always be entirely

[19] See his remarks about the brave person who acts in a sudden emergency (1117a17–22).

sure how to distinguish between what they decide to do and how they unthinkingly respond. And, of course, even what they thoughtfully do they might do because they could not possibly know the full implications of their actions; so on that ground they are not to be held accountable.

Responsibility for one's character

There are two further complications. The first comes from the Socratic and Platonic background. Socrates had maintained that while a person would willingly do good, they could not willingly do evil. Viciousness is not a state anyone would willingly be in. Aristotle does not accept this, and wishes to argue that if we can willingly be virtuous, we can equally willingly choose to be vicious. Second, we can put together two of Aristotle's claims which we have already seen: the first is that people might want quite different things because their emotional responses to things and situations have been very badly trained, or not trained at all; the second is that one is not to be exonerated simply on the grounds that one does not 'know the universal' – if, that is to say, one simply fails to see which things are to be aimed at in life. Together these positions amount to saying that some people just are like that through no fault of their own, but yet they should be blamed for their moral blindness. But surely there is a strong case to be made for saying that such people should be pitied, rather than blamed, because they have been brought up with defective moral standards? So is there not a good case for saying that at least some cases of viciousness are, and always were, quite beyond the person's control?

In III, 5 Aristotle considers this second objection, and vigorously rejects any attempt to excuse people along those lines, perhaps because he is more intent on combating the Socratic/Platonic position than on considering the psychology of development in children. Some of his arguments, however, are better than others. Here is a list of some of the less good ones:

(1) We as individuals, and legislators, praise people for being good, and encourage them to do good actions. But praise presupposes that they act willingly.

(2) We double penalties for people who do wrong while drunk, and we blame people for not knowing at least the simpler parts of the law.

(3) We blame people for negligence.

We here see the dangers of purely dialectical arguments, which take common sense, or even the considered judgements of the courts as likely to be correct. Even if they are a good starting point, they are, in the nature of the case, inconclusive. Here, the counter-argument to them all is that they simply beg the question at issue. While it is true that our practice assumes that people are accountable, it may be that, had we paid more attention to developmental psychology, we should have realised that it is psychologically impossible for some people, given their upbringing, to see things any differently from the way they do. So people who have been abused are very likely to abuse others. However much we abhor their behaviour, maybe they are not to be blamed, nor punished. Aristotle accepts that here and now such people may be incapable of doing better, but he still wants to insist, counter to Plato, that there must have been a time in the past when they *were* able to choose to be different. If this is right, then such people act in ignorance (rather than because of ignorance) because they are account-able for the state of ignorance in which they are. They are therefore blameworthy. Hence he says:

> What if someone argues that, while everyone aims at what appears [to them] to be good, they have no control over what does so appear: rather the end will appear to each person according to the type of person they are? But if each person is somehow accountable for his state of character, then they must also be somehow responsible for how things appear to them.
>
> (III, 5, 1114a31–1114b2)

The argument for this is given earlier in the chapter:

> So virtue is in our power, just as viciousness is. For whenever it is in our power to act, it is also in our power not to act, and conversely. So, if to act nobly is in our power, not to do so, and hence to act shamefully, is also in our power. But if it is in our power to do, or not to do, both noble and shameful acts, and

this is what is meant by being a good or a bad person, it follows that it is in our power to be good or bad. So the saying 'Nobody is willingly bad, or unwillingly blessed' is partly false and partly true. Nobody is unwillingly blessed, but people are willingly vicious.

(III, 5, 1113b6–17)

So he is directly concerned with rejecting the Socratic or Platonic view, and he does so by widening the scope of personal responsibility. His reply, then, is in effect to claim that:

(4)   If people were by nature equipped either to see or not to see such things aright, then virtue will be no more a subject for praise than vice is for blame. We are one way or another equally part-causes of both.

Aristotle assumes that the objection turns on people's natural qualities of character or the limits of rational decision making, rather than on what is often enough an inadequate moral education. We have seen that he is willing to admit that some people do suffer from natural defects or mental illness, which blind their moral perceptions (1141b29). But plainly he thinks that these are quite exceptional cases, which, since the persons involved could never have done anything to improve their situation, deserve pity and not blame. They act because of ignorance, and hence not willingly. These cases apart, human beings are by nature constituted in such a way as to leave open the possibility of developing a variety of habits, though not an unlimited variety. Human nature, then, puts some causal limits on what we are able to make of ourselves, but we too have a causal input into how we turn out. In the case of normal people who are wicked, he once again assumes that, even given their natural traits of character, they willingly contributed to their present state and so are accountable for that state. The argument rests on pointing out the cost that has to be paid for denying that vices are habits willingly formed: for we would then have to abandon giving anyone credit for their virtues either. Presumably he thinks that conclusion is untenable for two reasons: (1) it would run counter to too many of our ordinary common-sense views; (2) it would totally fail to respect the fact that human beings are distinguished from other animals precisely in being capable of practical thought, and especially of deciding to do something or not to.

In concentrating on the natural abilities of normal people, he does not sufficiently consider defective upbringing, which might surely be thought to be the most common reason for believing that people are not accountable for how their moral character developed. Elsewhere, there are passages where Aristotle clearly envisages that parents and the city as a whole might easily fail to provide the environment which is necessary if a person is to develop habits of virtue.[20] The point of the study of politics is to try to discover how a city can best contribute to moral training. It might be argued that if proper training is not provided, then the disadvantaged young persons can hardly be held accountable for how their characters develop. And it is not simply that their characters will be adversely affected. We have already seen that character defects make it difficult and sometimes impossible for people to see the moral quality of particular actions, and so to fail in practical wisdom. Practical wisdom and moral virtue are, after all, closely connected. But Aristotle never, so far as I can see, explicitly suggests that people with defective upbringing might be wholly or partially exonerated.

We can still ask whether Aristotle is correct in claiming that it would follow that, if we are not to be blamed for the vices resulting from an inadequate upbringing, then neither can we be praised for the virtues which arise from a good upbringing. Are the cases symmetrical? There might be good Aristotelian reasons for denying that there is the same symmetry here as there would be if we were constrained by natural necessity. He could argue that a good upbringing provides role-models, advice and instruction, and, in the last resort, threats of various kinds. We can, then, learn what our society approves and disapproves of, and, at least in an abstract way, come to see why it does so. Given all this, we can decide to take advice or refuse it, to act in ways which are admired and so come to know from our own experience what acting virtuously has to offer, or to refuse to act in these ways. We therefore cannot claim to be acting because of our ignorance. On the other hand, without such instruction and encouragement,

[20] See X, 9, as a whole, and especially 1179b4–1180a24.

it would be at least much more difficult to become good people, for two reasons. First, it may be difficult for us, perhaps impossible in practice though not in theory, even to begin to form a picture of a way of living which is quite different from anything we have seen in others; and second, there would be little encouragement of any kind, and hence no initial satisfaction in acting as a virtuous person would act.[21] In such circumstances, it could reasonably be argued that the young person acts because of their ignorance, and hence cannot be held accountable.

Decisions and freedom

Does Aristotle believe in freewill? So put, the question is not entirely clear; and some commentators have argued that in any case such a question is anachronistic.[22] Nevertheless, commentators have tried to see whether Aristotle's treatment of accountability and decision making might contain enough to enable us to see what he would have said had the question been put to him in its modern form. It is possible to defend all three possible answers: that there is not enough evidence to enable us to decide either way; that he does not believe in freewill; and that at least by implication he clearly does. I shall argue for this third view.

In the hope of clarifying somewhat a debate which is often very confusing, it will help to set out a common form of argument purporting to show that we cannot be responsible for any of our behaviour:

(1)   Everything that happens in the world is determined.
(2)   All our decisions are determined (*follows from (1)*).
(3)   Events which are determined could not have been other than they were.

---

[21] Recall that in the earlier stages of acquiring a virtuous disposition, the person will often have to act counter to their desires in order to act as the virtuous person would. They must, if they are to do so, in some way be able to present so acting as in some way good. Encouragement, and a sense of shame at falling short of people's expectations, play important roles in motivation in such cases.

[22] For a good rebuttal of this suggestion, see Sorabji [1980], ch. 15.

(4)   To choose freely requires that, precisely in those circumstances, we could have chosen otherwise.

(5)   Our choices are not free (*follows from (2), (3), and (4)*).

(6)   We cannot be accountable for anything which was not freely done.

(7)   We cannot be accountable for any of our behaviour (*follows from (5) and (6)*).

Responses to this argument are of three main types:

The first two responses both accept (2). They then draw different conclusions:

- *Incompatibilists* accept the argument in its entirety. Moral accountability is incompatible with determinism.
- *Compatibilists* accept (2) and (3); but they deny (4), and hence also deny (5) and (7). Moral accountability is compatible with determinism (and some would even say that it requires determinism).

The third response denies (1), (2), and (5); accepts (4) and (6), and denies (7):

- *Libertarians* believe that free choices are not determined; and that only this fact justifies us in holding people accountable for them.

First, then, some comments on (1). The determinist, as I shall use the term, holds that the state of the world at any instant *t necessitates* any event which occurs at $t + 1$; that is to say, what occurs at $t + 1$ occurs inevitably given the state of affairs at t.[23] It may be disputed whether or not (1) is true, and if it is not, then of course it cannot be used to support 2), which would then have to be argued on other grounds.[24]

---

[23] I put the matter this way rather than in terms of causes, since the term 'cause' is interpreted in several different ways, some of which do not require necessitation at all. My definition does not require, or deny, that the causal relationship must hold between events; and libertarians need not, on this definition, deny that all events have causes.

[24] Even if (1) is held to be false for at least some events in the world (notably some events in quantum physics), it could still be argued that it is true of all the ordinary events with which we are concerned in the present debate.

It might be argued, for instance, that all our decisions depend upon, and indeed are necessitated by, our beliefs and desires at the time.[25] Libertarians typically accept that beliefs and desires will *explain* our actions (though not all our behaviour), but deny that the explanation shows that actions are necessitated by one's beliefs and desires at the time.

As it stands (3) is ambiguous. A determinist can accept that in one sense the state of the world at $t + 1$ *could have* been different, provided only that things had been different at t. So, our decisions could indeed have been other than they were had our desires and beliefs at t been other than they were. In particular, we were capable of making different decisions, since we were capable of having different desires and/or beliefs. But of course it is also true that in a determinist world it was inevitable, given the state of the world at $t -1$ that our desires and beliefs at t were as they were. Indeed, working backwards in the same way, only if the starting conditions of the world had been different would things have worked out differently from the way they have. In that sense, our decisions *could not* have been other than they were.

Therefore (4) is highly contentious. It is intended to be stronger than the simple claim that, had our desires and/or beliefs been different, we would have chosen otherwise; it assumes that, even given our desires and beliefs at t, it is still open to us at t to choose in different ways; and it then claims that it is precisely this ability which is the defining characteristic of freedom. The alternative would be to argue that freedom simply requires that a choice be necessitated only by factors internal to the agent – for instance the agent's beliefs and desires rather than by anything outside the agent. On this latter definition of freedom, freedom is compatible with determinism; on the former definition, it is not.

Which of the above propositions (1)–(7) would Aristotle have accepted? It is a matter of dispute whether Aristotle would have accepted (1) even so far as concerns the physical world. He does distinguish between states of affairs that could not be other than they are, and those that could. But typically by that he means that there are potential

---

[25] For two very different types of argument for this conclusion, see Honderich [1973], especially pp.195–98, and Rudder Baker [1995], ch. 5.

changes in the world which will never be actualized (for example, my jacket could be torn on a nail; but in fact it will wear out without being torn). So, if things had been different, which in principle they could have been, the outcomes would also have been different. This in itself says nothing about whether determinism is true or not. There are passages elsewhere in his writings which some eminent commentators have taken to suggest that, in Aristotle's view, if there are exceptions to the scientific laws as we have so far formulated them, those exceptions could be captured in a modified law which would hold good always, because it would then exactly capture cases of necessitation in nature. And there is an argument which might suggest that Aristotle did not think one could ever ask about the starting conditions of the universe. But the upshot of all this is that it is simply not clear whether Aristotle believed (1) or not, even so far as concerns the physical world apart from human choices; but it is perhaps more probable that he did not.[26]

It is therefore equally doubtful that Aristotle believed (3); so the dispute turns in the end on the sense of 'free' required in (4). Clearly Aristotle believes that we can choose to do something or not. The question is, does he intend more by this than to say that, had our desires and beliefs at the time of choosing been different, then we would, inevitably, have chosen differently? Does he mean that, at a particular time, and given our desires and beliefs at that time, it is *still* open to us to make one or another choice? Given that the captain desired to save himself and his ship, and given what he knew about the storm and the threat it posed, was it in Aristotle's view *causally inevitable* that he chose to jettison the cargo? Was this choice just as unavoidable in the circumstances as is the behaviour of someone who is mad, or crazed with the bloodlust of battle, or suffering from the kind of natural defect or illness which makes them simply not accountable for what they do?

The question cannot be answered without at least some hesitation. Still, I think that there are some points which can be urged in favour of the view that Aristotle was a libertarian.

[26] Relevant texts are: *De Interpretatione* ch. 9, and especially 19a7–23, where my example comes from; *Metaphysics VI*, 2, 1027a20–27, which W. D. Ross interprets in the way I have given in the text, but which many others do not; and *De Generatione et Corruptione*, Book II, ch. 11, 337b26–338a3.

(1)   It must be accepted that phrases like 'it is up to the agent', 'willingly', 'is able to say Yes or No', and 'the origin is within the agent' which appear often enough in the texts, are not in themselves decisive. They are, however, suggestive in the contexts.

(2)   If I am right in interpreting some of the texts we have already considered as referring to compulsive behaviour (not everyone would accept this, though), then Aristotle clearly did not think the captain's behaviour was in that sense compulsive. He sharply distinguishes between the two cases from the point of view of blameworthiness, precisely on the grounds that the captain could choose either way. That he takes a libertarian view would be the simplest hypothesis to explain how Aristotle argues here. Were he a compatibilist, one would expect a different contrast to have been drawn, perhaps in terms of whether the choice was or was not derived from the person's beliefs.

(3)   For suppose that, in Aristotle's view, the outcome of captain's deliberation itself was causally inevitable, given what he wanted and what he knew about the dangers. That inevitable decision is internal to the captain in just the same way as the desires and beliefs of the mad are internal to them. Why, then does Aristotle think that the captain is accountable, but the mad are not?

(4)   One might try to reply to this difficulty by saying that the captain's beliefs can be changed by conversation with his first mate; but the beliefs of the mad are impervious to any argument, and *that*'s why the captain is different. But, at least in my own view, that simply makes the captain open to influence by something outside himself, and that influence is either causally ineffective, or causally decisive, depending on what the mate says. Deliberating is not then something which the captain does, but something which happens to him. I do not think that this is the picture Aristotle wishes us to form of how agents deliberate or choose.[27]

---

[27] I therefore agree with Sorabji [1980], ch. 15. For a variety of other views, see: Hardie [1968], ch. IX; Broadie [1991], ch. 3, pp.152–74.

On balance, then, it seems to me that Aristotle's texts read much more naturally if they are taken in a libertarian sense.[28]

Additional note on 'wanting'

Here are a few remarks about 'wanting', which Aristotle discusses in III, 4.[29] I put them here, so as not to disrupt the flow of argument about responsibility in the chapter as a whole. Aristotle considers wanting since it is part of the background to deliberation.

In translating the term as 'want', I am using 'want' as distinct from 'feel inclined to'. Thus, one can want to go to the dentist, without feeling inclined to go, or in that sense having a desire to go. As Aristotle points out, someone can want the impossible – a particular athlete can want to win a race, for example (1111b22–24). But when we make a decision, it is in view of something which we want. One difference between wanting and feeling inclined is that in wanting something we have *thoughts* about why it is worth having; and the other difference is that, while desires (say hunger, or sleepiness, or anger) naturally tend to make us behave in certain ways, merely wanting something does not (we might want a horse to win a race, but there is nothing we can do about it). When we decide, we decide to act upon a want, and hence to act to achieve an aim about which we have beliefs.

I am not, however, persuaded that wanting need involve clear beliefs about happiness or a conception of the good life as a whole.[30] To want something involves thinking of it as worth having in some

---

[28] A hundred years later, there was a lively debate explicitly on all these issues, focusing on the determinist views of one of the Stoic philosophers, Chrysippus. The easiest place to find this material is in Long and Sedley [1987], Volume 1, section 62, where key texts are translated, and a brief but excellent commentary provided. The very ambiguities which make it difficult to be sure where Aristotle stood on these issues are brought into the open and the battle-lines clearly drawn.

[29] The Greek word is *boulēsis* (not to be confused with *bouleusis*, 'deliberation'), and is often translated 'wish'.

[30] For the contrary view, see Irwin [1980], pp. 128–29. See also the criticisms of Irwin in Broadie [1991] pp. 106–08 with note 42, and pp. 232–38.

way or another; it would be good (from some point of view) if such and such were the case. So Aristotle makes it clear that we can want something only if it seems to us to be good; the good person will want what is truly good, while others will want all kinds of things which are not in fact good (see III, 4, especially 1113a22–26).

Wanting is presupposed by deliberation since, as Aristotle repeatedly says, one deliberates about how to achieve what one wants. But there is nothing in his text which suggests that we can only want one thing at a time (which would in any event be a very strange suggestion). There are many states of affairs of which we might believe that it would be good if things were like that. I want, if possible, to be kind as well as truthful. But in these particular circumstances I might realize that this want is unrealistic, and have to decide whether this is a time for being encouraging or being unambiguously truthful, and how precisely to do whichever it is that I decide is required.

Chapter 7

Moral failure

Relevant text: Book VII, chs 1–10

Problems of interpretation
- Which questions is Aristotle trying to answer?
- Is he offering just one explanation for one type of moral failure?
- How are his remarks about the practical syllogism to be read?

Critical issues
- Is Aristotle's view better than Hume's?
- Does Aristotle fail to grasp the key issue?

Why is moral failure problematic?

We are surely all conscious of our moral failures. Some of them we might put down to moral weakness, a lack of will-power or resolution; others we might think of as more coldly deliberate and calculated. Sometimes we try to conceal from ourselves what we are really doing. Sometimes perhaps we feel we simply cannot help ourselves, try as we might. Moral failures come in various sizes and shapes and degrees of badness. But they might not at first sight seem at all problematic, or philosophically puzzling. They are an obvious, if regrettable, feature of most of our lives.

We therefore need to make something of an effort to see why Aristotle, like Socrates and Plato before him, thought there was something deeply puzzling about moral failure – what he called *akrasia*, a word which suggests a lack of self-control.[1] The problem that has most interested commentators is one which Aristotle inherited from Plato, and ultimately from Socrates almost a century earlier. Socrates maintained that nobody knowingly does wrong.[2] And his reason was that to do wrong is to harm oneself, and nobody would knowingly wish to harm themselves. So people who apparently do wrong do so because they have misunderstood, or miscalculated the import of their action. Virtue is knowledge, and vice is ignorance. Plato was in fundamental agreement with this line of argument. But it may be that he was prepared to make some concessions; people could act against their moral *beliefs*, since these are unstable and easily undermined; but he still wished to maintain that people could not act against what they *know* to be right. Plato argued that the ultimate basis of ethics was the Form of Goodness itself, a transcendent immaterial entity whose supreme goodness was reflected in any goodness possessed by this-worldly virtues and persons and actions. The process of moral education consisted in using instances of good things to remind us of the Form of Goodness, with which our souls have been familiar before birth. Ideally, we gradually ascend to what is presented almost as a vision of Goodness itself. This knowledge of Goodness, once obtained, serves as a standard for assessing all our actions and traits

[1] Aristotle first deals with, and largely dismisses, what he takes to be problems of classifying various kinds of failing, and some not very deep philosophical conundrums. See VII, 1–2.

[2] It is not always easy to distinguish the historical Socrates (who left no writings) from Socrates as he appears as a character in Plato's dialogues. The view I take in the text draws the line in one plausible place.

of character, and hence as a touchstone for all our moral judgements. The suggestion is that, once the soul has been captivated by this vision, and hence been filled with true moral knowledge, it will then have no reason or motive whatever to pursue anything else in life except what is good. Socrates was right, moral failures are ultimately failures in knowledge.[3] Plato himself made more of the power of emotion and passion to influence our decisions, and to fight against our reason. But even he was unwilling to concede that knowledge in the full sense of the term could be overcome by passion, even if beliefs could be. It was still a commonplace of Plato's Academy that moral failure is less a matter of weakness than an instance of ignorance. After all, how could anyone knowingly choose less than the best for themselves?

Yet surely these conclusions are problematic, and they certainly seemed so at the time. Are we not all too often conscious of having knowingly, even deliberately, done wrong; and in such cases would we not admit that we are blameworthy? And if blameworthy, then surely we acted willingly, and hence knowingly? Aristotle himself would have had particular reasons for trying to resolve this puzzle. After all, his account of moral training is much less narrowly intellectualist than that offered by Socrates. If we need to train our emotions before we can rely on our moral *judgements* (since practical wisdom and moral virtue depend upon one another), then a lack of good moral training would lead to our being unable to form correct moral judgements. So the problem we saw at the end of the previous chapter reappears here: how can we be blameworthy if we never had a chance to know any better? Is moral failure down to ignorance after all?

In explaining what he intends to do in the first ten chapters of Book VII, Aristotle gives one of his most explicit accounts of the

[3] For the ascent to knowledge of the Good Itself, see Plato, *Symposium,* 211; for the general conclusion, *Protagoras*, 352–58, and *Republic*, 439–41. It is worth noting that in saying nobody willingly does wrong, the word I have translated 'willingly' is the same word (*hekōn*) that is used by Aristotle in Book III; and Plato's word for 'does wrong', *hamartanei*, could equally well mean 'gets things wrong' and hence 'makes a mistake', thus tying in with the notion of ignorance.

philosophical method which he will use here, as he has done so often elsewhere in his writings. He says that he is going to consider three character-traits which have not so far been fully discussed, moral weakness, softness and brutishness (with which we can contrast self-control, endurance, and – for want of a better term – superhuman goodness).

> With regard to these, as with the rest, we must set down what seems to be true and start by considering the puzzles, and in this way demonstrate the truth ideally of all our common beliefs about them, or, failing that, at least of most of them including the most central ones. For if the difficulties are resolved and our common beliefs remain, that would amount to a sufficient proof of them.
>
> (VII, 1, 1145b2–7)

This full-dress programme reflects both the importance Aristotle attached to the subject, and the difficulty which he and his predecessors thought would be encountered in trying to give a satisfactory account of moral failure.

Aristotle's solution: one interpretation

Aristotle puts a question which he takes to be central to approaching all these issues. Unfortunately, there is no one agreed view of precisely what this question is, nor of the answer which he offers. For the sake of clarity, I shall outline as simply and straightforwardly as I can the view which I take on the whole to be the best. In the next section I will try to defend it in more detail against other possible interpretations of the text.

There are two clues to Aristotle's own position to be found in the way he sets out the puzzles: at 1145b21 he says, 'One might be unsure about in what way the person who lacks self-control has a true grasp of what they are doing.' Returning to the same point at the start of VII, 3, he says, 'The first thing to ask is whether [those who lack self-control] act knowingly or not, and in what way knowingly' (1146b8–9). Aristotle also remarks that to say nobody knowingly does wrong goes against what seems to be the most obvious facts of our experience (1145b27–28).[4] In all three places, the implication surely is that the wrongdoer must in some way act knowingly, even if it is not clear exactly in what way. But if the person in some way acts knowingly (though we still have to see how this can be true), then Aristotle cannot in the end accept the Socratic claim that 'nobody knowingly does wrong'. The trouble with this is that at least in one place he seems to say that Socrates was right after all. So we need to be careful.

Aristotle dismisses as irrelevant what may be Plato's suggestion that there is less of a problem if one talks about the agent acting contrary to his beliefs rather than contrary to his knowledge. Aristotle disagrees that the strength of one's conviction depends upon whether it is merely a belief or whether it is also an instance of knowledge; so it would be just as easy to act against the one as the other. So the difficulties must be approached from some other direction.

In what precise sense, if any, can someone who does wrong be said to know what they are doing? This is the central question and the one which must be answered first before attempting to consider the differences between various kinds of moral failure (1146b8). To approach it, Aristotle proposes four ways in which someone might be said both to know and not to know. The implication of this approach is, I think, twofold. First, it is going to turn out that moral failure does involve knowing what one is doing, but only with some qualifications; second, that the different ways in which someone can 'know and not know' might be relevant since there are different kinds of moral failure. Here is a list of them:

---

[4] The point of chapter 2 is to demonstrate why there are genuine problems to be resolved, as he makes clear in his summary at the beginning of chapter 3 (1146b5–7). Texts from chapter 2 need not be reliable evidence for how Aristotle himself would have framed the issues, nor for what Aristotle's own solution is. Rather, the issues should be approached from the opposite direction. Once we have determined what Aristotle goes on to say on his own behalf, we can then look back on this chapter and see which of the arguments in it he might have accepted. Even so, the way in which he makes the points I have here mentioned in the text does suggest that these at least represent Aristotle's own views of the state of the debate, rather than simply reflecting opinions which others might have.

(1) We can either bear in mind what we know, or not bear it in mind. It would be strange to do wrong while bearing it in mind that what one is doing is wrong: but not strange to do wrong while not bearing it in mind (1146b31–35).[5]

(2) One can know both premises of a practical syllogism, but use the major, and not use the minor. For example, one might know, and make use of the truth that dry foods are good for people: but either not know, or not act upon, the truth that this food here is dry. This would not be strange, but the other [using both the major and the minor] would be (1146b35–1147a10).

(3) One can also know and not know something either:
  (a) in the way that someone asleep or drunk or mad does;
  (b) in the way that someone overcome by strong feelings does;
  (c) in the way that someone knows what he has been told, but has not as yet assimilated what he has been told;
  (d) in the way in which an actor knows his lines (1147a 10–24).

(4) One can know all the following statements:

(a1) What contains sugar is bad for me	(b1) What contains sugar is pleasant
(a2) This contains sugar	(b2) This contains sugar
(a3) I ought not to eat this	(b3) This would be pleasant to eat

(1147a24–1147b2)

Throughout the discussion, it seems to me clear that Aristotle is trying to defend the common-sense view that one can do something wrong and know that it is wrong. He does this by invoking various versions of the distinction set out in (1), which therefore gives the general outline of what is to follow.[6] As we shall see, he does not think that all instances of moral failure are exactly alike.

[5] 'Bearing in mind' translates the verb *theōrein*, which is the active consideration of what one knows. The technical sense of the noun *theōria* in Book X has the same connotation.

[6] Unfortunately, Aristotle expresses himself slightly differently in three different places: first, one can know and not use (1146b32): second, know and not consider (1146b33): third, know and not activate one's knowledge (1147a7). It is not clear

In (1) the central contrast is between knowing something and bearing it in mind. Aristotle says that there is no problem in saying that someone knows stealing to be wrong, but, paying no attention to that knowledge, steals nonetheless. That is exactly how we would generally think of moral failure. What would be strange would be for someone to steal while at that moment claiming to bear in mind their belief that stealing is wrong. 'Bearing in mind' here is equivalent to 'making use of' or 'acting upon'. So we have the broad outline of Aristotle's interpretation. As announced, he does *not* follow Plato in saying that moral failure is to be explained by ignorance; rather, the person knows full well, but in one way or another, pays no heed to what they know.

Now consider (2), and take a more obviously moral example instead of the one he gives. We are to imagine a situation in which someone knows that stealing is wrong, and still takes pens and computer discs home from work. Aristotle considers two possibilities.[7] Maybe the person genuinely does not think that this is stealing; or maybe he knows that it is, but chooses not to consider that fact. In the first case, though he knows that stealing is wrong, he does not believe that what he is doing counts as stealing (though it does indeed amount to stealing). I have already argued in the previous chapter that although Aristotle sometimes presents the minor premise (e.g. 'This man is my father' in the Oedipus case) as a purely factual matter about which someone can be mistaken, there are other cases in which a mistake about the minor premise is a moral mistake. Here we have just such an instance: failing to see taking these things home from work as stealing from one's employer is a moral failure, evidence of an inadequate grasp of what stealing involves. So there are two possibilities: in both the person might sincerely say, 'Of course it is wrong to steal'

---

whether or not these expressions are intended to be equivalent (which I think they are) nor precisely what each contrast involves: 'know and not keep in mind' is perhaps the central notion.

[7] It is not entirely clear whether Aristotle offers just one possibility but is unsure how it is to be described – 'not having' or 'not acting upon' – or whether he offers two separate possibilities. I think the two are intended to be genuinely different.

– thus heeding/using their knowledge of the major premise – while still sincerely believing that he is not in this instance stealing at all; or, a person might know very well that they are stealing, but decide not to look at the action in that light ('they'll never miss this amount'). In either case, as Aristotle says, the person heeds only the major premise (that stealing is wrong) but either does not know the minor (a failure in moral perception), or does not act on it (he prefers not to think of it at the time). Either way, he can be said both to know that stealing is wrong, but to steal nevertheless. And that is another kind of moral failure, one in which there is no explicit mention of desire at all.

We can all think of other types of case in which we know things and pay no attention to what we know. Aristotle mentions some of these in (3), pointing out that they are different from the ways of 'knowing and not knowing' which he has already considered (1147a12). His examples are: being asleep, being drunk, being mad; indeed, he goes on to say, we are in that kind of state when in the grip of a strong emotion, when anger or sexual desire and other such feelings involve bodily changes which even make some people go mad. Obviously, he says, *akrasia* is like this. Presumably, in saying this, he means that the *straightforward* case of *akrasia* is comparable to sleep, drunkenness or madness, and not necessarily that *all* cases of moral failure are best thought of in this way.

Aristotle then pre-empts a possible objection, that the comparison with those asleep or dead drunk, or mad is not a good one, since people who fail morally will be quite capable of exhibiting their knowledge of moral principles. That proves nothing, Aristotle says: people mouthing moral principles to which they pay no heed are either like those in the grip of strong emotions who can still quote Empedocles,[8] or they are like people who can repeat what they have just learnt but not yet assimilated, or like actors repeating their lines. The point of these examples is that in none of them is the person really stating his beliefs, or using them; at most he is just uttering words.

[8] Perhaps quoting, ironically enough, lines from a work on purity of soul! See Gauthier and Jolif [1970], p.608.

Finally, in (4), Aristotle says that we can give an explanation of moral failure by considering it 'from the point of view of nature'. In this context, the phrase is probably meant to introduce a psychological explanation of how the combination of knowing and not paying any heed to comes about. He begins by reminding us of his general account of reasoning. Just as, in theoretical matters, once one has put the major and minor premise together and drawn the conclusion, the soul of necessity asserts that conclusion, so in practical matters, when one puts the universal premise together with the perception of the particular instance and draws the conclusion, then one acts on that conclusion if one is able and not prevented.

Now the obvious case of moral failure is where someone is led by desire to do what they know to be wrong. Aristotle offers two accounts which someone might give of why they did what they did when confronted with, say, a bar of chocolate. The diabetic might very well accept the whole of the argument (a1)–(a3), and hence know that (a3) is the conclusion which anyone of practical wisdom would reach in his situation. But in a moment of weakness he pays no heed to that conclusion or indeed to that argument as a whole, since the perception of the chocolate as sweet stimulates his desire, and hence 'drags him' to see the situation in terms of (b1)–(b3). Seeing the situation in this way, however, still gives him a reason for acting as he does – none of the statements (b1)–(b3) is false, and none of them contradicts anything in (a1)–(a3). There is, then, nothing wrong with the argument in (b1)–(b3) in itself. What has happened is that the person's desires have led him to focus upon what is true but in that situation is either not morally significant or certainly not morally decisive. Aristotle concludes:

> So the moral failure comes about in a way under the influence of reason and belief. The belief is not in itself contrary to right reasoning, though it happens to be in this case; it is the desire, not the belief which is unreasonable.

> (VII, 3, 1147a35–b3)

The beliefs (that sweets are pleasant to eat, and that this is sweet) are true, and the argument using these beliefs is valid. In itself, then, there is nothing irrational (if that is taken to mean illogical) in this line of thought; but in this instance (where the person is diabetic, say) this is still not 'correct thinking' (*orthos logos*); the desire which leads to this train of thought is unreasonable. This is exactly the conclusion which, at the start of the discussion, Aristotle led us to expect. The person *does* know that what he is doing is wrong, at least in some sense of 'know'; furthermore, the person does not straightforwardly assent to a *contradiction*; but, despite knowing how he should have looked at the matter, he still chose to look at it in a different, and unreasonable, light, because, seen in that light, he can give himself a coherent reason for acting which fits in with what he desires.

A more detailed defence

The account I have given is far from uncontroversial: indeed, I doubt if it is possible to give an interpretation of this passage which every scholar would accept! In particular, I have argued that Aristotle is not intent on offering just one account of moral failure. I have also argued that though Aristotle thinks that Plato's view of moral failure is not wholly mistaken, since *some* instances of moral failure are as Plato says they are, and fit the 'standard' use of the term 'moral weakness' since in these cases one is unduly influenced by desire. But he does not think that Plato gives nearly enough weight to the common-sense view that of course we can do wrong knowing full well what we are doing, and even doing so deliberately. I have at least suggested that not all moral failure has to be ascribed to the influence of desires.

A good example of a competing view is offered by Gosling.[9] On this view, the four stages outlined above represent not four different types of moral weakness, but four steps in focusing on the precise problem: (1) above is offered as unproblematic: obviously enough, we can have knowledge of what we should do and simply not use it; (2) is also unproblematic, in that one can know and use the major premise of a practical syllogism; the problem would arise only when one claimed to use the minor premise as well, and still did wrong; (3) finally gives the problematic case, and suggests that in the case of *akrasia* the person knows that they are doing wrong only in the ways

[9] Gosling [1990], chs III and IV.

in which those asleep or drunk can be said to know; (4) gives a psycho-logical explanation of how this comes about. Aristotle is not giving accounts of different types of moral failure, only one of which is *akrasia* in the strict sense, as my own interpretation would have it; he is speaking throughout only of *akrasia* in the strict sense, calling atten-tion to one specific kind of 'knowing-and-not-knowing' and relating this kind of knowing-and-not-knowing to psychology.

In the face of this interpretation, my own view needs consider-able explicit defence, and the attempt to do this will surely reveal why the passage has been such a source of difficulty and controversy. The details are just not clear.

Several types of culpable failure?

I have suggested above that Aristotle in fact thinks there are several different ways in which someone might do what they know (or believe – it makes no difference) to be wrong. Indeed, much of the second part of Book VII (from chapter 4 onwards) consists in trying to make plain the subtle differences between various types of character, and between the kinds of failure that is characteristic of each. Not all these failures are blameworthy – not, for instance, the brutish behaviour resulting from physical defect or mental illness. Of the kinds of failure which are blameworthy, he has various things to say. The question is, is he already dealing with some of those different types of moral failure here in the passage from 1146b31–1147a24, or just with one central case, which can be looked at from several angles?

The first thing to notice is that at VII, 3, 1146b31 Aristotle, having dismissed as irrelevant the suggestion that it might be belief rather than knowledge which fails, goes on to state what it is that *will* be relevant. His reply to the difficulties starts here and is followed by three further suggestions, each introduced by the same word 'again'.[10] It is clear that he expects all four to be relevant, in contrast to the suggestion dismissed at 1146b25; and the question to which all four suggestions are relevant is the one referred to at 1146b25, and spelt out at 1146b8–9: once a person has reached a conclusion about how

---

[10] In Greek *eti*; it occurs at 1146b35, and in 1147a at lines 10 and 24.

they should act, if they then fail to act accordingly, in what sense if any can they be said to know what they are doing? Moreover, all four suggestions are variations on the same theme, since all have to do with ways in which one can simultaneously have knowledge and not attend to the knowledge which one has. It is the sense of 'knowingly' which we are trying to determine, and *not whether* someone can knowingly do wrong at all, nor *why* it is that they do wrong.

It seems to me that the four elements are meant to be parallel to one another, and hence that they give *different* variations to the know-and-not-know move, to illustrate different forms of moral failure, only one of which is *akrasia*. I suggest that the train of thought goes like this:

(1) We need a distinction between knowing and heeding what one knows.

(2) This distinction can be applied to the different elements in practical reasoning as represented by the schema of the practical syllogism, and this will point to some kinds of moral failure.

(3) Sometimes knowledge is not heeded because a person is swept away by desire. This is moral weakness, *akrasia* as the term is normally used.

(4) But if one looks to the psychological explanation of why sometimes knowledge is not heeded even when it is readily available, one finds that desire alters the way in which one focuses on the various aspects of the situation.

As against this, though, it must be admitted that mention of different kinds of *akrasia* turns up explicitly only later, at 1147b20.

The next question concerns the precise relevance of the examples of the person asleep, the drunk, the learner who has not yet assimilated what he has been told, and the actor. Ideally we would want them all to be like the other three suggestions, and to illustrate ways of knowing-and-not-knowing. But they don't. The learner does not yet properly know what it is that he repeats by rote; and the actor need not believe any of the things he says. But perhaps this is to stretch too far the point of the comparison, since there is a sense in which the learner knows what he has learnt (since he can repeat it) and the actor knows his lines, but in another sense neither knows in the way required. In none of the comparisons given in (3) does the required knowledge make any difference there and then. I suggest that these comparisons are used simply to illustrate that key feature of this kind of moral failure. Someone can not merely know, but can even repeat in so many words, the correct view about what they should do, without thereby having it available so that they can act upon it. The drunk can fix you with a bleary eye and say, 'My wife's a wonderful woman, I ought to treat her with more respect', and genuinely mean it; yet his drawing that conclusion will not make the slightest difference to his behaviour. So it is in the case of *akrasia*. Now it is clear that Aristotle thinks that *akrasia* is blameworthy; and we have already seen that actions done in ignorance (as distinct from those which are done because of ignorance) are also blameworthy. Perhaps the implication here, then, is that someone who gives way to fury or lust or drunkenness is responsible for getting themselves into the state in which their knowledge of what they should do is no longer effectively available to them. In the heat of the moment, they simply cannot think straight, but they are still blameworthy for any wrong they do while in that state.

The passage from 1147b6–17 then goes on to say that how someone recovers their equilibrium and their understanding of what they did is the same kind of question as how someone gets over a hangover, and thus seems linked to the illustrations given in (3). But this raises a further issue. How are we to take the example of knowing and not knowing given in (4) above? There are two broad alternatives. First, it is intended to be a physiological explanation of the drunkenness/madness examples given in (3). In that case it explains what Aristotle takes to be the straightforward case of *akrasia*, and (4) is linked directly to the paragraph about recovering one's equilibrium. Second, it is a description of another type of moral failure, *not* straightforward *akrasia*, and hence not directly linked to the passage about recovery.

In favour of the first alternative is that one might expect the passage about recovery to follow on immediately; and, furthermore, one might wish to connect the physiological explanation mentioned in (4) with the fact that it is physiologists who explain the recovery of one's equilibrium, and with the fact that anger and lust produce obvious physical changes. In short, everything from 1147a11 to 1147b17 is all of a piece, and is all concerned with straightforward *akrasia*.

But there are counter-arguments available, which might tell in favour of the second alternative. The way Aristotle marks four key sentences of the text (see note 7 above) strongly suggests that there are four equal possibilities, not three plus a long explanation of the third. Moreover, the conclusion of (4) is *not* that the person is overcome by desire to the extent which would support the analogies of sleep, drunkenness, or the actor repeating his lines, even in the vague sense in which I have just suggested these analogies are to be taken. The conclusion of (4) is, as we have already seen (this time with my italics):

> So the moral failure comes about *in a way under the influence of reason and belief.* The belief is not in itself contrary to right reasoning, though it happens to be in this case; it is the desire, not the belief which is unreasonable.

> (VII, 3, 1147a35–b3)

It is very hard to see how, if the point had to do with being carried away by desire (as it would be, if (4) is just a restatement of (3) in psychological terms), Aristotle could say that moral failure comes about in a way under the influence of reason, which, he goes on to remark, explains why animals are incapable of moral failure (1147b4).

A powerful second counter-argument is to be found later on in the text. In chapter 8, 1151a20–28, he says:

> There is the kind of person who is swept away by passion contrary to right reasoning. Passion so rules them that they do not act in accordance with right reasoning, but does not so sway them that they come to believe that they should pursue these pleasures without restraint. Here we have the person who lacks self-control; such a person is better than someone who is self-indulgent, and cannot without qualification be said to be bad, for the best part of them, their starting point,[11] is preserved.

[11] This slightly odd expression must refer either to their reason, or to the moral principle involved; either could be said to be the origin of an action.

This careful description of the person who lacks self-control explicitly distinguishes him from the person who is carried away by their feelings. Here the person who lacks self-control is not at all like the drunk or the sleeper; they are perfectly clear headed and wide-awake to the implications of what they are doing.

On balance, though there is no open and shut case to be made, it seems to me that these two texts strongly point to an interpretation of (4) which does not suggest that the kind of moral failure involved is just a physiological re-description of (3). Instead, we should try to find an account of moral failure in which the person is perfectly capable of thinking, and still chooses to act contrary to what they think would be best. I believe that such an interpretation best fits the text of (4).

The practical syllogisms

The way in which I have set out the text under (4) above assumes that Aristotle thinks that there are two syllogisms involved, which share one common premise, that the food contains sugar. Nevertheless, the fact that the food contains sugar is seen quite differently in the two cases: in the first, because the food is sugary it is seen as dangerous (e.g. because I am diabetic) and therefore as establishing that the food is to be avoided; in the second, it is seen as pleasant, and hence as nice to eat.

Some careful attention must be given to what Aristotle says about these conclusions:

> When one [belief] is produced from these two [beliefs], the soul thereupon must assert that conclusion or, in practical matters, act at once. So for example:
>
>> One should taste whatever is sweet
>> This is sweet
>
> (this second being one of the particulars); the person who is able and not prevented will at once act accordingly. But whenever the person has the universal belief which is telling us not to taste, and also the other, that everything which is sweet is pleasant, and this is a sweet thing, and this second is the one which is

active, and a desire happens to be present, then one set of reasons is telling us to avoid it, while desire is urging us to taste it. Desire can move each of our bodily parts. So the moral failure comes about *in a way under the influence of reason and belief.* The belief is not in itself contrary to right reasoning, though it happens to be in this case; it is the desire, not the belief which is unreasonable.

(VII, 3, 1147a26–b3)

Not the clearest of statements. Still, though not everyone would agree, several things seem to me to emerge from this text: (a) *Two* conclusions are simultaneously available to the person, one that this sweet thing should not be eaten and the other that it should be eaten; (b) Despite the first sentence of the text, it therefore cannot be the case that to know that such a conclusion is available is already to act upon that conclusion, since the person has as yet not done anything: (c) The possible conclusions must be along these lines: 'I shouldn't eat this' and 'This would be nice to eat'; and in each case 'because it contains sugar' is the relevant feature of the particular; (d) Exactly how it is relevant depends upon the point of view from which I look at the situation as a whole – as dangerous to me as a diabetic, or as delightful to me who have a passion for chocolate. (e) The presence of the desire is not sufficient to explain why the person eats the chocolate – for a self-controlled person also has the desire, is capable of reading the situation in either of two ways, and in fact does not eat the chocolate. (f) Since the person who is guilty of a moral failure acts contrary to what they have concluded they should do, we must suppose that, no matter which way the person chooses to act in the example Aristotle here gives, he has reached the conclusion that he should not eat the chocolate.

If I look at the situation from the point of view of the chocolate addict, it is not necessarily the case that I am swept off my feet by a passion for chocolate. (I *might*, of course, suffer from bulimia, and not be able to resist at all: but in that case, Aristotle might say, I would deserve pity rather than blame, and could not properly be described as lacking in self-control.) In thinking how pleasant the chocolate would be, I do not cease to know that it is dangerous and to have that knowledge available, together with the conclusion that I really shouldn't eat it; but I pay no heed to that knowledge, which therefore plays no part in explaining what I am doing. I could very well say, 'I know I shouldn't, but just this once . . .', without it being true to say that I am simply repeating the words like a drunk or a dreamer, unless this is simply taken to mean that what I say makes no difference to what I do. That is the answer to the question, 'In what sense can someone who does wrong be said to know that what he is doing is wrong?' I can know perfectly well, and not want to heed that knowledge. I have argued all the way through this book that Aristotle's key insight is that everything depends on how one 'reads' an individual situation – upon one's moral perceptiveness. Which factors are relevant, which are more important, which if any is of over-riding importance? I will be aware that it is perfectly possible to read the situation in different ways, even if some of these ways cannot properly be justified.

We can now compare and contrast the person who has self-control (the *enkratēs*) with the person who lacks self-control (the *akratēs*). Each of these two has at their disposal both ways of reading the situation. If asked why he did not eat the chocolate, the self-controlled person would of course say that he did not eat it because it was dangerous for him to do so; the person who lacks self-control would say that he ate it because it was really nice sweet chocolate. Both can therefore give reasons, as Aristotle points out: 'they act under the influence of belief' – and, he might have added, true belief. Neither makes any assertion which the other denies – they do not strictly speaking contradict one another. The reason why they do not contradict one another is that they ended up looking at the situation in different terms. Aristotle is trying to explain the sense in which someone can be said to do wrong knowingly. That is the commonly held belief which he thinks can be shown to be correct, at least once it has been tidied up a bit. The tidying up consists in pointing out the several different ways in which knowing is compatible with other states – with not paying attention to, or not being in a fit state to pay attention to, or not seeing the full implications of, or, as here, choosing to look at a situation from a different standpoint because of the presence of a desire. But the presence of the desire in case (4) does not, in contrast with the person who is described in (3), sweep someone off his feet, or render his moral knowledge unavailable to him at the time. Indeed, Aristotle carefully describes someone who has reached a conclusion about what should be done – has made a *prohairesis* – and chooses to act in a way which contradicts that very conclusion.

Does Aristotle defend Socrates, or common sense?

If I argue for this interpretation, I still have to account for the very difficult passage at 1147b9–17, where even the translation is in dispute:

> Since the last proposition[12] is an opinion about what is perceptible[13] and is what leads to action, then it is either not possessed by someone when they are influenced by a desire, or they possess it in such a way that possessing it does not amount to knowing it, just like the drunk who recites Empedocles. And since the last term is not universal nor an object of knowledge in the way that the universal term is, even the result that Socrates wanted seems to follow; for being affected in this way does not come about in the presence of what is agreed to be knowledge in the fullest sense. It is not this kind of knowledge but a grasp of what is perceptible which is dragged around by desire.

I have already pointed out that I have to take this passage (which follows on the remarks about how the drunk can recover) as a commentary on (3) which describes straightforward *akrasia*, in which the person is carried away by their feelings. It is not a commentary on (4), in which the person is not carried away, but can see quite clearly at the time of deciding what to do.

---

[12] The Greek could mean 'the last *premise*' and hence refer to 'This is sweet' in the example. But since it is the conclusion of the argument, not the minor premise, which Aristotle has already said is what leads to action, it seems to me that the translation I have given is preferable. Aristotle is talking about the statement 'I should not eat this'.

[13] I take it that 'perceptible' here is used in the broad sense, in which what is perceived is the chocolate as dangerous to health, or as nice to eat. See VI, 8, 1142a25–30.

The contrast which runs through this entire passage is that between knowledge of a universal and a grasp of what is perceptible. I think this is best interpreted as referring to the contrast between knowing, for example, that 'I shouldn't punch people in the face just because they have made a provocative remark', and 'This is a time to walk away quietly before things get out of hand'. The first is an abstract, theoretical principle; the second involves 'seeing' the particular situation as involving an application of that principle. Aristotle has earlier remarked that emotional imbalance does not on the whole upset one's judgement about geometry; but it easily can and often does upset one's moral judgement.[14] Maybe his point here is that it is not one's theoretical knowledge that violence is wrong which is upset; it is one's grip on the fact that this potentially violent situation is one to walk away from right now. So the crucial insight, upon which right action would have depended, is either not there, or not used. So the person can well say, and mean, 'I really shouldn't let him get to me like this!', and in *that* sense know that they should not be acting as they are. But the *practical* grasp which leads to action is, as Socrates always maintained, not there.

So, does Aristotle think Socrates was right all along? He has already described Socrates's view as 'contrary to the obvious facts' (1145b28), and I do not believe he really makes much of a concession here. He says that it might seem that *even* Socrates's view would follow; but all that he concedes is that there is *a* kind of knowledge which is not upset by desire – and that's at least one thing Socrates wanted to say (1145b23–24). The person who is influenced by desire 'does not have, or rather does not use' his understanding of the particular situation. The reference to the drunk and Empedocles is to be taken to indicate that the relevant knowledge is there but not accessible once one has let fury take over. So in the end Aristotle takes himself to have explained the sense in which a person can be said to know what they are doing when they act wrongly. As he promised, he has defended what most of us would have said about such cases; but he has also shown what it was in Socrates's view that could at a pinch be defended, namely that one's theoretical grasp of morals may remain unaffected by desires.

[14] See VI, 5, 1140b13–16.

Can we say why some people act wrongly when they need not have?

Aristotle is *not* trying to explain why someone acts wrongly rather than rightly. Many commentators, since they think that is just what he should have been explaining, insist on finding such an explanation, and proceed to find it in the influence of desire. Desires, they suggest, are sometimes stronger than one's rational wanting to do the right thing. Even if the notion of desires having in some sense a predetermined strength were clear (which to my mind it is not), I do not think that this is Aristotle's point at all. The reason is simple. Desire cannot be the differentiating factor, since, just like the diabetic who gives in, the self-controlled diabetic also experienced the desire to eat the chocolate: had he not, he would have been virtuous rather than self-controlled. We need to distinguish between two different questions:

- Why did he eat the chocolate? *Answer*: Because he felt like eating something sweet; and
- Why did this feeling lead him to eat, but the same feeling did not lead the self-controlled person to eat? *Answer*: There is nothing more to be said about that except that it was up to him to do one or the other, and he made his choice.

The person who is guilty of a moral failure and the person who exercises self-control are usually very much in the same state of mind. Unlike the vicious person (whose moral judgement has been totally corrupted), they do know what they ought to do; unlike the virtuous person, they do not feel inclined to do what they see they should do. I argued in the preceding chapter that Aristotle is in fact a libertarian about freedom. The point is relevant here. Suppose, in a tricky and embarrassing situation someone hesitates between avoiding confronting someone, and properly confronting them, difficult as that will be. On Aristotle's view, there and then the person is equally capable of choosing either way. Moreover, whichever way they choose, they will have an *explanation* for that choice; 'Because the right thing to do was to grasp the nettle there and then', or, 'Because it would have shattered his confidence', or simply 'Because I couldn't face it'. Even when someone shies away from doing what needs to be done, they do so, as Aristotle says, 'in a way for a reason'. But this explanation need not be, and in Aristotle's view usually isn't, a deterministic one, somehow couched in terms of the strongest desire inevitably winning out. There is no explanation of why I did *this rather than that*, except that I so chose. *Sometimes*, to be sure, I might just have been psychologically unable to have a confrontation there and then; but that cannot always be the case, or Aristotle's account of self-control would make no sense. I can often choose, despite strong desires. I can choose to act in a way contrary to what I see to be best, provided only that I can tell myself *some* story, give some kind of reason for thinking that choice would be a good thing from at least one point of view. I can choose what I think would be for the best without any feelings or inclinations at all.[15] And, finally, there is the kind of moral mistake perhaps most typical of those whose moral training is as yet incomplete. I can choose to do what I have been told is wrong, even when I believe what I have been told, simply because that belief falls short of the judgement which characterizes the person of practical wisdom.

As we have seen, Aristotle does in general think that we are responsible for not having developed the moral virtues which we should have fostered. We are therefore ultimately responsible for the ways in which inappropriate desires can provide us with a motive for choosing to look at the situation differently, or can cloud our judgement, or can on occasion even sweep us off our feet. So even in the case in which moral failure is most similar to drunkenness, Aristotle does not accept that it is on that account blameless. But what of the

---

[15] The notion that only an inclination can motivate us to action is Hume's, but not Aristotle's. (See the discussion of 'wanting', p. 142) By definition, what I choose to do is what I most want. But there is no need to explain 'most want' in terms of 'have the strongest inclination for'. Many choices are made without either emotions or inclinations being involved at all. I need to have a check-up at the dentist, so I decide to do that on Saturday rather than weed the garden. If I choose to go to the dentist, I do so because I think that would be the most convenient, or that perhaps someone else could weed the garden. It is highly artificial to suggest that each possible alternative represents a *desire* with an already fixed 'strength', and still more artificial to suggest that my choosing is the causally inevitable predominance of the inclination with the greatest strength.

situation in which we do clearly see that what we propose to do is wrong, but do it nonetheless? Maybe we simply choose not to heed our best judgement; or we feel like doing something else without it being remotely true that we were swept off our feet by desire. It would seem that this must be possible, in Aristotle's view. The only difference, he says, between an instance of moral failure, and an instance of moral self-control is that:

> The person who exhibits moral weakness desires what they do, but it does not represent their moral conclusion (*prohairesis*); the person who exhibits self-control, by contrast, acts on their moral conclusion, not in accordance with desire.
>
> (III, 2, 1111b12–14)

To say this is to describe what happens. It is not an attempt to explain how *that* particular choice, whichever it was, came to be made.

Relationships
with others

Relevant texts: Books VIII, IX, V

Problems of interpretation
- Which relationships does Aristotle include?
- Is Aristotle an ethical egoist?

Critical issue
- Does Aristotle in effect abandon the link between morality and human nature?

It is time to correct an impression which might have been conveyed by the very list of topics that we have so far discussed. The focus has been on what it is for a person to live a fulfilled life, what traits of characters the person needs to develop in order to do so success-fully, and how a person comes to make moral decisions well or badly, as the case may be. It would be easy to suppose that Aristotle shares the highly individualistic standpoint which characterizes much of contemporary

167

Western ethics; or even to conclude that Aristotle held one or another version of ethical egoism. Neither conclusion would be justifiable; but the evidence for each needs to be discussed. So what does he say about relationships with others?

Aristotelian relationships

It is usual to speak of the section of the *Ethics* which includes Books VIII and IX as Aristotle's discussion of friendship. As is so often the case, though, the common translation is slightly misleading. So in order to appreciate what he has to say, we have to think about the most appropriate translation for the term *philia*. The word appears in what is effectively the title for the long section of the *Ethics* which starts at 1155a3. It is clear enough that 'friendship' covers too narrow a range to be a good fit for the Greek term *philia*. *Philia* has many of the connotations of 'relationship' as we use the term in speaking of the relationships we have with people; and the corresponding verb *philein* means something like 'to get on well with', or 'to like'. We might hope to get on well with a wide variety of people: our family, our close friends, our business partners, neighbours, fellow members of the cricket club, people at the leisure centre, mates down the pub, the local shopkeepers. We have different relationships with all these people, but they could all be described by Aristotle as our *philoi* – people we get on well with as distinct from merely have dealings with; and the various good relationships we have with them are relationships of what Aristotle would have called *philia*. The first thing to notice about Books VIII and IX, then, is the wide variety of relationships which Aristotle includes.[1] *Philia* applies to a rather broader spectrum of relationships than 'friendship' does in English; and *philein* someone is to like and get on well with them, but not necessarily to love them, or

---

[1] A representative sample: young lovers (1156b2), lifelong friends (1156b12), cities with one another (1157a26), political or business contacts (1158a28), parents and children (1158b20), fellow-voyagers and fellow-soldiers (1159b28), members of the same religious society, or of the same dining club (1160a19), or of the same tribe (1161b14), a cobbler and the person who buys from him (1163b35).

even to think of them as friends in our sense of that word. Aristotle goes so far as to say that there is some kind of *philia* in any form of community (VIII, 9), by the mere fact of it being a community as distinct from a mere chance collection of people.

As minimally necessary conditions for *philia* Aristotle suggests that these relationships must be mutual, be mutually recognized, and involve mutual goodwill (VIII, 3, 1155b26–56a5). Aristotle is therefore not willing to say that one can have a relationship of *philia* with an inanimate object – wine, for instance – since it cannot return one's affection and there is no chance of the relationship being mutual. And (one of Aristotle's comparatively rare jokes, perhaps) the only sense in which one could wish well to a bottle of wine would be to wish that it be well kept so that one could have it later. But he apparently leaves open the possibility of a properly mutual relationship with other ensouled things, such as one's pet dog or cat (1155b27–31).[2]

In Book IV he gives an example which, I think, goes somewhat further. He makes a distinction between simply getting along with someone and liking them, and at least in this passage maintains that *philia* requires that we like someone rather than that we simply get along with them.[3]

Aristotle classifies relationships according to what they are based upon. He thinks there are three basic types:

(1)   Relationships based on mutual advantage.
(2)   Relationships based on mutual pleasure.
(3)   Relationships based on mutual admiration.

He does not suggest that these never overlap; indeed, it is his view that the third type of relationship will also be an instance of each of

[2] He has earlier dismissed as irrelevant to his present purpose scientific speculations about the role of Love and Strife in the Cosmos (1155b1ff); perhaps he regards such language as simply metaphorical, as we might speak metaphorically of gravitational or magnetic 'attraction' or 'repulsion'.

[3] 1126b17–23, 1166b30–35. See also Cooper [1980] pp.305–08, and the references he collects in note 9 on p.336. I have the impression that on p.316 Cooper insists that *philia* requires rather more in the way of feeling a liking for someone than I imply in the text.

the first two types as well, though its distinguishing feature is that it is based on an admiration for the qualities of the friend's character. This third type of relationship is the best and most perfect kind of friendship.

The reasons for saying this are several: (a) A friendship of this kind is based on the intrinsic qualities of the friend, and not on whether they happen to be good fun to be with, or useful. (b) Friendships based on admiration for someone's personal qualities are more likely to endure than friendships based on pleasure or mutual advantage. Whether someone can continue to give pleasure or offer other benefits depends very much upon changing circumstances. People can cease to be attractive; tastes and amusements can change; a person may no longer be in a position to do the kind of favours which were so useful. But the virtues that characterize the good person are by their very nature enduring, and are admirable in all circumstances. (c) The basis of such friendships is admirable without qualification. In contrast, the members of a pornography ring may get on with one another on the basis of the pleasures they can provide for one another; and the members of a gang may find it worth working together for their share in the profits from drug smuggling. But the basis for these relationships is not good without qualification, and indeed is bad overall however good it might be from some limited standpoint. In contrast, those friendships which depend upon morally admirable characters cannot be criticized from any point of view (VIII, 3–6).

More tricky is how exactly we are to understand what Aristotle says about goodwill:

> So people in a relationship must have goodwill for each other, know of each other's goodwill, and wish good things for one another, on one of the three grounds already mentioned. These grounds differ from one another in kind. So then do the ways of relating, and the kinds of relationship. There are therefore three types of relationship, corresponding to the three grounds which are their objects.
>
> (VIII, 2, 1156a3–8)

The second half of this paragraph is clear enough from what we have already said. The first part is not so clear. Aristotle has already remarked that 'it is commonly said that one should wish for good things for a friend for the friend's sake' (1155b31). How does that remark tie in with what is apparently said here, that people should wish good things for another because one's friend is useful (or gives pleasure, or is thoroughly admirable)?

There are several points to be made. (a) The grounds for the friendship appear in the answers which would be given to some question like 'What is there between you and Tony?' So it might be that Tony is a very useful person to know; or that he is good fun to play tennis with, or that he is someone I really like and trust and admire. These answers both explain why I have any relationship with Tony at all, and define what kind of relationship it is. (b) Given that I have such a relationship and to that extent like and get on well with Tony, Aristotle assumes that there must be a certain degree of mutual goodwill, since without goodwill there simply is no relationship at all. To have goodwill for someone is to wish them well and to be prepared to do things for them for their sake, although no doubt how much goodwill one can presume upon in any relationship will vary with the nature of the relationship itself. (c) To have goodwill towards Tony is a feature of the relationship which will naturally find expression from time to time. It does not necessarily follow that when I do something for Tony's sake, I am doing it in order to maintain the relationship, or for the sake of some future advantage or pleasure to be obtained.

I therefore suggest that the final clause of the first sentence of the text I have cited above ('on one of the three grounds already mentioned') relates to the whole of the earlier part of the sentence, rather than explaining the immediately preceding clause about wishing good for the other person. That is to say, it suggests that the way in which *all* the characteristics of the relationship work out will depend upon the basis on which the relationship as a whole is founded. The depth and extent and nature of my goodwill and the ways in which that goodwill is naturally expressed will all vary with the type of relationship. But in each kind of friendship the goodwill is directed to the good of the other person, for that person's sake.[4]

[4] For a slightly different version of this, see Cooper [1980], especially pp.308–15.

Is Aristotle an ethical egoist?

In taking the line I have just suggested, I have by implication begun to make the case for saying that Aristotle at least cannot without qualification be described as an egoist in the modern sense. On the other hand, the considerable stress which he seems to lay on developing one's capacities and living a fulfilled life might still suggest that the ultimate focus of ethics is indeed upon oneself rather than upon others. So is Aristotle after all an egoist?

The question is not entirely clear, however, until we have tried to clarify what we might mean by 'egoism'. One way to do this is to decide how best to use the term 'altruism', since egoism and altruism are normally taken to be mutually exclusive. Consider, then, four possible accounts of an altruistic action:

(A1) An altruistic action is an action done to benefit another from which the agent derives no benefit.

(A2) An altruistic action is an action done to benefit another from which there is no foreseen benefit to the agent.

(A3) An altruistic action is an action which the agent performs to benefit someone else without considering whether he will benefit or not.

(A4) An altruistic action is an action which the agent performs principally for the sake of producing some benefit for someone else.

We may reasonably decide not to adopt (A1) on the grounds that it is too far from our normal usage, which would suggest that whether or not an action is altruistic depends on what the agent believes at the time. In contrast, the criterion offered in (A1) is independent of what the agent might think. (A2) avoids this objection, but might still be thought to be too restrictive on other grounds. On the basis of (A2), even the most unself-regarding parents could not perform an altruistic action towards their children, not even if they believed that no sacrifice should be spared in order to bring them up well, if they also thought that to be good parents would be among the most fulfilling things they could possibly do. (A2) is so much more demanding than ordinary usage that it should be adopted as a definition only if there are good reasons for supposing ordinary usage is very confused or in some other way unhelpful.

On the other hand (A3) seems much closer to the way in which we would normally use the word. It is thus an improvement upon (A2). It also seems preferable to (A4) which I think is too weak. I therefore propose to define an altruistic action in terms of (A3). If one then defines ethical egoism as the view that denies that one ever has a duty to perform an altruistic action, then ethical egoism turns out to be:

(E1) One has a duty to perform an action only if it is believed to benefit oneself.

This, however, is a very weak form of ethical egoism. It does not even deny that it is permissible to act for the good of someone else; it merely says that one never has a duty to act solely for the benefit of someone else.

(E2) One may not perform an action unless one believes it will benefit oneself.

This is much stronger than (E1), in that it denies that the prospect of conferring some benefit on another can ever be a sufficient reason for doing something. It is incompatible with altruism as defined by (A2). However (E2) is still weaker than:

(E3) One may perform only that action which one believes will maximally benefit oneself.

There is no one correct account of egoism. Each of these different principles can be said to capture a plausible view which can reasonably be said to be egoist in spirit.[5] They are sufficiently different from one another to make it worth asking whether any of them corresponds to Aristotle's account.

We need to recall what Aristotle says about *eudaimonia*. The only ultimately justifiable reason for doing anything is that acting in

---

[5] For the sake of simplicity I am assuming that, in each of these three principles, we are speaking about the actions available to a particular agent in the circumstances obtaining at that time.

that way will contribute to living a fulfilled life. We can, of course, be mistaken in our view of what a fulfilled life requires, as we can be mistaken in our view of what will in fact contribute to living such a life. We are unfortunately capable of deciding to act in a way which we know will not in fact contribute to living such a life. In these various ways our actions can be unjustifiable; and we may or may not be blameworthy for doing what cannot in the end be justified. Still, living a fulfilled life is not just something we should do, it is something which we all naturally desire to do – indeed it would not *be* a fulfilled life were this not so. If, then, the word 'benefit' as it occurs in (E1), (E2) and (E3) is understood as 'whatever contributes to living a fulfilled life', then it seems that Aristotle subscribes at least to (E2), and hence to (E1). To act as one should is to act according to the intellectual and moral virtues: and to act virtuously is what living a fulfilled life consists in. Moreover, since the fulfilled life is complete and self-sufficient, nothing can possibly be an improvement upon it: so it seems that Aristotle must subscribe to (E3) as well. So he does, in just the sense we have outlined, and for the reasons we have given. Aristotle, in IX, 8 asks whether one ought to love oneself or others most of all (1168a28); his answer involves distinguishing between the vulgar sense of 'looking after number one', as we might put it, and true love of one's self. The vulgar think of looking after themselves in terms of acquiring possessions and power and honours and pleasures; and since these goods are in limited supply, one person will acquire them only at the expense of others. Truly to love one's self, in contrast, is to love the best and most controlling part of one's self, that which most defines what a person is (1169a2). It comes as no surprise to discover that true self-love consists in respect for one's mind.

> The self-lover in the fullest sense is quite a different kind of person from the self-lover who comes in for criticism, just as a life lived in accordance with reason is quite different from one ruled by feelings, and desiring what is fine is quite different from desiring what seems to be to one's advantage. Those who are outstanding in their eagerness to do what is fine are welcomed by everyone with praise. When everyone competes to do what is fine and tries to do the best actions, then everything will come

about for the common good, and for each individual too there will be the greatest benefits, since that is just how virtue is.

(IX, 8, 1169a3–11)

There are two key moves in this argument. One is the definition of what is truly beneficial for one's self in terms of what is fine, noble and virtuous rather than in terms of riches, pleasures and honours; and the other is the consequent suggestion that there is no reason why true self-lovers should have to compete with one another for personal fulfilment in the way in which people might have to compete for other kinds of goods. There is nothing about the fulfilled life to suggest that it can be lived only at someone else's expense.

To say that the fulfilled life is a life in which one pursues the noble and fine and lives according to the virtues in itself says nothing about what such a life consists in. One has to go on to fill in the details in terms of courage and honesty and temperance, and, in particular, of the virtues involved in liking people and getting on well with them. At this point, Aristotle, as we have clearly seen, insists on the importance of wishing someone well for their sake rather than one's own. IX, 8 concludes with a long and beautiful account of the nobility of self-sacrifice for others' sake even at the cost of one's life, on the grounds that the person who is called upon to make such a sacrifice gains something beyond price. Once he says that, Aristotle clearly accepts even (E3). But now (E3) seems very different, since it is explicitly shorn of what would normally be thought to be most characteristic of egoism, the claim that the egoist will at times be justified in promoting his own advantage *at the expense of others*.

Two criticisms will at once suggest themselves, the first based on Aristotle's own account of why we do things, and the second based on a more pessimistic view of the inevitability of damaging competition.

Aristotle believes that everything we do is done for a purpose, and that fulfilment is the ultimate end for the sake of which we do everything we do. I have argued above (Chapter 3) that this is to be interpreted as meaning that the link to fulfilment explains why something is worth doing, by giving the *point* of doing it. Well then, someone might argue, even the things one does out of goodwill towards one's friends and the people one likes are not *ultimately* done for the sake of those people, but for the sake of our personal self-fulfilment. Is this not egoism in a fairly strong sense, despite what has just been said? Plausible though it might sound at first hearing, I nevertheless think that this objection fails. Morally virtuous activities are worth performing because they are noble and fine things to do; they are worth doing for their own sake, and because living in that way just is living a fulfilled life. That last occurrence of 'because', relating an activity to the living of a fulfilled life, explains *why* an activity is properly described as virtuous. Now an act of goodwill done for a friend because she is a friend, is just such an activity. It is done for her sake: and as such is worth doing both in itself, and because it plays its part in the living of a fulfilled life. There is no conflict at all in saying that the kindness is performed for the sake of one's friend, and that being kind to one's friends is in itself a worthwhile thing to do; nor in saying that things are worth doing because they contribute to a fulfilled life.[6]

In general, Aristotle's position is that living a life of virtuous activity is fulfilling, and that in general there is no reason why someone should be able to live such a life only at someone else's expense. On the contrary, good relationships, and especially friendships based on admiration for the good qualities of one's friend, bring the best out of people. However, there are two ways in which this otherwise optimistic hope might prove illusory. Aristotle believes that living a fulfilled life and being able to practise the virtues requires at least a basic standard of well-being and leisure.[7] If people are forced to subsist below this minimum level, then living a morally admirable life, let alone a life with time for reflection, might prove very difficult or even

[6] Kraut [1989], ch. 2, contains a good and full discussion of these issues, covering both the *Ethics* and the *Politics*. On p.137, he disagrees with my argument here. He argues that if acting for her sake is worth doing only because it is fulfilling, then the fact that it is done for her sake does not of itself provide a reason for doing it. To my mind, 'doing it for her sake' neither justifies the action nor gives a reason for doing it, but rather *characterizes* it as an act of friendship. The justification and the reason for doing it is that an act of friendship is virtuous, and so worth doing in itself. Because it is worth doing, it can form part of a fulfilling life.

[7] I, 9, 1099a31–b8.

impossible. If people have to compete with one another for the scarce resources required for minimal human subsistence, then it will be the case that one person will be able to live a fulfilled life only by acting in such a way that someone else has no such chance. So it might appear once again that Aristotle is committed at least at this level to the kind of competitive self-regard characteristic of egoism.

His reply to this might be along the same lines as we have seen already. Nothing in Aristotle's general view suggests that even in the case of scarcity we may ever act other than as justice requires. The situation is parallel to the one he has already discussed in IX, 9 where someone might be asked to perform an action of heroic self-sacrifice for the sake of others. Aristotle firmly maintains that the value of performing a fine and noble action outweighs all the more material losses which are incurred. It is true that the almost lyrical praise of altruism at the end of IX, 8 might seem to be ever so slightly clouded by the remark at 1169a22, to the effect that the good person will prefer the short but intense *pleasure* of giving their life for someone else to the quieter delights of a more humdrum existence. But perhaps this remark is to be read in the light of Aristotle's view that the value of any pleasure depends upon the activity in which the pleasure is to be found, not the other way round.[8] So once again, the egoist challenge is sidestepped, by defining what is valuable for oneself in such a way that it need not conflict with what is in a different sense valuable for others.

The radical nature of this position needs to be fully grasped. It has its roots in Plato's famous dictum that the good person cannot be harmed, and his consequent identification of the fulfilled life with the life of virtue. In a very similar way Aristotle in speaking of heroic self-sacrifice says calmly enough, 'Not unreasonably, then, is a person thought to be admirable when they choose what is fine at the cost of everything else' (1169a31–32). It will be recalled that at the end of the Function Argument in I, 7, Aristotle seems almost to abandon the biological approach which one might have expected from him. Instead of arguing that human fulfilment consists in the integrated functioning of the various powers inherent in human nature, Aristotle insisted that

[8] See Chapter 9.

it consists in the proper exercise of the highest and most distinctive of these powers, the human mind. One consequence of this we have already seen, is the special position he gives to *theōria* the exercise of reason in theoretical matters. More surprisingly, perhaps, the exercise of reason even in practical matters turns out to owe less than one might have supposed to the biological roots of human nature. Of course moral virtues such as temperance, courage and generosity consist in a balanced set of desires and emotional responses, and these emotions are, in Aristotle's view, firmly rooted in our biology. But, at least in extreme situations, the morally admirable life has a value and a beauty which simply cannot be cashed in terms of the satisfaction of any other desires at all. What this shows, I believe, is that even in less extreme cases in which someone behaving generously, or temperately, or honestly, acts in accordance with their (virtuous) inclinations, what is *morally* significant is that they do so because to act in such a way is fine and noble. If Aristotle intends us to see that what is fine and noble is an irreducibly moral quality of actions, then it becomes more difficult to see why he ever bothered to invoke anything like a Function Argument at all. An unsympathetic critic might point out that what looked like a promising and helpful proposal to ground ethics in the sciences of human biology and psychology seems, in the end, to have ended up with nothing more than an appeal to a moral sense – a kind of perceptiveness of the sort which Bentham might have described as 'caprice'. Instead of a comparatively obvious appeal to human well-being, what Aristotle offers us is a notion of fulfilment discovered only by *phronēsis* – an alleged ability to perceive what is fine and noble – whose workings are, it turns out, beyond rational scrutiny.

I suppose that Aristotle would reply that the basis of ethics is complex, not simple. Of course human fulfilment presupposes in general terms that people are in good physical, mental and emotional health; and it is wrong to treat people in such a manner as to destroy or impair any of these basic human functions. But these features of human nature reveal only part of the story. It is precisely the appeal to the Function Argument which leads us to see that specifically *human* fulfilment involves the mind – theoretical and practical – which in an important sense *is* our 'self' (1169a1). To say that our mind is our self implies not just that to look after one's self involves caring for one's mental health; it means that our self is essentially relational, and relational to other selves. It is part of practical wisdom to see the crucial truth that human beings are by nature such as to find their fulfilment in relationship to others; and this realization profoundly affects both our notion of individual fulfilment and our perception of the kinds of demands which the life of virtue might make upon us. Perhaps he regards what is fine and noble as characteristic features of the fulfilled life precisely because the fulfilled life is lived in a community, and the actions which a fulfilled life requires of us have a community dimension.

> Perhaps it is just absurd to make out that someone living like a hermit could be happy. Nobody would choose to possess all good things, and yet to be on their own. A human being is social, naturally fitted to live with others.
>
> (IX, 9, 1169b16–19)

By nature we need relationships with others, of various kinds and depths. This natural fact has the consequence that what is distinctive about human fulfilment is that there are demands upon us which need not coincide with what might promote our individual well-being narrowly understood. It is no accident of careless editing that almost two entire books of the *Ethics* are taken up with the discussion of the relationships between human beings. The discussion of vulgar and true self-love in IX, 8, and the arguments to show that human beings need relationships of true friendship in IX, 9, are central to a correct appreciation of the earlier discussions which might otherwise seem to focus on humans as isolable individuals. Once we see this, we see the fulfilled life not just as satisfying, but as fine and noble.

Flexibility, relationships and justice

The two books on interpersonal relationships contain a large number of detailed examples in which Aristotle considers a wide variety of possible transactions. He deals with relationships between equals and between unequals, between good people and between bad people; the difference it makes whether a relationship is based on mutual advantage or mutual pleasure; when and how to break off a relationship when the people concerned have changed over the course of time.

In IX, 2, after listing a typical set of questions to which the answers are not at all obvious, Aristotle says:

> It is not at all easy to give precise answers to all these questions, is it? There are so many features of all sorts which make a difference – sometimes important and sometimes only small – to what is fine and to what is unavoidable. It is not hard to see that not everything should be given back to the same person; that favours given should usually be repaid before one indulges one's cronies – so one should repay a loan to a creditor rather than lend the money to a companion.
>
> But even this is not always true. For instance, if someone has ransomed you from kidnappers should you ransom him in return, no matter who he is? Or suppose not that he has been captured, but that he asks you to repay the ransom he gave for you, should you repay him rather than [using the money to] ransom your father?
>
> (IX, 2, 1164b27–1165a1)

Here we have a good example of Aristotle's general point that one should not expect in ethics the kind of precision which one might hope for in physics. Not that one cannot attempt to formulate at least some general principles. Of course one can, and throughout his discussions in VIII and IX Aristotle does it all the time. But one cannot expect even these principles to hold good in every case.[9]

> To ask how a man should behave towards his wife or in general how one should conduct any relationship with someone else seems to be the same as asking how one should live one's life justly. The answer is plainly different if one is dealing with a friend or with a stranger, with a companion, or a contemporary.
>
> (VIII,12, 1162a29–33)

[9] Thomas Aquinas, in very much the same spirit, remarks that the more detailed the principles one tries to formulate, the less obvious they are, and the less likely they are to hold good in every case (*Summa Theologiae*, I, 94, 4).

What is just also varies: it is not the same for parents towards their children as for brothers towards one another, nor the same towards companions as towards fellow-citizens, and similarly for other kinds of relationship.

(VIII, 9, 1159b35–1160a2)

These two texts make much the same point, this time linking problems about relationships with the notion of justice.[10] There are no very simple, general answers to be given. And, as V, 10 makes clear, the law itself, when applied strictly to particular cases, will at times produce results which are unjust. It therefore needs to be supplemented by what Aristotle terms *epieikeia*, a sense of what is fair and reasonable in an individual situation. *Epieikeia* can be regarded as one application of *phronēsis,* practical wisdom at work in legal contexts. Like practical wisdom, it is a matter of perception rather than principle.

Human beings are not machines. They are far more malleable and flexible in their patterns of behaviour both as individuals and in their mutual relationships. For this reason, ethics, in Aristotle's view, is not and cannot be like physics or astronomy. In particular, the notion of rationality in ethics cannot be just the same as it is in the sciences. At least ideally, Aristotle thought, explanations in science could be exhibited with logical rigour as conclusions which followed validly from premises whose necessary truth was beyond question. In ethics, Aristotle does not abandon the notion that actions can be explained by appeal to a practical syllogism. The conclusions of practical syllogisms, too, should follow validly from the premises. But the premises themselves, even ideally, do not express necessary truths which are

[10] I do not propose to comment in detail upon the treatment of justice in Book V. Suffice it to say that Aristotle identifies two different senses of 'just'. The first is totally general, and is coterminous with 'morally admirable'. Aristotle suggests that the laws (at least in an ideal state) will reinforce its publicly accepted morality, so that 'unjust', in this general sense, is equivalent to 'unlawful'. The second sense of 'just' identifies justice as a particular virtue alongside courage and temperance. Justice is exhibited both in just distribution of benefits, and in the righting of previous wrongs or injuries. In this sense it is contrasted both with trying to obtain more than one's share, and with unfairness.

therefore true and relevant in every case. Again, there is a sense in which Aristotle might agree that moral rationality is *somehow* related to maximizing expected benefits. But he accepts this only on condition that the notion of 'benefit' be understood in terms of virtuous conduct, rather than in some less contentious way. To grasp the notion of virtuous conduct is to recognize that, on occasion, an act of self-sacrifice can bring the greatest benefits of all.

Chapter 9

Pleasure and
the good life

Relevant texts:
Book VII, chs 11–15; Book X, chs 1–5

Problems of interpretation
- How is pleasure connected with
  eudaimonia?
- What precisely is pleasure?

Critical issues
- Is the fulfilled life necessarily pleasurable?
- Is whether we live a fulfilled life or not
  partly a matter of luck?

In translating *eudaimonia* as 'fulfilment', I have been
trying to capture several strands in its meaning. The
morally admirable life involves the development and
exercise of our natural capacities, and especially those
which characterize us as humans. It is fulfilling in the
sense that a person might fulfil their early promise.

'Fulfilment' is also a good translation since it suggests something which cannot be improved upon. But it also has at least some overtones of satisfaction. Even if fulfilment is not directly a feeling like pleasure or enjoyment, could we really say that a life was a fulfilled life if it were not also at least broadly speaking an enjoyable life? Is fulfilment a particular kind of pleasure?

Pleasure is discussed in two different places in the *Ethics*, once in Book VII at the end of the treatment of moral failure, and once at the start of Book X, introducing the final definitive discussion of *eudaimonia*. Neither discussion refers to the other, and it remains something of a puzzle why they are both included in the *Ethics* at all. This puzzle provides one of the most obvious reminders that Aristotle wrote two treatises on ethics. Book VII is one of the books which is common to both the *Nicomachaean Ethics* and the *Eudemian Ethics* as those books have come down to us; Book X appears only in the *Nicomachaean Ethics*. Was the original home of Book VII in the *Eudemian Ethics* or not, and was it written earlier or later than Book X? Commentators have more commonly taken the view that the Book X passage is the later, and have detected a more detailed and sophisticated discussion of the issues than is to be found in Book VII. But this view is by no means beyond challenge, and a good case can be made for dating the two passages in the reverse order.[1] I shall not attempt to settle these issues here; I take the view that the differences between the two passages are not so radical as to indicate any important shift in Aristotle's position. They may well reflect the fact that discussions of the issues involved had a slightly different focus depending on who was actively involved at different times.

Each passage fits well enough into its immediate context. In Book VII, where Aristotle has already discussed the role that desires, and especially bodily desires, have to play in cases of moral failure, it makes good sense to discuss pleasure. So at the beginning of VII, 11 Aristotle says he has to discuss pleasure, since virtue and vice are concerned with what people find pleasurable and painful; and most people think that a fulfilled life must be pleasurable. Yet, since moral failure

[1] See Gosling and Taylor [1982], chs 11 and 15 for an excellent and detailed account of the various possibilities.

is often occasioned by a misdirected desire for pleasure, it might well seem that pleasure is morally suspect, or at least that many pleasures are morally bad. At any rate, the highest good clearly cannot be pleasure, given the link between pleasure and moral failure. At the beginning of Book X, Aristotle repeats the same point about the connection between pleasures and the moral virtues. Moral education, in both its methods and its results, depends upon encouraging people to take pleasure in what is fine and noble, and to feel discomfort at what is base. Besides, pleasure and pain are very important when it comes to living a fulfilled life. So, reasonably enough, the focus in VII is on whether some pleasures, far from being bad and leading us astray, might actually be good and somehow contribute to the fulfilled life; and in X, the introduction to his final thoughts on *eudaimonia* consists of asking whether pleasure might not be *the* good. Of course, Aristotle has already in I, 5 brusquely dismissed the life of pleasure-seeking as fit only for brutes, and he can hardly be asking us here to reconsider *that* judgement. But, he now asks, is there *no* sense in which a fulfilled life could be described as the pleasantest? Is fulfilment not delightful after all? Should we expect the morally admirable life to be great fun? To be enjoyable? Satisfying?

The issues as they appeared to Aristotle

Eudoxus

Eudoxus was a philosopher who came to Plato's Academy at about the same time as Aristotle first went there. Aristotle gives his opinions and arguments a good airing in X, 2.

> Eudoxus thought that pleasure was *the* good, because he saw that all animals, rational and non-rational, aim at it. Moreover, in any domain it is the fitting which is worthy of choice, and the most fitting which is most worthy of choice. The very fact that everything is drawn to the same thing points to the fact that it is best (for each thing finds what is best for it, just as it finds its own proper food), and that what is good for everything – what everything aims at – is the good ... He thought the same result

followed from consideration of the opposite: pain in itself is to be avoided by all, so the parallel would be that pleasure in itself is choiceworthy. Again, what is most choiceworthy is what is not chosen because of or for the sake of something else. And this everyone would admit is how it is with pleasure. Nobody would ever ask what is the point of pleasure, since it is worth choosing simply for its own sake.

(X, 2, 1172b9–23)

Some of the phrases which Aristotle uses in this thumbnail sketch of Eudoxus are worth noticing: 'what all things aim at' is exactly the phrase which Aristotle himself uses to conclude the first sentence of his *Ethics*: '. . . so it has been well said that the good is what everything aims at'. Again, Aristotle claims that *eudaimonia* is complete, precisely because it is chosen for its own sake and not for the sake of anything else. It makes no sense to ask what one wants a fulfilled life *for*. One might be forgiven for concluding that Aristotle must surely endorse the position which he attributes here to Eudoxus. But things are not so simple. In the middle of the passage I have just cited, Aristotle inserts a cautionary remark. People were swayed by what Eudoxus said, he suggests, not so much because of what he said, but because Eudoxus had a reputation of being a sober and virtuous man rather than a mere pleasure-seeker. The suggestion is that Eudoxus's arguments could easily be represented as an encouragement to a life devoted to the pursuit of pleasure, despite how Eudoxus himself interpreted them in practice. So one question, to which we shall have to return, is precisely how far Aristotle does accept Eudoxus; and one way of sharpening that question is by asking exactly what Aristotle takes the relationship to be between pleasure and living a fulfilled life. Is there no sense in which a fulfilled life must be the most pleasant life one could have? What exactly is the difference between aiming at fulfilment and aiming at a life of pleasure?

The physiology and psychology of pleasure

Everyone knows what pleasure is – until one tries to define it. When we think of the variety of instances, we perhaps begin to realize that it is not going to be at all easy to give a clear account. Consider some examples: having a hot bath at the end of a tiring walk; spending an evening with a close friend one has not seen for some time; having one's aching muscles expertly massaged; mountaineering; listening to music; solving a crossword puzzle; having a philosophical argument; playing rugby; playing chess; gardening. Even if these are all activities which give one pleasure, it is surely quite implausible to say that there is one experience which they all give. Certainly there is no one *sensation* which is produced by all these; and even using such a vague term as 'feeling' does not help. There is no one feeling experienced when playing rugby and when spending an evening with a friend or solving the crossword. At most one might say that these are all things one can enjoy doing. But that simply demonstrates the enormous flexibility of the term 'enjoy'. The two Greek words *hēdonē* and *hēdesthai*, which correspond more or less to 'pleasure' and 'to enjoy', are just as flexible as their English equivalents.[2]

The Greek philosophers made one attempt at explaining the nature of pleasure by relating it to a physiological process, and in particular to the process of replenishing some deficiency or meeting some physical need. Thus the pleasure of downing a pint consists in making good a lack of fluids in the body. As a refinement on this view, it might be suggested that the change need not be to supplement a deficiency, but rather to restore the balance required by nature. If one is convinced by this as an account of the delights of slaking one's thirst, or restoring one's tired muscles, it is tempting to try to extend the theory to cover pleasures which are not, or at least not obviously, physical pleasures at all. Perhaps, for instance, the pleasure of seeing one's long absent friend is the process of making up for a lack of affection, and listening to music is a kind of mental massage?

This last suggestion marks in fact two shifts. The first is the shift from a mere physiological change to a *perceived* physiological change. Not just any change will be a pleasure; not even any change which repairs a defect, or fills up a deficiency. The slow healing of a wound,

---

[2] *Hēdonē*, like its English derivative 'hedonism', can suggest that the pleasures are rather disreputable, or that the pursuit of pleasure is all too single-minded; but, as in English, it can equally well have a perfectly good sense.

for instance, is not in itself a pleasurable process. The change has to be perceived: and that is tantamount to accepting that pleasure, even bodily pleasure, somehow involves more than a purely physical process. The second shift comes with the recognition that when it comes to pleasures which are not bodily pleasures, any talk of repairing defects or filling up deficiencies or restoring balances is a metaphorical rather than a strictly literal account.[3] So caution needs to be exercised when non-physical pleasures are explained in terms of the change from deprivation to fullness. The physical model may indeed be enlightening, but must not be unduly pressed.

General moral arguments

Many of the same arguments of a broadly moral character which we might think of as telling against basing morality upon the pursuit of pleasure were current in Aristotle's day. Hedonism has a bad name with us, just as the pursuit of *hēdonē* had for many Greeks. Morality requires us to do our duty, and as often as not requires that we avoid pleasures in order to do as we should. In any event, many pleasures are undesirable; and some pleasures are not merely undesirable, they are positively corrupt or perverted. Moreover a life devoted to the pursuit of pleasure is very likely to miss out on many of the most worthwhile activities.

Aristotle's comments on the moral arguments

At the beginning of VII, 13, Aristotle briskly says that such arguments and the others which are usually advanced simply fail to show that pleasure is not good. They do not show even that it is not *the* good.

He dismisses, almost in a series of one-liners, many of the moral arguments aimed at showing that pleasure cannot be good. 'Good' can be said quite generally and without qualification; or it can be said in relation to particular individuals and circumstances. The same applies,

---

[3] At least this is true in many cases. There may, of course, be instances where mental states are altered by purely physical means, and feelings of depression, say, are replaced by feelings of well-being by means of appropriate drugs.

he says, to what can be said to be natural, or to processes and comings-to-be (if these are what pleasures are). Some of these seem to be bad without qualification; others only to be bad for a particular thing in particular circumstances. Some procedures which are in general bad can even be good in certain situations. Take surgery, for instance: being cut open is in general bad; but might be very helpful for someone who is ill. To put it in a nutshell, Aristotle thinks that most of the people who argue that pleasure is always bad are guilty of wild over-generalization. Of course some pleasures can have bad consequences; and of course some pleasures can distract us from what we ought to be doing. So the temperate person does not pursue any and all plea-sures, but he does pursue some.[4]

Neither does Aristotle accept the particular kind of moralistic high-mindedness which would claim that at least bodily pleasures are shameful, or even downright bad, and that only the higher pleasures ought to be sought after. If these pleasures are not good, he asks, why is it that the corresponding physical pains are so awful? For what is contrary to an evil is a good (VII, 14, 1154a10–11). He gives his own opinion, which is neither prudishly disapproving, nor uncritically permissive:

> Or is it that necessary [bodily] pleasures are good to the extent only that what is not bad is good? or are they [positively] good up to a point?
>
> In the case of those states and processes in which one cannot have too much of a good thing, so neither can there be too much pleasure involved in them. But where it is possible to have too much of a good thing, so it is possible to have too much pleasure. Now one can have too much in the way of bodily goods, and a nasty person is so not because he [enjoys] the neces-sary pleasures, but because he goes after what is too much. After all, everyone enjoys nice foods and wines and sex, but not all enjoy these as they should.
>
> (VII, 14, 1154a11–18)

---

[4] The common objections are given at VII, 11, 1152b8–24; and the brisk dismissals of most of them come in VII, 12, 1153a17–35. Between these passages is a longer discussion which will be considered below.

Perhaps friendship is a good example of a state in which one cannot have too much of a good thing, so one cannot enjoy one's friendships too much. But, as Aristotle's discussion of temperance has explained, it is possible to be too captivated by good bodily pleasures. Still, that is not to say that the temperate person does not enjoy food, wine, sex, or aromatherapy, or that these are at most grudgingly admitted as not being definitely wrong. These pleasures are positively good. Why, then, are people so apt to be so wrong in estimating their worth? Aristotle concludes by offering some explanations, in terms of their intensity, their sometimes disreputable nature, and their connection with the remedying of the imperfections of our natural constitution.

So much for the moral arguments intended to show that pleasure is not good at all. They do not merely fail to establish that conclusion; they do not even show that there might not be a pleasure which is *the* good. But there are arguments of quite a different sort, metaphysical rather than moral, which need more detailed discussion.

The argument from opposites

One reason for holding that no pleasure is good is because one is already committed to the view that the only good state is a state involving neither pleasure nor pain. The more metaphysical reasons for this position need not concern us for the moment. But there are more commonplace reasons too. Here are some. Both pleasures and pains might be thought of as perturbations of a desirable meditative calm, or as liable to cloud one's moral judgement. One might imagine a defence of this position being offered perhaps by a Buddhist monk. Again, pleasure might seem to be inherently unstable, always likely to get out of control, to lead us astray, to be almost dangerously addictive. A quite different set of reasons can also be given for denying that pleasure is good. Some philosophers wished to hold that pleasure in itself was neither good nor bad, even if we are not sure precisely why they thought so in every case. Speusippus, who took over the direction of the Academy after Plato's death in 347, is one such. About his views Aristotle makes the following somewhat cryptic remarks:

Now, that pain is bad and to be avoided is also generally agreed. One kind of pain is bad without qualification, another is bad because it gets in the way. But the opposite of what is in itself to be avoided and bad is good. So one has to say that pleasure is a good thing. Speusippus's proposed counter-argument – that just as the greater is opposed both to the less and to the equal – does not work. For he would not be prepared to admit that pleasure is evil.

(VII, 13, 1153b4–7)

Plainly, a fair amount needs to be filled in if we are to reconstruct Speusippus's position. Presumably he wanted to maintain that pleasure is not good. When his critics said that pain obviously is evil, and pleasure is opposed to pain, so pleasure must be good, Speusippus must have tried to argue that pleasure could be opposed both to pain (and so not evil) and to good (because pleasure is neither good nor evil, but neutral.) Aristotle says that this is a mistake, and that if pleasure is opposed to good it must be evil, however much Speusippus might like to wriggle. But why would Aristotle think that followed?

They deny that, just because pain is an evil, it follows that pleasure is good. For one evil can be contrasted with another, and yet both be contrasted with what is neither good nor bad but neutral. This is a fair point, but it is mistakenly applied to this discussion. If both were evil, both should be avoided; if neither is, then neither should be avoided, or they should be avoided equally. But in fact they clearly avoid the one because it is evil, and choose the other because it is good. And that's exactly the contrast between them.

(X, 2, 1173a5–13)

So Aristotle's criticism is that Speusippus is inconsistent, in that he wishes to maintain on the one hand that pleasure and pain are both in the same evaluative category (neutral), while still saying that pain is bad and to be avoided, while pleasure is not.[5]

---

[5] Gosling and Taylor [1982] pp. 228–34 are unconvinced that the two passages I have quoted here can be meant as criticisms of one and the same philosophical

Still, surely the inconsistency in the position described in this second passage is really too glaring to have been believed by anyone? Maybe not. One might, perhaps, believe that only stable states were in the proper sense good or bad; but that processes which had these states as their end-products, while not in themselves good or bad, might still be able to be ranked in order of preference, according to which direction they were moving in. So, one might think, perhaps, that pleasure was experienced when one was in transition to a good state, say, health, or understanding some difficult argument, or having established a friendship; and that pain was experienced when one was in the process of becoming ill, or breaking up a valuable relationship, or becoming confused about something. In this case, the dispute with Aristotle would be about whether 'good' and 'bad' should apply not only to final states, but also to the processes, when one was worth choosing and the other worth avoiding. Aristotle would want to say that such processes, too, are good or bad, not perhaps in themselves, but in a qualified sense, because of the results which they lead to. If this is the problem, then it seems to be one of terminology rather than of substance.

But two deeper questions underlie this difference of opinion:

- Why should only stable states be in the full sense good or bad?
- Is it true that pleasure and pain are perceived transitional processes?

There is a long passage in Plato's dialogue *Philebus* (53c–55a) in which Plato quotes the opinions of those who say that all pleasures are processes rather than states or, as Plato puts it, 'instances of becoming, rather than being' (53c4). Clearly, Plato says, someone who holds this position will make fun of anyone who says that pleasure is good, thereby saying that the fulfilled life consists in pleasures. For, the argument goes, it is our goals, the ends we aim at, which are properly said to be good; the processes by which such results come about should be called something other than good. (Perhaps Plato

view. I think that they can, but it is not easy to be sure how to reconstruct either of Aristotle's two highly condensed and elliptical remarks. It may be that the passage in Book X is not about Speusippus at all, but about someone who also tried to maintain a different version of the neutrality view.

might be happy with 'useful', or 'effective'.) So the person who pursues pleasure is aiming at a life of becoming rather than being, a life of travelling hopefully but never arriving. Plato does not wholly endorse this argument, since he thinks that some pleasures, in particular pleasures of the mind, need not be processes, nor involve filling up some physical deficiency in the way in which bodily pleasures might be thought to do. But he does seem to think that it is a good argument against those who think that pleasures just are perceived processes of physical restoration. Surely it is the state of restoration, the re-established balance which is worth having, not the process of getting to that state.

Something along these lines is in all likelihood the kind of position which Aristotle criticizes. Pleasure is not good: only the restored natural balance is good; but pleasure is still contrasted with pain, since it is a process moving in the right rather than in the wrong direction. Aristotle's reply to this argument is that even if pleasure might not be good without qualification, it must still be good precisely in so far as it is contrasted with pain, and will lead to a good end-result.

But Aristotle does not in any case accept that pleasure is a perceived transitional process:

> Furthermore, there is no need to admit that something else is better than pleasure, in the way that some suggest that an end-result is better than a process. For pleasures are not processes, nor do all of them even involve processes; they are states of final actualization. They don't come about when we are on the way to being something, but when some capacity is exercised. Not all pleasures aim at an end different from themselves, but only those enjoyed by people who are being led to the perfection of their nature.
>
> So it is not correct to say that pleasure is a perceived transitional process; rather it should be described as the exercise of a natural disposition; and instead of 'perceived', it would be better to say 'effortless'.

> (VII, 12, 1153a7–15)

One way of seeing what Aristotle means is to consider what happens when one uses one's mind. Obviously, learning something involves a process, and might be pleasurable. Even in this case, though, Aristotle wants to say that it is not the *process* as such which is pleasurable, but the exercise of one's natural ability. This pleasure is already there even when the process of learning is not complete.[6] It is the achievement, incomplete as it is, which is pleasurable, not the process as such. And of course, once the process is complete and one has mastered what has been learnt, then there is a pleasure in that state, too. Moreover, it is not as though one watches what one is doing, and sees that it is pleasant. That's the point of Aristotle's suggestion that we should drop the whole notion of pleasure as some kind of perceiving. It is the activity itself which is the pleasure, not some separate perception of that activity. Enjoyment is not standing back and saying 'I really am enjoying this'; enjoyment consists in effortlessly doing what one is doing.[7]

Aristotle's own view: arguments and problems

Pleasure is not a process

In Book X, Aristotle produces more detailed arguments in favour of the view that pleasure is not a process.[8]

- Processes progress quickly or slowly; pleasure does not.
- Pleasure is complete at any instant, processes are not.

---

[6] It is essential to Aristotle's general account of a process that once it is under way, something has already been achieved while more remains to be achieved. If someone is building a house, some of it has already been built even though more remains to be done.

[7] I suggest 'effortless' instead of the more usual translation 'unimpeded', as conveying something of the overtones of Aristotle's idea. It is that the exercise of a natural capacity is pleasant when nothing gets in the way of doing it well, and one does not have to *try*.

[8] I shall not consider here the arguments in 1173b5–20. These seem to be directed against the view that pleasures just are bodily processes, rather than *perceived* bodily processes. Quite why he should bother refuting this rather primitive position here, when it had been refuted by Plato in the *Philebus* and when the improved version is already in Book VII, is far from clear.

These two arguments fit into a general distinction which Aristotle draws in several places and contexts in his works, between process and actuality. Some examples which are not directly connected with ethics are these: building a house is a process: a built house is an actuality; each stage of the building process is the actualization of what previously was only potentially present (for instance, the foundations realize part of the architect's plans) and yet is still essentially incomplete; when I see something, there takes place a process in my eyes and nervous system; but that process is distinct from the psychological activity of perceiving which is an activity but not a process at all.

The application to the case of pleasure goes like this. One cannot enjoy oneself quickly or slowly, though processes such as healing, or quenching one's thirst, or learning a language can take place quickly or slowly. And even if one enjoys having a drink after a stint of long, hot and thirsty work, it is not the process of quenching which is the enjoyment, but what is at any stage actual in that process (the wetness in one's dry palate, the coolness on one's tongue, and so on). Even though, from one point of view, these are no more than stages in the overall process of quenching one's thirst, each of them from another point of view can be seen as an *achieved* state; and it is that feature which explains the pleasure involved. Similarly with non-physical pleasures. One might enjoy the challenge of having one's mind stretched when one is learning a language, or trying to solve a problem. While it is true that the learning and the working towards a solution are processes, being stretched, and using one's mind are actualities; and it is these which explain the enjoyment. Hence, too, the second of the two points which Aristotle makes. Even if the process is at some moment still incomplete, it does not at all follow that the enjoyment is incomplete. One can, of course, enjoy something more or enjoy something less: but one is either enjoying something or one is not; Aristotle does not think that there is a process of coming-to-enjoy, any more than there is a process of coming-to-see a tree (1174a13–b14).

Aristotle's position that pleasure is not a process is not restricted to bodily pleasures, though he thinks that the theory which would identify pleasure with some process was perhaps suggested to previous philosophers because they concentrated too narrowly on physical pleasures (1173b13–21). But it is worth noticing that in trying to explain Aristotle's view, I have found it natural sometimes to speak of a pleasure, and sometimes to speak of enjoyment, or the activity of enjoying something. We do – or did – have a very general use of 'pleasure' in English: as in 'It gives me great pleasure to introduce this evening's speaker', or when one requests the pleasure of someone's company. Such expressions now have a slightly formal and indeed old-fashioned ring to them. In the eighteenth century, though, this broad use of 'pleasure' was less unusual, and it is important to remember this when reading a classical statement of utilitarianism such as we find in Jeremy Bentham. When he discusses happiness in terms of maximizing pleasure, it is easy for a modern reader to understand him in just the mistaken, narrowly physical way to which Aristotle calls our attention. Bentham classifies pleasures as physical, political, moral and religious, a broad spectrum indeed, so broad that the use of the one word 'pleasure' seems to us today hardly possible. We might wish to speak of pleasures, and of things we enjoy, and of things in which we might take satisfaction, or from which we might look for consolation. Even Bentham found his terminology needed some defence in the face of his contemporaries:

> For these four objects, which in their nature have so much in common, it seemed of use to find a common name. It seemed of use, in the first place, for the convenience of giving a name to certain pleasures and pains, for which a name equally characteristic could hardly otherwise have been found; in the second place, for the sake of holding up the efficacy of certain moral forces, the influence of which is apt not to be sufficiently attended to.[9]

Bentham's point corresponds to some of the concerns of Aristotle. Bentham for his own utilitarian reasons wished to emphasise the importance of considerations of morality, politics and religion, and to show how these, too, could be incorporated into his hedonic

[9] Bentham [1789], ch. III, xii. For a fuller discussion of the notion of pleasure, especially in connection with Bentham and J. S. Mill and the controversies and misunderstandings to which their views gave rise, see Crisp [1997], ch. 2.

calculus. That critics of Bentham and of his disciple J. S. Mill were still inclined to suppose that the centrality of pleasure in their account of ethics implied that they were reducing human beings to the level of pigs, illustrates just the point which Aristotle makes in suggesting that people have developed mistaken accounts of pleasure because the word *hēdonē* is vulgarly associated mostly with bodily pleasures. We shall have to return to this point later.

Pleasure as the perfection of an activity

Aristotle's own account of what pleasure is, or what enjoying some-thing consists in, is difficult to grasp, and even he himself seems to be rather groping for a satisfactory way to explain what he has in mind. He first proposes an analogy. Suppose we ask: When is a faculty like hearing, or sight, functioning at its best?

> Every faculty of perception is active in relation to its perceptible object, and completely active when it is in good condition in relation to the finest of the things which are within its scope.
>
> (X, 4, 1174b14–16)

So the most complete exercise of, say, sight is when someone whose sight is in perfect working order looks at the best thing which can be seen. It is clear enough what is meant by saying that the faculty itself must be in good order. But what is meant by 'the best' of the things which fall within its scope? What are the best things a human eye can see, or a human ear can hear? Perhaps Aristotle has in mind something perfectly beautiful – a marvellous statue, or a lovely melody; but he might just conceivably mean something which is incredibly intricately made, or a complex sound generated by a full orchestra; in general, something which stretches the capabilities of the relevant sense to their utmost. The text is too vague for us to be sure, but the general point is clear enough.

Now for the point. Such an activity, Aristotle says, would also be the most perfect and the most pleasant:

> Every perception has its pleasure, as does every instance of thinking or study. The most perfect activity is the most pleasant,

and what makes it the most perfect is the relation of the well-ordered faculty to its most noble object. Pleasure makes the activity perfect. But it does not make the activity perfect in the same way as the perceived object and the faculty of perception do when they are both good, any more than a doctor and health contribute in the same way to someone being healthy ... Pleasure makes the activity perfect not as an intrinsic quality of the activity does, but as a supervenient perfection, like the bloom of youth.

(X, 4, 1174b20–33)

Much controversy has centred around the precise interpretation of this passage.[10] Perhaps the best interpretation goes like this. Imagine the perfect exercise of a faculty in good order, working on the best of its objects: perhaps the clear-sighted contemplation of a Monet masterpiece, or listening with total clarity to Brahms's Fourth Symphony. In setting up these examples, I have already incorporated the explanations of why each of these two activities might be described as perfect. The capacity is a natural one, in good working order: the object in question is in each case wonderful. So the question is, 'What more is added to this state of affairs by enjoyment?' I think the comparison Aristotle has in mind is captured by asking the parallel question, 'If one says of a young person that they are in perfect health, what more is added by saying that they have all the sparkle of youth?' Is the sparkle more than the fact that they are healthy? Well, old people too can be in excellent health, but would not, alas, thereby have the sparkle of youth, or perhaps any sparkle at all. It is only in the young that perfect health amounts to a sparkle. Perfect health in the young is even better than it is in the old. So, though in one way the sparkle of youth is an additional property over and above simple health, it still is just part and parcel of a young person being healthy. So, I think Aristotle means, enjoying something just is part and parcel of performing a natural activity at its best. It can be *thought of* as something different and additional, since one can explain what is meant by everything –

---

[10] For the details, see Gosling and Taylor [1982] pp.209–13, and ch. 13; or (taking the opposite view) Gauthier and Jolif [1970], II, 2, pp.838–43.

faculty and object – being at their best, without having to mention pleasure or enjoyment. But in fact to perform such a perfect activity just is to enjoy doing so. So pleasures, or instances of enjoyment, are such things as the thrill of singing something really well; or being in such a good physical, emotional, and spiritual state that one feels on top of the world; or being excited by grasping some new idea one has read in a book; or relaxing quietly with a close friend. In enjoying such activities, one is not doing two different things, performing the activity and enjoying it. To perform effortlessly a natural activity at its best just *is* to enjoy it.

Are some pleasures not really pleasures?

Aristotle gives a summary of various arguments in X, 3:

> When people [wishing to argue that pleasure is not good] give as examples the shameful pleasures, one could reply by saying that these are not pleasant. The mere fact that they are pleasant to people of a depraved disposition should not lead us to think that they are pleasant to anyone else, any more than we would think so in the case of things which are healthy, or sweet, or bitter to those who are sick, or again in the case of things which appear white to people suffering from eye-disease. Alternatively, one could say that the pleasures are worth choosing, but not when they come from these particular sources, as we might say in the case of riches provided they don't come from cheating; or health but not when it requires us to eat absolutely *anything*. Or perhaps pleasures differ in species; those which have a good source are different in kind from those deriving from a shameful source. It is simply not possible for some-one who is not just to enjoy the pleasures of the just person, or to enjoy the pleasures of art if one is not versed in the arts, and similarly with the rest.

(X, 3, 1173b20–31)

At the end of this chapter, he says that 'these are the views which are advanced', so he does not explicitly endorse any of them. As usual, they are the starting points of a discussion, to be taken as serious clues to the truth, but not endorsed uncritically. The general point of the arguments he cites is clear enough: in questions of taste and pleasure, the reliable judge is the person whose perceptions and responses are not skewed or warped by ignorance or disease. But when the question is pressed further, Aristotle offers us three totally different possible replies. So, when someone claims to enjoy a disgraceful or shameful activity, which of the following comments is correct?

(1)   It is not a pleasure at all, and his enjoyment is illusory.
(2)   It is a pleasure just like the pleasure of the good person: but one should not choose to have pleasures from such sources.
(3)   It is a pleasure, but of a completely different kind from the pleasures of the good person. The depraved person simply has no access to the good person's pleasures.

The first of these is a view which was defended by Plato, surprising as it may sound.[11] He makes Protarchus in the *Philebus* defend what one might think to be a far better alternative account, that when a pleasure involves a false belief, it is the belief which is false, but it is not the case that the pleasure is illusory. Suppose someone is enjoying thinking about the news that his enemy has been humiliated; if it turns out that no such humiliation has taken place, it does not follow that the enjoyment was not genuinely enjoyment, though perhaps it might be said to be false in the sense in which a false friend can mislead one. Yet, despite having spelt out this argument in a very plausible way Plato will have none of it. Nor, it seems will Aristotle:

> If things which are irksome to the good man seem pleasant to someone else, that is not surprising; for people can be destroyed and corrupted in many ways. Such things are not pleasant except to such people in such a state. It is quite obvious that these disgraceful pleasures should not be described as pleasures except to the corrupted.

(X, 5, 1176a19–24)

---

[11] *Philebus*, 36c–42b.

Even in this passage, though, things are not wholly clear. Do disgraceful pleasures only *seem* pleasant to the perverted: or *are* they pleasant to the perverted? So is the conclusion that such experiences should not be described as pleasures at all (perhaps, instead, 'what the perverted think of as pleasures'), or that they should be described as 'pleasures, but only to the perverted'?

I can see no other text in which Aristotle defends the view he mentions under (2) above. But there certainly are texts which defend (3). 'Nobody would choose to live with the thoughts of a child throughout their whole life even if they derived the greatest possible enjoyment from the things that children enjoy, nor to enjoy doing something shameful, even if they were never to suffer any subsequent pain as a result' (1174a1–4). This passage occurs among the 'things that people say', though perhaps we can detect that Aristotle in fact approves of this line of argument. More seriously, though, what is at stake in this discussion, however odd it might seem at first to more modern ears, is Aristotle's whole theory of what pleasure/enjoyment consists in. For if pleasure consists in a natural activity well-performed with the best of objects, then it would seem that the pleasures of the perverted cannot be pleasures at all.

The solution which he offers in X, 5 is something of a compromise. Here are some key texts which give the main steps in his argument:

> For this reason, pleasures seem also to be different in species. Things which are different in species are, we think, completed by similarly different things. This is seen both with natural things and with artefacts, such as animals, trees, a painting, a statue, a house, a tool. In the same way, activities which differ in species are completed by things which are different in species. The activities of thought are different from those of perception, and they differ in kind from one another, as do the pleasures which complete them.
>
> (1175a21–28)

> Since activities differ in appropriateness and badness, and some of them are choiceworthy, others to be avoided, and others neutral, just the same is true of pleasures. Each activity has its

own proper pleasure; the pleasure which is proper to an appropriate activity is appropriate, and that proper to a bad activity is a bad pleasure.

(1175b24–28)

The pleasures of different species of animal are different in kind. Still, it is reasonable to suppose that those of the same species are not so different, even though in the case of human beings they do vary more than a little. The same things please some people and displease others, and things which are painful and disliked by some are pleasant and liked by others. The same happens with sweet things. The same things do not seem sweet to the person with a fever and to the person in good health, nor do the same things seem hot to someone who is weak and to someone who is fit. So too in other cases. But in all these instances, what is actually the case is what seems so to the good person. If this is right, as it seems to be, and it is virtue and the good person who, as such, is the measure of all things, then those things actually are pleasures which seem so to such a person, and those things actually are enjoyable which that person delights in.

(1176a8–19)

So whether the activities of the perfect and blessed person are one or more than one, the pleasures which complete those activities could above all others be said to be properly human pleasures, and the rest will be pleasures only in a secondary and minimal sense, as are the corresponding activities.

(1176a26–29)

The key move is made in the first of these texts. 'Pleasure' does not denote one particular kind of experience, but a range of different types of experience, as different in kind as are the corresponding activities. This move makes it easier for Aristotle to suggest that the moral quality of any pleasure is just that of the pleasurable activity of which the pleasure is the completion. But the most controversial step is taken in the long passage which is the third of my quotations. This requires some more detailed comment.

The passage is preceded by the remark that each species of animal has its proper *ergon*, to which its proper pleasures correspond (1176a3). It is not hard to see in this an allusion to the Function Argument in I, 7, and which Aristotle is going to repeat only a few pages further on here in Book X. What is specific to the fulfilment of human beings is the good performance of those activities which are specific to humans. But those activities well-performed will, of course, be perfected and crowned by their own specifically human delight.

As we have already seen, though, the difficulty with the Function Argument in general is that human nature seems rather more flexible and malleable than that of other organisms. It is not just when we are ill that our perceptions, and hence our pleasures, can be distorted. It is that we are capable of learning to enjoy quite different pleasures and pains even when we are in good health. After all, as Aristotle often points out, education in virtue proceeds by using pleasures and pains, and virtues are distinguished from vices precisely by the things that a person has acquired the habit of enjoying or finding painful.[12] Here, he explicitly admits that human beings can differ from one another quite markedly in this respect. Humans are capable, it would seem, of enjoying both looking at great art and using heroin, a lifelong successful marriage and child abuse. So which pleasures are truly so called? Just as Aristotle fills out the Function Argument with its associated doctrine about the moral virtues by saying that the test for which patterns of emotional response are virtues and which are vices is the judgement of the person of practical wisdom, so here, with complete consistency, he claims that which pleasures are truly good is determined by what the good person enjoys. The phrase 'and of all these things it is the good person who is the measure' is clearly intended to recall the famous saying of Protagoras. Protagoras was perhaps a follower of Heraclitus, whom Aristotle mentions here only a few lines above the text we are considering. Heraclitus, some 150 years before Aristotle, had said that asses prefer chaff to gold, a remark which perhaps inspired Protagoras, a couple of generations later, to say that 'each human being is the measure of all things, of those that are that they are, and those that are not that they are not'. What is good,

---

[12] See, for instance, 1104b8–16.

admirable, or worth enjoying is determined by the judgement of each individual.[13] It is just this view that Aristotle thinks is radically mistaken, and which he denies here as it is applied to pleasure. The standard is not individual judgement, but the judgement of the good person.

Sickness can warp our judgement. So can lack of moral virtue. Does Aristotle therefore conclude that the pleasures of the depraved are not truly pleasures and that the depraved are mistaken in thinking that they enjoy them? In the end Aristotle does not quite go so far. He agrees that they can be described as 'pleasures', but claims that the word is now being used in a secondary and very minimal sense. Perhaps he means something along these lines. Consider someone who is severely short-sighted and astigmatic. Does he see things? Well, Aristotle might say, of course he does; but though it is a kind of seeing, it is not seeing in the full sense of the word at all, but seeing only in a secondary and minimalist sense. The depraved are warped by comparison with how human nature ideally should be (though, of course, not to the extent that they simply do not count as human beings). Similarly, their pleasures are not enjoyable in the way that pleasures are which come from the perfect exercise of natural capacities; but the activities of the depraved are still human. (If we describe people as 'animals' or 'couch potatoes', these are colourful metaphors rather than literal descriptions.) Since their activities are human in the minimalist sense of being performed by a member of the human race, so their pleasures are pleasures, but Aristotle hesitates to use the term for something so different in kind from the pleasures of the good person.

The difficulty with this entire line of argument is that everything depends on identifying the person of practical wisdom; and this is a difficulty which, as we concluded at the end of Chapter 5, Aristotle does not really address head on, let alone solve. Still, his discussion

[13] Plato, too, attacks Protagoras, and associates his views with those of Heraclitus, in the central section of his *Theaetetus*, 152–83. The way in which Protagoras's dictum is treated at 152a strongly suggests that it was taken to mean not that it is man, as distinct, say, from horses or pigs, who is the measure of all things, but that each *individual* human is.

of pleasures and enjoyment does perhaps advance matters at least a little. For it provides us with one more angle from which we can consider the lives of people around us. In our search for role-models, exemplars of the fulfilled life, we can look at what people do; we can listen to the explanations they give for what they do and see if those explanations make coherent sense to us; we can consider their lives in terms of health, emotional balance, the kinds of friendships which they have, and the way they see their role in contributing to society; and we can look at what they enjoy and where they look for satisfaction, fun, and pleasure. This last provides us with yet another 'take' on our moral world. Of course it remains true that we still need some framework which will enable us to make interpretative sense of what we see when we look around at our fellow humans in this kind of way. In Aristotle's view, we have ourselves to construct that framework inductively, developing simultaneously our principles and our judgements on individual actions, situations, and ways of enjoying ourselves. He does not for one minute believe that we are by nature equipped to do this infallibly. Moral insight presupposes moral virtue, and moral virtues, far from being part of our natural endowment, require the proper training from an early age. Few if any of us have had a perfect moral education. Still, perhaps optimistically, perhaps also reasonably enough, he does seem to think that most of us, by one means or another, are equipped to get most of it right most of the time: witness the respect he has for the *endoxa*, the reflective views of most people, be they ordinary citizens, philosophers, or sages; witness too the confidence he has that, starting from those reflective views, we can both effectively criticize and build upon them.

Is the fulfilled life enjoyable?

Aristotle's answer to this question is surely obvious enough. The question is, is it clearly satisfactory?

Since the fulfilled life has already been defined in terms of exercising our most specifically human capacities well (*kat' aretēn*, 'in accordance with virtue'), it follows from Aristotle's definition of pleasure that such a life will be pleasant, enjoyable, satisfying. Perhaps one needs to use several words like that, to take account of the fact that a fulfilled life will contain several activities, and that the pleasures associated with these activities are different in kind. They are completed, rounded off, in different ways which these various words attempt to capture.

> One might well think that everyone desires pleasure, since all aim at staying alive. Staying alive is an activity, and each person is active about those things, and by the means, that he most loves. The lover of music uses his hearing to listen to sounds, the lover of learning his powers of thought to consider questions of scholarship, and so on with the rest. Pleasure completes the activities, and hence completes the life which people long for. Reasonably, then, people aim at pleasure, since for each of us it rounds off living, and is worth choosing. Do we choose to carry on living for the sake of the pleasure it brings, or do we choose pleasure for the sake of living? That question we must leave for the moment. But the two seem to be inseparably bound together, since there is no pleasure without activity, and it is activity which is rounded off by pleasure.
>
> (X, 4, 1175a10–21)

In a similar context, after outlining the Function Argument in I, 7, Aristotle in I, 8 considers whether his account of *eudaimonia* squares with what people in general believe.

> Most people's pleasures conflict, since they are not by nature pleasant, whereas the lovers of what is noble enjoy those things which are pleasant by nature. Such are the activities in accordance with virtue, which are pleasant in themselves and also pleasant to such people. Their life does not need pleasure as a kind of add-on, since it contains pleasure in itself. In addition to what we have already said, the person who does not enjoy noble actions is not even a good person, nor would anyone describe as just someone who did not enjoy behaving justly, nor liberal a person who did not enjoy acting liberally.
>
> (I, 9, 1099a11–20)

Here, Aristotle uses the notion of what is 'pleasant by nature', which corresponds, I think, to the pleasures which the good person enjoys mentioned in Book X. The trouble with his view, however, is that it is not at all obvious that virtuous actions are all pleasant by nature. In particular, there are difficulties with courageous actions; but the point is quite a general one. Suppose that, to be generous, I donate a kidney to give to someone whose life is in danger. Is that action *enjoyable* or *pleasant*? If, in seeking to be honest with someone, I have to tell them some very uncomfortable truths, or if, in seeking to do what is just, I have to fire someone with a young wife and family wholly dependent on him, are such virtuous actions satisfying or pleasant? Indeed, would the person who enjoyed having to do such things be a good person at all? So, does the brave person enjoy putting himself in danger?

Aristotle defines courage idealistically enough:

Courage is a mean between instances of foolhardiness and timidity, in the ways we have described, and it endures out of choice because to do so is noble, and not to do so would be base.

(III, 7, 1116a10–13)

And even more gloriously, in speaking of the love of one's friends and how this is also a love of one's self, he says:

In fact the good person will do many things for the sake of their friends and their country, and even give up their lives for them; they will give up money and honours, anything at all that people fight to get, to obtain for themselves what is noble. They far prefer to enjoy that for a short time than to have a long period of calm, to live nobly for a year than to spend many years in an undistinguished life, a single great and noble deed to many small ones.

(IX, 8, 1169a18–25)

As with all the virtues, the decisive motive in such actions is that they are done because to do them is noble; and, according to Aristotle's official view, what is noble is enjoyable. But it is precisely part of courage that it is *not* fearlessness. It is being appropriately afraid, given the circumstances. Now being afraid can hardly be thought of as an enjoyable state.[14] In III, 9, Aristotle openly admits this; and, taking the example of a boxer, he suggests that the boxer endures the blows for the sake of the honours that come with winning. What his general account requires, and what unfortunately he does *not* say, is that the boxer enjoys himself while being punched, any more than the brave man enjoys being in peril of his life. Instead, he says, 'The end proposed by courage, pleasant as it is, appears to be obscured by the circumstances' (1117a35–b2), and he concludes:

> So it is not the case that in all the virtues the activity is enjoyable, except to the extent that the end proposed is attained.
>
> (III, 9, 1117b15–16)

With that admission, a glorious but highly counter-intuitive position is in effect abandoned. Aristotle can indeed maintain that a fulfilled life is noble, in many ways satisfying, enjoyable, and pleasant. It is all of these things just because it consists in living at one's best, without effort, with all one's capacities harmoniously actualized to the fullest of their capabilities. But it is not always so. Plainly in the case of courage and, I suggest, in other cases as well, the most he can argue is that the good person will willingly choose what is noble, however painful or costly or difficult it might be. But there is an enormous difference between acting willingly and enjoying what one is doing. We too can say that we were happy to do something for someone, without at all suggesting that doing it was pleasant or enjoyable.

A final footnote. Aristotle, idealist though in many ways he is, shows few signs of holding that whether my life is fulfilled or not is something which lies wholly within my own control. To live a blameless, virtuous life does not guarantee fulfilment.

> Still, happiness clearly stands in need of external goods too, as we said. For it is impossible or at any rate difficult to do noble deeds without assistance. Many things are done by using as instruments one's friends, or money, or influence. And there are some things lack of which spoils our happiness – good birth,

[14] Except perhaps in borderline cases like being on a roller-coaster in a fairground; do people who enjoy the ride experience fear at all?

good children, and good looks. A person is not likely to be completely fulfilled if they are unpleasant to look at, or are of low birth, or are on their own, or if they have no family. Maybe it is even less likely if their children or their friends are good-for-nothings, or were good but are no longer alive. As we said, a fulfilled life seems to require prosperity of this kind. That is why some people link a fulfilled life to luck, whereas others link it to virtue.

(I, 8, 1099a31–b8)

In fact Aristotle wishes to say both that the key element in living a fulfilled life is the performance of virtuous actions, and that our fulfilment is to some extent at the mercy of chance events beyond our control. If someone lives virtuously, their sense of fulfilment will be proof at least against comparatively minor reversals of fortune. True, serious misfortunes will indeed shake them. Even in these, though, they will remain constant and virtuous, and hence will retain the key component in human fulfilment. For that reason, even in this condition in which someone cannot be said to be living a fulfilled life, they still cannot be said to be wretched (I, 11, 1100b23–1101a16).

Chapter 10

Aristotle's moral world and ours

Depending to some extent on how one selects passages in his text to emphasize, and to some extent on the examples one gives to illustrate what Aristotle has in mind, it is possible to present Aristotle's views as by and large fairly typical of the mainstream tradition of Europe at least from his time to our own, or as really quite strange and in many respects foreign. By way of summing up, it may help to consider the distance between Aristotle and ourselves as well as the similarities between his views and ours.

Culture: acceptance and criticism

Some unusual Athenian virtues

From III, 6 to the end of IV, Aristotle discusses several virtues, including courage, temperance, generosity, magnificence, wittiness, mildness, friendliness. We have already looked at what he says about different kinds of relationship, and about justice. Most contemporary European readers would, I imagine, find much of what

he says relatively unsurprising and reasonable enough, whatever disagreements they might have on points of detail. But every so often one suddenly finds oneself having to remember that Aristotle's world was very definitely not just like ours, and that the virtues and vices which he could count on his audience to recognize are not exactly the same ones which we might take for granted.

So, we can all recognize the buffoon who will do anything to get a laugh, however crude or embarrassing he has to be in order to do so (1128a33–b1), or the people who make a show of their austerity (1127b22–28), or the people whose wealth and power simply makes them arrogant and inclined to throw their weight around (1124a27–30). The cast of characters, each with their faults, who walk through the Athens of Book IV are with us still – the skinflints, the ostentatiously wealthy, flatterers, extortionate moneylenders, and the rest. But surely some of the others are strangers. Take, for instance, Aristotle's Magnificent Man, described in IV, 2, or the Magnanimous Man of IV, 3. Though we can think of great philanthropists nearer our own time – Rowntree or Carnegie, Nuffield or Bill Gates – the picture Aristotle paints seems somehow to differ in emphasis. The Magnificent Man spends large sums of money on the kinds of public benefactions which need such expenditure: providing an effective warship for the navy; entertaining ambassadors from other cities; providing public feasts, sponsoring dramatic performances at festivals, and the like. But though Aristotle is careful to point out that the Magnificent Man is not ostentatious or vulgar, he still comes across perhaps as too much concerned with his own credit and honour to strike us as wholly admirable. Even more so does the Magnanimous Man, who justifiably sees himself as a Great Man, and is justifiably concerned with being honoured as such, and appropriately pleased when such honours are bestowed on him. He is above the petty concerns of more ordinary mortals, towards whom he is effortlessly superior; he speaks with a slow, calm and deep voice.

We might well feel that neither of these two exhibits any of the types of character that we might find entirely admirable. The sense of strangeness in the middle of much that is entirely familiar is reinforced when we recall that Aristotle thought that women were incapable of public responsibility, and that some humans were natural slaves, or that menial work was somehow dehumanizing. Such views are not merely strange, they are, from our point of view, shocking. How could he get such things so wrong?[1] Less dramatically, what would he have thought of some of the examples I have used in illustrating his discussion – visiting prisoners, volunteering to help in a hospice, to say nothing of women surgeons or barristers? What would he have made of a Mother Teresa or Francis of Assisi? So the question might arise whether, for all the detailed discussion of *eudaimonia* which Aristotle offers, and despite his account of practical wisdom and its relationship to the virtues of human character, his position as a whole is not seriously undermined by his lack of critical attention to those very virtues on which the whole edifice is based. We have already seen that Aristotle assumes that his students will have been well brought up, and that a good upbringing involves training one's emotional responses in such a way that the desired ones become second nature. So the entire system, the critic will urge, is geared to the less than critical perpetuation of the attitudes and judgements *already* accepted in Aristotle's elitist Athenian society.

Uncritical acceptance?

There are several possible responses to arguments of this kind, at least so far as they touch upon ethics, which can be sketched out as follows:

(1)   One is of necessity so immersed in one's own culture that it is simply not possible to criticize it.

(2)   One can recognize differences between cultures; but there is no neutral standpoint from which any neutral comparison between cultures or assessment of the overall standpoint of any culture can be made.

---

[1] *Politics* I, chs 1–6, and 13. It is not *simple* prejudice on Aristotle's part. He does have an argument, based on what he takes to be variations in the range of people's natural abilities; and he does consider different views. But, as I have already suggested in the context of children whose upbringing is inadequate, he fails to make adequate allowance for environmental and social influences, and is too ready to assume that differences are differences in natural abilities.

(3)   It is in principle possible to discover standards by which to assess any moral culture, including one's own.

It is plain that Aristotle does not accept (1) at all. Much of his method consists in assembling the variety of views on ethics and on politics which were current in his day, and trying to clarify, assess and put some order into them. He clearly believed that he had at his disposal the tools required to do this. He claimed to have shown the inevitability of the principle of non-contradiction, for instance; *any* culture will provide its members with *some* basis for sorting out and assessing beliefs, since not all beliefs can consistently be held together. He thought that the same general approach and expectations applied more broadly, and in particular could be applied also to ethics and politics. It is often possible to trace apparently irreconcilable beliefs back to some more fundamental positions which would be generally acceptable, and on that basis to reconstruct a position which respects the basic truths held by most people while yet remaining consistent.

This widely held position has much to commend it. Thus, it is easy enough to show that our grasp of the full implications of the language we use is highly incomplete, and that this is true across the board, in mathematics as in ethics. Even in mathematics, it is not always obvious which statements are contradictory and which are not; and the same goes for ethics, where our moral concepts are likely to be less accurately defined. Again, it is often the case that disagreement in ethics is based upon disagreement about factual matters whose relevance to ethics is not in dispute. Just what would in fact happen if a plant's genetic structure were modified in a particular way may be unknown or disputed; but people might still agree about the answer to be given to a hypothetical question about the ethics of developing such a plant if the consequences of doing so were clear. Again, we have reasonably clear views about the kinds of emotional involvement which are likely to cloud our moral judgement, as contrasted with the kinds of emotional involvement which give us a greater insight into a situation. We can to that extent test our capacity to be objective about a particular case, or type of case. And so on. In each of the above ways, it is possible for us to use the tools provided by our culture to assess individual beliefs, or sets of beliefs, held within that culture.

In contrast, (2) is a much more radical position, and is one way of formulating ethical relativism. The basic claim in (2) is connected with non-comparability, which can be manifested in a variety of ways. It might be claimed, for instance, that there is no action available in Britain in 2000 which is equivalent to having several wives in a West African village; indeed it might be held that the very concept 'wife' in English is a misleading word to use for an African relationship which is very unlike an English marriage. Again, it is possible to argue that each society defines for itself what is worthwhile in life, and that this vision of worthwhileness colours everything else. So, the argument would go, there is no reason to suppose that we, brought up as we are, would even begin to see the point of a completely different view of what was worthwhile in human living. From this perspective, what would be crucial to Aristotle's position would be his defence not merely of the formal conditions for *eudaimonia* (completeness, self-sufficiency), but his defence of his particular view of what the life of the fulfilled person consists in.[2] Aristotle needs to show more than that his fourth century Athenian view of the fulfilled life is one which would win acceptance among his contemporaries once they had sorted out their various unreflected opinions on the subject. He needs to show that there is no equally intelligible, and perhaps preferable, alternative.[3]

So he has to defend some version of (3); and this will involve him not merely in a defence of his view of *eudaimonia*, but will require a defence of his own view of rationality quite generally, in both its theoretical and its practical uses. It is not sufficient to show that one's position in ethics is rationally defensible unless one also shows that one has a rationally defensible way of thinking about reason itself.

[2] For an excellent contemporary discussion of these issues, and a vigorous defence of a relativist position, see Arrington [1989]. Chapters 5 and 6 are especially relevant to the problems I am discussing here.

[3] The most elaborate defence of Aristotle along these lines is in Irwin [1988], chs 16–22, which amount to a commentary on almost all the issues raised by the *Ethics* and by the *Politics* as well. See especially §§200–12 which contain some of the key elements in Irwin's account. For a less optimistic view of Aristotle's reliance on what is commonly believed as a starting point for his reflections, see Nussbaum [1982].

Aristotle's general line is to show that ethics and politics are based on a metaphysical understanding of what it is to be a human person: a rational agent with senses and emotions. He believes that his account of the life lived according to the moral and intellectual virtues constitutes the most fulfilling life available to humans. We cannot successfully pretend to be disembodied gods; so our rational agency must take into account the fact that we have desires and emotions. Ideally, then, our desires and emotions must themselves reflect true rather than false beliefs about ourselves and how we can interact with our world. So we need to train ourselves to have just those patterns of desire and emotional response whose satisfaction can be rationally justified. At the end of the day it is our capacity for rationally directing our lives which is central both to our conception of ourselves and to our notion of fulfilment. In IX, 4, Aristotle is drawing parallels between the relationship one has to a true friend and the relationship one has to oneself:

> As we have said, it seems that it is virtue and the good person which are the standard in each case. The good man is of one mind with himself, and desires the same things with the whole of his soul. He wishes for himself both what is good and what appears to be good, he acts accordingly (for it is characteristic of the good person to make efforts to achieve what is good), and does so for his own sake (since he does so for the sake of his thinking part, which seems to be what each person *is*). He wishes to live and to survive, especially that part of him with which he thinks. To exist is good for the good man, and everyone wants what is good for *himself*. Nobody would choose to have everything if that meant becoming someone else (it is God, in fact, who has everything). We want what is good only if we remain whatever we are – and that seems to be a being which thinks, or that more than anything else.

> (1166a12–23)

He believes that he can show that the following statements are true:

(1) That a human being is essentially a rational bodily agent, by nature equipped to function in a community.

(2)   A fulfilled life for such a being involves the development of all its essential capacities.

(3)   But the specific character of human fulfilment is the rationality which is to be found in the desires, emotions, and chosen activities which make up the life of a fulfilled human person.

(4)   Rationality in general requires that the conclusions of reason be consistent, and be explained in terms of starting points.

(5)   Theoretical rationality yields conclusions which are necessary: practical rationality does not do so, because of the variability of persons and circumstances.

(6)   The ethics yielded by (1)–(5) is compatible with most of our pre-reflective moral beliefs, and can explain why others of these beliefs are plausible but false.

In short, the function argument, the discussion of what it might be to have rationally justifiable desires and emotional responses, together with the formal requirements of the fulfilled life, combine to produce standards by which our moral beliefs can be assessed – standards which are defensible on general grounds and do not depend on our own particular cultural assumptions. It will not be surprising if moral beliefs which are deeply entrenched in our culture for the most part turn out to be true. But we need to be able to explain *why* other beliefs have been widely held when they turn out to be false. In particular, since we will in all likelihood disagree with Aristotle on several matters, some of them (the position of slaves and women, for instance) far from trivial, we will be interested to see whether what we take to be Aristotle's mistakes do not discredit his entire method of argument and approach. That in the case of women and slaves he so seriously underestimated their natural capacities might suggest that he made a factual mistake rather than one which calls into question his approach to ethics. But the very difficulty we have, in our own day as in Aristotle's, in distinguishing between innate and learnt characteristics, might suggest that we need to be more cautious than Aristotle was in making claims about the essential features of human beings and what follows from those features so far as human fulfilment is concerned. Perhaps, too, we need to take seriously the possibility that there may be very different ways of structuring a life, and structuring societies, each of which might promote human fulfilment. To the extent that such a pluralism is defensible, it might be that the Function Argument does suffice to exclude a strong version of ethical relativism which maintains that different moral codes are simply non-comparable. Any version of human fulfilment will have to be *human* fulfilment, and human nature is not indefinitely flexible. Fulfilled lives, and admirable societal structures will of necessity be comparable. But the comparisons may well not be simple or straightforward, and the moral views in which these various lives find verbal expression may well seem to be very diverse.

Virtues and principles

The amount of space which Aristotle devotes to a discussion of the various virtues – virtues of character and virtues of the mind – makes it reasonable to ask whether it is true, as is sometimes said, that he clearly held a version of what is now called 'virtue ethics'. The question is not so easy to answer, however. The reason is partly that it is not so clear quite what 'virtue ethics' is supposed to be; and partly that there are various ways of reading Aristotle.

Virtue ethics might be thought to embrace either or both of the following views:

- The proper focus of ethics should be on people's characters rather than on their actions.
- The best way to know what one should do is to think of how to behave virtuously, rather than thinking of how to follow a moral principle.

On the first account, what is morally important is to be a particular kind of person, and to have developed the particular traits of character which are the moral virtues. Moral philosophy, virtue ethicists might suggest, has been too long preoccupied with 'issues' and moral dilemmas. But the moral life is quite distorted if it is seen principally as problem solving or trying to deal with agonizing cases. What we normally focus upon in our friends or our children, or, for that matter, in people we find it hard to deal with, is their characters, the kind of people they are. And if asked how we thought of our own moral lives, we might much more naturally say that we would hope to be loyal, honest, generous, rather than say that we would hope to keep a set of rules, however admirable they might be, or to solve all kinds of difficult moral dilemmas.

The second claim of virtue ethics is more radical. It is not just a question of how we might naturally think of living a morally good life. It is an epistemological claim about how we can best discover what living a good life requires of us. We discover what to do by thinking about generosity, or fidelity, or honesty or fairness rather than, say, by doing a utilitarian calculation, or applying a Kantian test. Underlying this epistemological fact, it might also be argued, is the fact that it is virtuous dispositions which give us the required moral perceptiveness, rather than some abstract set of principles to which we subscribe.

Before asking whether or to what extent Aristotle might accept these points, we might note that the case in favour of virtue ethics is far from being open and shut. Of course it is true that the person who thinks in terms of moral principles will sooner or later have to deal with situations in which his principles conflict with one another, or where they seem too coarse grained to deal adequately with the circumstances with which he is faced. But it might equally be true that it will be hard to know whether this is a time for honesty or kindness, or to know exactly what kindness would require here and now. So it is not at all obvious that it is easier to think in virtue terms than in terms of principles. Moreover, the reason for this might be that it is not easy to tell when our emotional responses are balanced and appropriate, and hence not easy to tell which patterns of response are truly virtuous. Are virtuous responses defined in terms of the actions which they facilitate, or are right actions defined in terms of the virtues from which they spring?

How would Aristotle answer these questions? It is undeniable that he spends a great deal more time talking about virtues than he does about moral principles. Indeed, he is at pains to point out that moral principles are at best generalizations which are far from being true in every case, and that it is mistaken to look for the kind of exactitude in ethics which one can find in geometry, or even perhaps in physics. This might suggest that he is clearly in favour of a virtue ethics, and has little interest in moral principles. Such a conclusion would be far too hasty, however. To begin with, he defines the concept of virtue in terms of the decisions which a person of practical wisdom would make rather than the other way round. Again, when, for example in connection with justice or with friendship, he talks about the variations in persons and circumstances which make it difficult to know what to do, he expresses himself in terms of principles – for instance, he asks should one always repay debts no matter what other claims there might be on the use of the money. He does not, as I have done, often ask whether this is a time for truth or kindness, punctiliousness or loyalty. The reason seems clear enough. The disposition terms we use for virtues are even less definite than the descriptions we might seek to give of our actions. 'I surely had to use the money to ransom my father, even though I was due to pay it back today to the person from whom I borrowed it' is how Aristotle portrays someone thinking out what to do. We have to *think* what to do; and thinking results in just the kinds of action-descriptions which might be used to formulate moral principles.

On the other hand, Aristotle also makes it clear that in his view our ability to think clearly about practical decisions depends upon our emotional balance. Only the emotionally balanced person will be sensitive to all the morally significant features of the complex situations with which adults are commonly faced.

His final view is that one cannot be morally good in the full sense without practical wisdom, nor have practical wisdom without possessing the moral virtues (VI, 13, 1144b31–32). Practical wisdom involves a grasp both of universal principles and of individual situations; virtues are defined in terms of the responses which facilitate such a grasp, and motivate actions in which that grasp is expressed. At a pinch a person can on occasion exercise self-control, and do what needs to be done even when they cannot do it in the way that the good person does it. It is therefore not the case that *on each occasion* a correct moral assessment of what should be done requires moral virtue, though it is true that moral virtue is needed to get things right consistently, day in and day out. More significantly, the opposite alternative simply never appears as a possibility; Aristotle nowhere suggests that a person can do the right thing by relying only on their emotional responses. That is why even his well-trained and well brought up students need a course in moral philosophy. If anything, then, it seems to me that Aristotle is a rationalist who rightly sees the importance of the moral virtues, rather than a virtue-ethicist who is interested in playing down the role of reason and principles in ethics, or in shifting the focus from how people should behave to the kinds of characters people should have.

But his rationalism is not any kind of moral mathematics, nor does it derive from a view of reason which is quite divorced from the subject matter to which reasoned thought might be applied. Central to moral philosophy as Aristotle sees it is the ordinary everyday experience that people have of trying to live a good life. If one contrasts his approach with, say, Kant's or even Mill's, one is surely struck with the extent to which the arguments and issues he raises have the same recognizable shape as one's own patterns of moral thinking. Not for nothing does Aristotle insist both that ethics should start from what most of us would pre-philosophically have taken to be true, and that ethics is concerned with truth even though truth in ethics defies any attempt at exact formulation. He resists all attempts to force ethics into the narrow confines of a systematic theory, while still trying to show the ways in which common sense and culturally accepted opinions can be assessed, criticized or defended on broader philosophical grounds. Different though our culture is from the Athens in which Aristotle wrote, the assumptions he makes about the nature, scope and method of ethics are equally applicable in our own day. They have about them a down-to-earth common-sense quality, a recognizable fidelity to our normal moral practice, and a marvellously nuanced view of the interplay between emotional sensitivity, rational coherence, and philosophical backing. The *Ethics* displays a blend of the theoretical and the practical which itself exemplifies the virtues which Aristotle sought to encourage in his students and his readers.

Glossary

Many Greek words can be translated in several ways, depending on the context. Some of the terms which occur most frequently are traditionally translated in a particular way. I offer several alternatives, including the traditional ones, but I have placed first the translation which I take to be the best in most contexts.

akōn	unwilling(ly); *akousion*, an action unwillingly done
akrasia	moral failure, moral weakness, weakness of will
archē	a starting point, a first principle
aretē	virtue, any good characteristic, excellence; *kat'aretēn,* well, in accordance with virtue
boulēsis	want
bouleusis	deliberation, consideration, planning
endoxa	commonly held views
epieikeia	equity, ignoring the letter of the law in the interests of justice

ergon	function, job, work
eudaimonia	fulfilment, well-being, happiness
hēdonē	pleasure, enjoyment
hekōn	willing(ly); *hekousion,* an action willingly done
hexis	acquired disposition, acquired habit
logos	reason, definition, rule, argument
nous	the capacity for insight, intelligence
orthos logos	right reason
pathos	what is done to, or happens to someone, what is suffered
philia	personal relationship, friendship, a liking for someone
phronēsis	practical wisdom, moral discernment
prohairesis	choice, the conclusion of moral deliberation
sophia	intellectual ability in theoretical matters
sōphrosunē	moderation, temperance
technai	skills, craft
telos	aim, objective, end
theōria	thinking

Bibliography

This bibliography is not intended to be in any sense complete. It includes only those works which I take to be the most accessible to those coming to the subject for the first time.

Translations

Barnes, Jonathan (ed.) [1984] *The Complete Works of Aristotle: The Revised Oxford Translation*, Princeton University Press.

Irwin, Terence [1988] *Aristotle: Nicomachaean Ethics,* Hackett Publishing Co.

Books and Articles

Ackrill, J. L. [1980] 'Aristotle on *Eudaimonia*' in A. O. Rorty (ed.) *Essays on Aristotle's Ethics*, University of California Press, pp. 15–33.

Annas, Julia [1993] *The Morality of Happiness*, Oxford University Press.

Arrington, Robert L. [1989] *Rationalism, Realism, and Relativism: Perspectives in Contemporary Moral Epistemology*, Cornell University Press.

Austin, J. L. [1956] 'A Plea for Excuses' in *Proceedings of the Aristotelian Society*, Vol. 56: 1–30.

Bentham, Jeremy [1789] *An Introduction to the Principles of Morals and Legislation*, T. Payne & Son. See also H. L. A. Hart and F. Rosen (eds) [1995], Oxford University Press.

Broadie, Sarah [1991] *Ethics with Aristotle*, Oxford University Press.

Burnyeat, Miles [1980] 'Aristotle on Learning to be Good' in A. O. Rorty (ed.) *Essays on Aristotle's Ethics*, University of California Press, pp. 69–92.

Cooper, John M. [1975] *Reason and the Human Good in Aristotle*, Harvard University Press.

Cooper, John M. [1980] 'Aristotle on Friendship' in A. O. Rorty (ed.) *Essays on Aristotle's Ethics*, University of California Press, pp. 301–40.

Crisp, Roger [1997] *Mill on Utilitarianism*, Routledge.

Dahl, N. O. [1984] *Practical Reason, Aristotle, and Weakness of Will*, University of Minnesota.

Frankena, William K. [1939] 'The Naturalistic Fallacy' in *Mind*, Vol. 48: 464–77.

Gauthier, René and Jolif, Jean [1970] *Aristotle: L'Éthique à Nicomaque*, Nauwelaerts.

Gosling, J. C. B. [1975] *Plato: Philebus*, in Clarendon Plato Series, The Clarendon Press.

Gosling, J. C. B. [1990] *Weakness of the Will*, Routledge.

Gosling, J. C. B. and Taylor, C. C. W. [1982] *The Greeks on Pleasure*, The Clarendon Press.

Hardie, W. F. R. [1968] *Aristotle's Ethical Theory*, The Clarendon Press.

Heinaman, R. [1988] 'Eudaimonia and Self-Sufficiency in the Nicomachaean Ethics' in *Phronesis* 33: 31–53.

Honderich, Ted [1973] *Essays on Freedom and Action*, Routledge & Kegan Paul.

Irwin, Terence [1980] 'Reason and Responsibility in Aristotle' in A. O. Rorty (ed.) *Essays on Aristotle's Ethics*, University of California Press, pp. 117–55.

Irwin, Terence [1985] *Aristotle: Nicomachaean Ethics*, Hackett Publishing Co.

Irwin, Terence [1985b] 'Permanent Happiness: Aristotle and Solon' in J. Annas (ed.) *Oxford Studies in Ancient Philosophy, Volume III*, Oxford University Press, pp. 89–124.

Irwin, Terence [1988] *Aristotle's First Principles*, The Clarendon Press.

Kenny, Anthony [1978] *The Aristotelian Ethics*, The Clarendon Press.

Kenny, Anthony [1991] 'The Nicomachaean Conception of Happiness' in H. Blumenthal and H. Robinson (eds) *Oxford Studies in Ancient Philosophy*, Supplementary Volume, Oxford University Press, pp. 67–80.

Kenny, Anthony [1992] *Aristotle on the Perfect Life*, The Clarendon Press.

Kosman, L. A. [1980] 'Being Properly Affected: Virtues and Feelings in Aristotle's Ethics' in A. O. Rorty (ed.) *Essays on Aristotle's Ethics*, University of California Press, pp. 103–16.

Kraut, Richard [1989] *Aristotle on the Human Good*, Princeton University Press.

Long, A. A. and Sedley, D. N. [1987] *The Hellenistic Philosophers,* Cambridge University Press.

Midgley, Mary [1979] *Beast and Man*, Harvester Press.

Moore, G. E. [1903] *Principia Ethica*, Cambridge University Press.

Nussbaum, Martha [1982] 'Saving Aristotle's Appearances' in M. Schofield and M. C. Nussbaum (eds) *Language and Logos*, Cambridge University Press, pp. 267–93.

Rorty, Amélie Oksenberg (ed.) [1980] *Essays on Aristotle's Ethics*, University of California Press.

Rudder Baker, Lynne [1995] *Explaining Attitudes: A Practical Approach to the Mind*, Cambridge University Press.

Sherman, Nancy [1989] *The Fabric of Character: Aristotle's Theory of Virtue*, Clarendon Press.

Sorabji, Richard [1973] 'Aristotle on the Role of Intellect in Virtue' in *Proceedings of the Aristotelian Society* Vol. 74 [1973/4], 107–29, also in A. O. Rorty (ed.) *Essays on Aristotle's Ethics*, University of California Press, pp. 201–19.

Sorabji, Richard [1980] *Necessity, Cause, and Blame,* Duckworth.

Urmson, J. O. [1973] 'Aristotle's Doctrine of the Mean' in *American Philosophical Quarterly*, vol. 10: 223–30, also in A. O. Rorty (ed.) [1980] *Essays on Aristotle's Ethics*, University of California Press, pp. 157–70.

Woods, Michael [1992] *Aristotle: Eudemian Ethics: Books I, II, and VIII*, 2nd edition, Clarendon Press.

Index

Academy, and Aristotle 1,
10, 185; and Eudoxus
185; and Speusippus 2
accuracy, not possible in
ethics 16, 63–4, 67, 80,
92, 102, 122, 180,
217–19
Ackrill, J. L. 28–9
action, contrasted with
animal behaviour 147–8;
with compulsive
behaviour 119, 121; with
production 14, 55–6,
88–91, 94, 98; with
reflex 14, 119–29; under
a description 122–8
akrasia, see moral failure
Alexander the Great 2–3
altruism 172–5
animals, incapable of
action 130; of fulfilment
22, 50; of moral failure
158; of thought 38
Aquinas, Thomas 180n9

archē, moral starting point
73–4, 115; translation of
74n21
aretē, see virtue
Aristotle, parents of 1
Arrington, R. L. 215n1
Austin, J. L. 118n1

Bentham, J. 89, 178,
196–7
biology, Aristotle's interest
in 4–7; basis for ethics
24–6, 39–40, 44, 178
boulēsis, see wanting
Broadie, S. 43n23, 46n24,
46n25, 141n27, 142n30
brutishness 57n4, 120, 122,
148, 155
Burnyeat, M. F. 75

character, relation to
fulfilled life 26; relation
to virtues 57, 69;
responsibility for 133–7

229

children, limited responsibility of 130–7

choice, defined 69, 104; relation to virtue 69–70, 108, 113; *see also* conclusion, moral

Chrysippus the Stoic 142n28

common views 7, 44, 205, 213–14, 221; about the law 118–19; about moral failure 147–8; about pleasure 199–200; about virtues 66; use of in dialectic 7, 109n13, 134–5

compatibilism 138

compulsion, definition 118–21; exaggerated views of 118; relation to threat 122

compulsive behaviour 123

conclusion, moral 129–33; relation to moral failure 165–6; translates *prohairesis* 129n16, 162; *see also* choice

conditioning 72–3

consequentialism 89–90

Cooper, J. M. 169n3, 171n4

courage 20–8

Crisp, R. 196n9

dating of Aristotle's works 4, 10

deliberation 95, 103–5, 131–2; rapid 104n11, 132n19

desire, and moral failure 153–9

determinism 68, 70, 137–42, 165

diagram 65

dialectic, meaning 109; use of 134–5; *see also* common views

dilemma 77

disposition 54–5; *see also* habitual disposition

dominant/inclusive 27–8, 32–3, 39–41, 45, 47–8, 50

drunkenness 150–2, 156–7, 162–3

egoism 172–9

elitism 47, 213

emotion, definition of 58; and moral virtue 45, 56–7, 60–1, 67–8, 72; and practical wisdom 98, 109; role of, contrasted with Hume 112–14; source of insight 68, 75, 80, 107

Empedocles 152, 162, 163

end of action 14–16, 25, 27–31, 35; in relation to skill 100; *see also* Function Argument

endoxa, *see* common views

endurance, limits of human 120, 123

epieikeia 181

ergon, *see* Function Argument

ethics, contrasted with physics, 16–17

eudaimonia, translation of 22–4, 89n2, 92–3, 183–4; *see also* fulfilled life

Eudemian Ethics 9, 65n15, 123n10, 125–6n13, 184

Eudoxus, on pleasure 185–6

Euripides, examples of alleged excuses 119

experience, required for practical wisdom 18, 81, 98, 111n14

external goods, in relation to fulfilment 209

forms, general theory of 5–6, 24, 26n3; of the Good 24, 26n3, 146

Frankena, W. K. 42n22

free will 137–42, 164
friendship, *see* personal relationships
fulfilled life 21–51; as active 22, 26; coherent 29, 92–3, 109; complete 31–2; sufficient 32–3; not possible for animals 25; not product of good actions 89; nor of theoretical knowledge 106; popular views of 24, 90; relationship to egoism 199–205
Function Argument 36–41, 43–4, 47n4, 57, 60, 79, 90, 115; in relation to pleasure 201–6, 214–17; in relation to self-love 174, 177–8

Gauthier, R. A. 119n3, 152n8, 198n10
God, *see* prime mover
Gosling, J. 154, 184n1, 191n5, 198n10

habitual disposition 55, 64
habituation 75
Hardie, W. F. R. 27–8, 63n14, 141n27
hēdonē translation 187n2; *see also* pleasure
Heinaman, R. 30n6
hekōn/akōn, *see* willingly/unwillingly
Heraclitus 203–4
hexis, *see* habitual disposition
Honderich, T. 139n25
human nature, as basis for ethics, 44, 116, 183, 216–18
Hume, D., differing from Aristotle on emotions 112–14, 165n15

ignorance, and acting because of acting in 126–8, 135; moral 128, 136–7; and redescription of actions 125–8; of universal or particular 127–8, 133; and vice 146
individualism 167
indoctrination 78–81
induction in ethics 74–5, 99–100
insight 99
intuitionism, in ethics 115–16
Irwin, T. H. 5, 116n19, 120n6, 128n15, 142n30, 215n2

Jolif, Y. 119n3, 152n8, 181n10
judgement, as criterion for virtue 64
justice 56, 180–2; general and particular 208

Kant, I. 41n20; on emotions 114–15, 221
Kenny, Sir Anthony 9–10, 46n24
Kosman, L. A. 63n13
Kraut, R. 29, 50n28, 176n6

leisure 176
libertarianism 164–5
logos, various meanings of 63–4
luck 208–9
Lyceum 3

Macedon 1–3, 15n2; Philip of 1–2
mean, as defines moral virtue 61–4
means, and ends 30–1, 85; deliberation about 103–12
Midgley, M. 38n16
Mill, J. S. 40, 196–7, 221
moderation 59–61, 63
Moore, G. E. 41–2

moral failure 145–66; *akrasia* 146;
and brutishness 120; and desire
164–5; and ignorance 147; and
pleasure 185
moral training 17–18, 55, 58–61,
70–8; Plato's view of 146–8; and
pleasures 184–5, 203

natural defects 135
naturalistic fallacy 41–3
Nicomachus 3, 9, 10
noble actions 25; as aim of life
174–9, 206–8; and politics 75;
and practical wisdom 89, 93,
106–8
nous, *see* insight
Nussbaum, M. 215n2

Oedipus 126–7, 151
origin of action 119, 121, 122,
128–9, 141
orthos logos, *see* right reason
Orwell, G. 120

parental influence 72–3, 133–5
particulars and universals 86, 94–5;
ignorance of 126–8, 133; in
practical syllogisms 150, 152–3,
159, 162; universals from
particulars 101–2, 105
pathos 57n5
perception, moral 58, 64, 98–109,
128, 152, 161–2, 178, 219
peripatetics 3
personal relationships 167–82;
conditions for 169; essential to
human nature 178–9, 190;
require goodwill 170–1;
translation of *philia* 168; types
of 170

perversions, *see* brutishness
pets 169
philia, *see* personal relationships
phronēsis, *see* practical wisdom
Plato, founder of Academy 1; on
pleasure 192–3; on the soul
33–5; philosophical interests 4,
5, 7–8; relationship to Aristotle
4, 5, 7–8, 13, 16, 24, 26n3,
134, 146–7, 149, 151, 154–5,
177
pleasure 183–209; broadly
understood 195–6; distinct from
fulfilment 24–5, 43; from the
highest good 25–6, 185–6; from
process 193–7; from any single
experience 187, 202; 'false'
pleasures 199–205; 'higher'
pleasures 24–5, 40, 60, 189–90;
'necessary' pleasures 189–90;
physiology of 187–8; related to
moral failure 184; to moral
virtue 177, 184, 205–9;
Aristotle's final view of 197–8;
Plato's view of 192–3;
Speusippus on 190–2
Politics 13, 128n15
politics, as highest science, 15–16,
24; influence of 72, 136
practical syllogism, related to
means/ends 86, 88, 94–102;
related to moral failure 150, 153,
159–61; *see also* particulars and
universals
practical wisdom 83–116; and
change 87; and fulfilment 47;
and the good life 84, 93, 178;
and moral virtue 64, 76, 77, 84;
and skill 88–94; and the young
18; result of training 84

practice, as aim of the *Ethics* 13–14, 17–19, 71
prime mover 46, 47, 48, 50
process 194–5
prohairesis, see conclusion, moral
Protagoras 203–4
Pythias (daughter) 3
Pythias (wife) 2

racism 7, 44
regret 124–5
relativism 213–18
Republic, Plato's 13, 34n10, 147n3
reputation 24, 212
responsibility 117–43
riches 23, 174–5
right reason 64, 71, 87–8, 154, 160
Ross, W. D. 140n26
Rudder Baker, L. 139n25

scarcity 176–7
science 87, 89, 99–100
self-control 18, 67, 113; contrasted with moral failure 146, 161–4; in Hume 113
self-sacrifice 24, 76n16, 201–4, 209
skills 55; contrasted with intellectual virtue 85, 88–94; with moral virtue 55–6; misuse of 90
slaves 202–3, 217
Socrates 1, 5; views on wrongdoing 133, 146, 160–2
sophia 87
sōphrosunē 59n9; *see also* moderation

Sorabji, R. 120n6, 125–6n13, 137n22, 141n27
soul, Aristotle's view of 8, 34–5, 47, 60; Plato's view of 33–4
Speusippus 2; views on pleasure 190–2

Taylor, C. C. W. 184n1, 191n5, 198n10
technai, see skills
telos, see end of action
temperance *see* moderation
theōria 46–51, 92, 150n5, 178
theory, importance of 49–50, 87; involves universal principles 111; and practical application 93–6, 98, 106, 163
threat 121–3
truth, in ethics 79, 114

universals, *see* particulars and universals
Urmson, J. O. 63n13

virtue ethics 218–21
virtue, intellectual 83–116; instances of 101n9; training in 71, 80
virtue, moral 53–81; 23–4, 54, 55, 57; criterion of 64–7, 203; relation to functioning well 37–40, 43–5; to knowledge 166, 170, 172; to pleasure and pain 211; required by practical reason 71, 106–9; unity of 76–7, 109–12; some unusual 212

wanting 142–3
willingly/unwillingly, translation of *hekōn/akōn* 118; not willingly

124; used of actions as done at the time 109–12, 141; used by Plato 147 n3
women, rights of 7; abilities of 212–3, 217

Woods, M. J. 65n15

young people 17–19, 99

Index of Aristotelian texts cited

Where the textual reference is given in **bold** type, the text is printed out in full on the page.

De Interpretatione		**1097b14–20**	32–3
19a7–23	140n26	1097b28–1098a18	37–8
		1098a20–4	45
De Generatione et		**1098a34–b4**	73–4
Corruptione		**1099a1120**	206
337b26–338a3	140n26	1099a29–31	25, 42n18
Topics		**1099a31–b8**	176n7, 208–9
100b21	5n2		
		1100b23–1101a16	209
Metaphysics		1101b16–18	130n17
1027a20–7	140n26	1102a16–25	35n12
Nicomachaean Ethics		*Book II*	
		1103a14–25	55n1
Book I		1103b6–25	55n2
1094a18–22	28	**1103b21–5**	72, 78
1094b11–12	16	**1103b26–31**	13, 67, 70
1094b14–16	17		
1095a2–11	18	**1103b34–1104a10**	64
1095a12	14	1104b8–16	203n12
1095a19	22	1104b9	58n5
1095b4–8	74–5	1105a17–b5	55
1096a10–12	25n2	**1105b7–18**	13

⌐4	69
⌐24–5	69
⌐b36–1107a2	56–74
⌐7a28–33	65
⌐07a34	65n15
⌐107b1–4	62
⌐107b8–14	62
1108a9–19	65
1109b14–23	63–4

Book III

1109b35	118
1110a1–4	119
1110a9–19	121–3
1110a23–6	120
1110b2–3	119
1110b9–17	119
1110b18	124
1110b20	124
1110b24–1111a1	126–8
1111a10–13	124, 138
1111a15–20	131
1111a19–21	124
1111a26	120n4
1111b4–6	129–30n16
1111b10	131
1111b12–14	166
1111b20–9	131
1111b22–4	142
1111b26–9	104
1111b28–30	105
1112a15–16	104
1112b11–12	104
1112b20–4	100n8
1113a22–6	143
1113b2–4	104
1113b6–17	135
1114a31–b2	134–5
1114b16–25	73n19
1114b31–1115a3	73n19

1116a10–13	207
1116b33–6	121
1117a17–22	131, 132n19
1117a35–b2	208
1117b15–16	208
1117b27–1118b27	59n10
1118a23–1119a20	59–61

Book IV

1124a27–30	212
1126b17–23	169n3
1127b22–8	212
1128a33–b1	212

Book VI

1138b25–34	87–8
1139a22–3	69
1139a21–6	104–5
1140a25–8	93, 104
1140b4–6	93
1140b13–16	163n14
1141a16–20	46
1141b2–8	46–7
1141b12–22	95–102
1141b29	135
1142a11–15	18
1142a11–18	99
1142a20–3	99
1142a23–30	99–101
1142a25–30	162n13
1142b26–8	104n11
1142b31–3	108
1143a32–b5	101–2
1143b11–14	5n2
1143b14–17	87n1
1144a6–9	107
1144a13–19	98–9
1144a26–b1	106–8
1144b26–32	71
1144b31–2	220
1144b32–1145a2	76–7, 109–12

Book VII

1145b2–7	5n2, 148
1145b21	148
1145b23–4	163
1145b27–8	149, 163
1146b5–7	149n4
1146b8–9	148–9, 165
1146b25	155
1146b31	155
1146b31–1147b2	150–66
1146b31–5	150, 165n8
1146b32–3	150n6, 160n4
1146b35–1147a10	150, 155
1147a7	150n6
1147a11–b17	158
1147a10–24	150, 165n8
1147a26–b3	150, 160
1147a35–b3	153–4, 158
1147b4	168
1147b6–17	157, 162
1147b20	156
1148b15–1149a3	57n4
1150b8–16	120
1151a20–8	158–9
1152b1	58n5
1152b8–24	189n4
1153a7–15	193
1153a17–35	189n3
1153b47	191
1154a10–11	189
1154a11–18	189

Book VIII

1155a3	168
1155b1	169n2
1155b26–1156a5	169
1155b27–31	169n2
1155b31	171
1156a3–8	170
1156b2	168n1

1156b12	168n1
1157a26–8	168n1
1158a28	168n1
1158b20	168n1
1159b28	168n1
1159b35–1160a2	181
1160a19	168n1
1161b14	168n1
1162a29–33	180

Book IX

1163b35	168n1
1164b27–1165a1	180
1166a12–23	216
1166b30–5	169n3
1168a28	174
1166b30–5	169n3
1169a1–2	174, 178
1169a3–11	174–8
1169a18–25	177, 207
1169a31–2	177
1169b16–19	179

Book X

1172a22	58n5
1172b9–23	186
1173a5–13	191
1173b5–20	194n8
1173b20–31	199
1174a14	201
1174a13–b14	195
1174b14–16	197
1174b20–33	198
1175a10–21	206
1175a21–8	201
1175a24–8	201–2
1176a3	203
1176a26–9	202–5
1176a19–24	200
1177a11	22

/	46n25	*Eudemian Ethics*	
1–4	47	1220b23–1221a14	65n15
926–9	47	1224a25–6	123n10
a20	48		
8a23–b4	129–30n16	*Politics*	
78b7–32	47, 48, 50	I, 1–6, 13	213n1
79b4–1180a24	136n20	1280a31–4	128n15
180b57	73		
1180b13–28	92n4	*Rhetoric*	
1181a12	49	1373b25–1374a15	125n12